www.ingramcontent.com/pod-product-compliance
Lightning Source LLC
Chambersburg PA
CBHW080744250426
43671CB00038B/2863

I0322224

www.ingramcontent.com/pod-product-compliance
Lightning Source LLC
Chambersburg PA
CBHW081218230426
43666CB00015B/2787
9780874418316

Alef Bet Quest

TEACHER'S EDITION

BY DINA MAIBEN

Techniques for Students With Special Learning Needs:
Lisa Friedman

Editorial Consultants:
Sarah Gluck
Ellen J. Rank

Book and Cover Design: Itzhack Shelomi
Project Editor: Terry S. Kaye

Springfield, New Jersey
www.behrmanhouse.com
ISBN: 978-0-87441-831-6
Manufactured in the United States of America

CONTENTS

PURPOSE OF *ALEF BET QUEST*

Welcome to *Alef Bet Quest*, a multimedia Hebrew decoding experience!

Teaching children to read and fostering their emerging literacy is the teacher's most important task in any language or culture. Participation in Jewish holiday celebrations, communal worship, and life-cycle events often requires the ability to decode Hebrew accurately and fluently. As a teacher of Hebrew reading, you have been entrusted with a sacred responsibility. *Alef Bet Quest* will assist you in this important and challenging work.

Alef Bet Quest facilitates the learner's acquisition of basic Hebrew decoding skills, using the instructional sequences that researchers in Israel have found to be most effective. (For more information on this research, visit www.AlefBetQuest.com.)

All twenty lessons in *Alef Bet Quest* are designed to follow these seven steps:

1. Reviewing recently learned key words, consonants, and vowels
2. Introducing new key words, consonants, and vowels
3. Making sound-symbol associations of new letters and vowels through a multi-sensory presentation and phoneme analysis
4. Direct instruction of difficult concepts
5. Reading practice of letter and vowel combinations ("Word Building" and "I Can Read Hebrew!")
6. Completing activities
7. Assessment

If you are using the *Alef Bet Quest Companion Reader* in conjunction with the primer, you should consider including the optional oral Hebrew language lesson offered in the techniques for each lesson in this guide.

HOW IS *ALEF BET QUEST* DIFFERENT FROM OTHER PRIMERS?

Alef Bet Quest is the first Hebrew primer to combine the best practices of Hebrew reading instruction with the best of today's technology, integrating phonics mastery with computerized learning. It is designed to teach young students to decode Hebrew accurately and fluently, while cutting-edge technology brings the language to life in animated computer activities and games.

Alef Bet Quest:

1. **Stands on a solid foundation of research on Hebrew reading instruction and second language acquisition.** All elements of instruction and drill—from the presentation of key words to the sequence of letter introduction—follow innovative methods of Hebrew reading. For example, when more than one symbol represents a single sound (such as ס and שׂ—*s* sound), they are taught together. Researchers have found that when such symbols are introduced separately, students tend to remember one symbol but not the other. In contrast, they concluded that visually similar symbols (like ד and ר) should be widely separated, allowing the learner to become completely at ease with one before having to make the fine visual distinction required to recognize the other. Researchers have found, too, that introducing symbols that represent *similar*, but not *identical*, sounds together (like ס, ז, and צ), or one right after the other, actually *increases* the likelihood that students will confuse them. These types of letters are introduced far apart to decrease this likelihood. By the same token, when a single vowel symbol is used for multiple purposes, these purposes are treated separately and are presented far apart. For example, the three different uses of the *sh'va* (ְ) are presented in three different lessons (Lessons 10, 13, and 20). Likewise, the two different uses of *kamatz* (ָ) are taught separately (Lesson 1 and Lesson 19).

To best facilitate sound-symbol associations, letters that represent two sounds are treated as separate phonetic items. For example, בּ and ב (a single letter that represents two sounds; in English *b* as in ball and *v* as in video) are visually similar but they do not make the same sound. They are therefore treated as two phonetic items and are introduced far apart (בּ in Lesson 2 and ב in Lesson 10).

Note: *Alef Bet Quest* teaches decoding. *Decoding* is the ability to decipher Hebrew syllables, words, phrases, and sentences phonetically and accurately (translating symbols into sounds).

Reading is the process of translating visual symbols into meaningful language. Although the terms "decoding" and "reading" are not synonymous, in this guide they are often used interchangeably as it is more common to say "read Hebrew" than "decode Hebrew."

2. **Introduces all new Hebrew consonants and vowels through Hebrew "key words."** Each lesson opens with between one and three key words or phrases. These words often reflect the child's direct experience, providing young learners with Hebrew vocabulary that is immediately accessible (רֶגֶל, גֶּשֶׁם, מִשְׁפָּחָה). Some key words represent basic Jewish concepts that are connected to Jewish holidays or ritual (שַׁמָּשׁ, שׁוֹפָר, בִּימָה). After students are introduced to a key word, they break it down into its component sounds. This is known as phoneme analysis, and it helps students to better understand the relationship between the printed Hebrew letter or vowel and its sound. Finally, the key words provide a means of verifying every component sound (phoneme), such as שׁ or ַ. If students are unsure about a particular letter or vowel, you can review the key word that contains that symbol as a way of reminding students about its sound.
3. **Uses a multi-sensory approach to introducing letters and vowels, appealing to the widest range of learners.** Students learn in different ways. The three primary modalities (or sensory pathways) of learning are visual, auditory, and kinesthetic or tactile. By employing a multi-sensory approach to decoding—in other words, students see, hear-say, and use their hands or bodies to integrate new phonic items—more students in the class are able to master the material. The multi-sensory approach, a teaching method developed by Beth Slingerland, founder of the Slingerland Institute for Literacy in Washington State, is the recommended approach in *Alef Bet Quest*. A complete description of this procedure can be found in the "Multi-Sensory Approach to Hebrew Phonics" on page 11.
4. **Is the first Hebrew primer with a fully integrated digital application.** Students will delight in using their new skills when playing online video games and searching for clues in the digital application, "The Quest for the Golden Kiddush Cup." Students also practice their new decoding skills with computer-based, read-aloud activities (students hear both American *and* Israeli accents). The digital application, which takes the form of a treasure hunt in modern Israel, is fully integrated with the textbook. An activity or puzzle at the end of each lesson in the book ("Clue to the Quest") provides students with clues for scoring bonus points in a computer game. Students are motivated to use the software at home—creating additional practice time and opportunities. They can even e-mail their online lesson summaries directly to you! For more about the digital application, see "Using the Digital Application" on page 13.
5. **Focuses on individual vowels and vowel patterns through tightly structured reading drills.** Phoneme analysis is followed by reading drills that encourage learners to use their newly acquired skills with a variety of practice words. In early lessons, "Word Building" activities provide students with syllable drills and syllable building. Reading drills are composed entirely of real Hebrew words ("I Can Read Hebrew!"). Both the syllable and word-reading drills focus on individual vowels and vowel patterns. They follow patterns of rhyme and rhythm that assist beginning readers in recognizing the patterns of Hebrew words.
6. **Emphasizes phrase and sentence reading.** The ability to decode individual words is just the first step in teaching students to blend fluent phrases and fluently recite passages. Every lesson contains reading practice consisting of phrases and complete sentences. Students who also complete the *Alef Bet Quest Companion Reader* will be able to read many of these sentences with full comprehension.
7. **Builds a bridge between Hebrew decoding and siddur reading.** Beginning in Lesson 1, many reading drills contain Hebrew words that are drawn from the siddur and maḥzor. By Lesson 12 the drills are composed largely of siddur words. The use of siddur vocabulary from the earliest stage helps students become familiar with prayer words they will encounter throughout their lives. To further bridge the gap between reading words and prayer recitation, full passages of the Shabbat blessings, Hatikvah, and the Four Questions appear in Lessons 18 and 19.
8. **Provides direct instruction for difficult reading rules.** Students learning to read Hebrew will encounter rules and exceptions that are foreign to native English readers. For example, beginning Hebrew readers often have difficulty with directionality. They forget that Hebrew is read from right to left. An activity early in Lesson 1 assists students in determining where Hebrew words begin.

STRUCTURE OF THE PUPIL EDITION

Each of the twenty lessons in *Alef Bet Quest* contains the following features:

Key Words Each lesson opens with between one and three key words, each accompanied by a picture that illustrates the meaning. Children learn second language vocabulary best through direct association between a new word and the item it represents. Of the 42 key words in *Alef Bet Quest,* there are only two instances in which translations, rather than illustrations, are used.

"What's New?" Immediately under the key words, this feature presents the lesson's new letters and vowels. The names of new letters are included in English.

"Letters You Know" and **"Vowels You Know"** A review of all the previous letters and vowels follows (except in Lesson 1). The letters appear here in *alef-bet* order.

"Word Building" These drills appear only in the first four lessons and focus on individual Hebrew syllables, providing practice with Consonant-Vowel (C-V) and Consonant-Vowel-Consonant (C-V-C) syllables as well as syllable blending.

"I Can Read Hebrew!" Every lesson contains reading activities composed of real Hebrew words, and, in later chapters, phrases and sentences.

"I Can Write Hebrew!" Here students practice writing the new Hebrew letters and key words. For beginning readers, the act of writing the letter in block print provides kinesthetic reinforcement. A companion script writing workbook is also available. Visit www.behrmanhouse.com for more information.

"Clue to the Quest" Each lesson ends with a reading riddle, crossword, word search, or other puzzle whose answer allows students to earn bonus points in the digital application, "The Quest for the Golden Kiddush Cup." The integrated computer application allows you to extend classroom learning into the home with homework students like to do!

Alef Bet Quest also contains a variety of features that enhance student mastery of Hebrew decoding skills:

- **"Letter Hint," "Vowel Hint," "Letter-Vowel Hint"** These sections provide students with clues, such as mnemonics (ר is Round), for remembering the sounds of letters, vowels, and special combinations.
- **"Super Reading Secret"** Here students receive direct instruction in key aspects of Hebrew reading, such as how to break words into individual syllables.
- **"Odd Letter Out"** In early lessons, these selections incorporate general sound-symbol recognition. In later lessons, they focus on visual discrimination skills. For example, students may be asked to circle the letter that makes a different sound in the following row of items: תּ ט ת ה ת ט תּ
- **"Sound Check"** Students identify Hebrew homonyms (words that sound the same but are spelled differently). This is an important skill for developing Hebrew phonological awareness (a sensitivity to and understanding of the sounds of language) and phonemic awareness (the ability to recognize, isolate, and manipulate those sounds). Students may also be asked to isolate sounds within a word. This skill is known as auditory segmentation, an essential skill for learning to read phonetically.
- **"Rhyme Time"** The ability to identify words that rhyme is an important aspect of phonemic awareness, requiring beginning readers to recognize repeating patterns in print.
- **"The 'Write' Letter," "The 'Write' Word"** Students review letters and vocabulary as they select and write the correct letters or words that match illustrations in an activity.
- **"Picture This"** Students identify the Hebrew words that describe a picture.

STRUCTURE OF THE TEACHER'S EDITION

This Teacher's Edition contains the entire text of *Alef Bet Quest* in a reduced format. The pages are annotated with instructional techniques and suggestions for activities that correspond to features in the student book. The information and suggestions included here will assist you in developing your lesson plan. You need not follow every suggestion presented; rather, the guide provides you with several options from which you may choose. You know best what will work with your group of students and your teaching style.

Each chapter in the section beginning on page 17 of this guide contains the following sections:

Pages in Student Text

Key Words

New Letters Whenever two letters represent a single sound, they are taught together (ת תּ ט). As a result, up to three letters may be taught in a single lesson. After Lesson 4, no more than one new consonant sound is presented in any single lesson.

New Vowels With the exception of Lesson 20, only one new vowel sound is introduced in any lesson. However, single vowel sounds may be represented by as many as three symbols in Hebrew (◌ֲ ◌ַ ◌ָ). With one exception, all symbols that represent a single vowel sound are taught together. The exception is ◌ֵ, which remains controversial in North American Hebrew pronunciation. In some places, this vowel is pronounced *eh*, identical to the pronunciation of ◌ֶ and ◌ֱ. In other places, ◌ֵ is pronounced *ay*. Because ◌ֵ can take either pronunciation, we do not teach it with the other vowel signs that represent its sound. Therefore, ◌ֵ appears by itself, and teachers are directed to teach it according to the pronunciation in their community.

Recommended Instructional Materials This is a list of Phonics Flash Cards (numbered flash cards that contain the individual letters and vowels taught in each lesson), and Word Cards (numbered word cards that contain the key words taught in each lesson), and other materials and props for teaching the lesson. For a master list of Phonics Flash Cards and Word Cards, see page 12 in this guide. You can also find black-line masters for the cards in Appendices A and B on pages 107 and 113.

Review (except Lesson 1) This section describes a game or other activity that reviews previous material before presenting the new information contained in the lesson.

Set Induction An activity introduces and helps students relate to the central concepts in the new lesson, such as the idea that multiple symbols can represent a single sound.

Introducing the Key Words and Deducing Their Sound-Symbol Associations *Alef Bet Quest* promotes a multi-sensory approach to Hebrew decoding, integrating auditory, visual, and kinesthetic or tactile information and using all three of these modalities (or sensory pathways) to help all learners master Hebrew reading. You can find a full explanation of how to use this multi-sensory approach on page 11 of this guide.

Oral Language Lesson (Optional) Each chapter of the guide includes a short, modern Hebrew language lesson to integrate with the key words. Although optional, the oral Hebrew language instruction is strongly recommended. Include it for any class that is also using the *Alef Bet Quest Companion Reader*.

Techniques for Individual Activities For every activity in the student text, you will find directions and, in many cases, the theoretical basis for its inclusion in the book. For example, some activities focus on training students to hear the component sounds of Hebrew words. Others are designed to help students develop the ability to distinguish between letters that look similar. As the teacher, you may find it helpful to know what skill students are practicing in order to assess students' progress and remediate when necessary.

Clue to the Quest In addition to providing guidance about the final activity in each lesson, this section also includes challenge questions to help heighten student interest and motivation for using the digital application at home. It will also help you follow up on students' use of the software.

Assessment The most important procedure in an individual assessment of Hebrew reading is listening to each student's reading of unfamiliar material and completing an error analysis. Appendix C on page 123 in this guide contains a placement test that you can use to evaluate new students who enter the program late or to provide an overall picture of the class or grade in the middle or at the end of the year. A reading assessment for each lesson follows.

It is important that you organize your time so that you can evaluate each student individually at least every three lessons. You may need to provide more frequent assessment for students who are having difficulty with the material. Complete instructions for assessment and basic error analysis are included on page 9.

There are three ways to assess students' progress in the software:

1. Log on to www.behrmanhouse.com and click the blue "Assessment" button at the bottom left of the screen. Click on *Alef Bet Quest.* Put in your class's serial number. Review your students' results.
2. Students can print out a lesson summary when they have completed all the activities in a lesson and bring it in to class.
3. Students can e-mail the lesson summary directly to you. You may wish to set up a separate e-mail account to receive this information.

Inform your students how often you intend to assess their progress online. You may wish to check their progress each time you assign an activity or after they complete a chapter in the book.

PACING

Many variables contribute to the pace at which a class completes an instructional program. Students have different levels of ability, teachers have different styles, and schools vary in the number of instructional hours devoted to Hebrew. You will have to decide how slowly or quickly you want your class to move through the text. However, you should plan to complete *Alef Bet Quest* within one school year.

The twenty lessons in *Alef Bet Quest* consist of four to six pages each. Certain aspects of Hebrew phonics are more complicated than others and will require more time for mastery. For example, there are different uses of ְ, and students may need multiple sessions before they master each use. Similarly, the second pronunciation of ָ (*oh*) is taught with ֳ and the double-duty dot (מֹשֶׁה) in Lesson 19. Despite the fact that this lesson is five pages long, the complexity of the material makes it a more difficult, and therefore a more time-consuming, lesson than others of the same length.

Instructional time is the scarcest and most precious resource in Hebrew education. Deciding how you will spend your time is critical when planning lessons. Ideally, every lesson should include the following five components:

1. An activity that reviews previous material
2. An activity that introduces the new concepts or sets the tone for the lesson
3. Presentation of new material
4. Reinforcement of new material
5. A closing activity that summarizes or reinforces the lesson's content and prepares students for the next session

The amount of time you spend on each component will depend on the overall amount of time available to you for Hebrew instruction and on your goals for the lesson. Preparing your lessons in advance will help you manage your time so that you and your students can successfully meet your goals. Remember that the computer application provides you with an exceptional tool for extending class time with fun, online learning that can be completed at home.

Your lesson plans should include your goals for the lesson, the instructional materials you will need, specific activities you plan to use with time estimates for each, homework and assignments in the digital application, and any other relevant notes.

Once-a-Week Hebrew Instruction

If your class meets one to one-and-a-half hours per week for twenty-eight to thirty weeks, you should aim to complete one lesson per week on average. Lessons 10, 13, and 17 may each require two class sessions, as the contents of those lessons are complex. Similarly, Lesson 19 includes two long reading passages, to which you may want to devote extra time for student mastery. Depending on the makeup of your class and your school's overall goals for Hebrew, you may want to use the *Alef Bet Quest Companion Reader* concurrently with *Alef Bet Quest,* or you may choose to reserve it until after students have mastered the basics of Hebrew phonetic decoding. It is an excellent reinforcement tool.

Twice-a-Week Hebrew Instruction

If your class meets two or more hours per week for thirty weeks, you should allow two to three sessions per chapter. Consider incorporating the *Alef Bet Quest Companion Reader* as part of the regular classroom routine or use it upon completion of the primer.

THE HOME-SCHOOL CONNECTION

A partnership between home and school can help your students reach their greatest potential. Make every effort to facilitate this partnership. A significant number of parents cannot read Hebrew and are therefore unable to assist their children with Hebrew reading homework. *Alef Bet Quest* has taken a bold and innovative approach to solving this problem: the digital application. Students will enjoy playing the interactive games, which review and practice the reading skills they have learned in class. Students can hear the reading passages read aloud—in American and Israeli accents! The activities are self-correcting. And the results are easily accessible to you. Parents can even join in the fun. They may even learn to read Hebrew themselves!

You may wish to e-mail or send home a letter after the first day of class telling parents about *Alef Bet Quest* and introducing them to the computer program. Explain that you will be able to assess their child's progress online. (See "Assessment," page 9, and "Using the Digital Application," page 13.) You can find a sample letter to parents at www.behrmanhouse.com. Click on "Educators," "In the Classroom," then "Letters to Parents about Digital Applications." The letter contains steps for using the software, including sign-on instructions, and a link to a demo site for parents to try out the digital application themselves.

THE FIRST DAY OF SCHOOL

Setting the Stage

Before the first day of school decorate the classroom with Hebrew posters and an *alef-bet* chart. Label classroom objects, such as כִּסֵּא and שֻׁלְחָן, with their Hebrew names. Try to display ritual objects such as a ḥanukkiyah, a shofar, or a Kiddush cup, as well as Israeli goods and products such as a soda bottle and package labels.

On the first day of class, play a tape or CD of Hebrew songs (such as *Shiru Shalom Ivrit* or *Z'man LaShir*, both available from Behrman House) as the students enter the room and find seats.

Oral Language Lesson (Optional)

If you are using the *Alef Bet Quest Companion Reader* or you want to enrich your program with oral language, and you are comfortable using Hebrew, begin the first class with the following lesson. Take attendance, asking students to respond in Hebrew when you call their names. Teach them the following words:

שְׁמִי ____________ שָׁלוֹם פֹּה לֹא פֹּה

If a student is absent, the class can respond:

לֹא פֹּה ____________

Introducing the Book and the Digital Application

Distribute the books and allow students a few minutes to examine them. Show students the cover and ask what they think the book is about. (*Hebrew, alef bet, learning to read Hebrew, Israel*) Explain that by the end of the year they will be able to read every Hebrew word in the book. They will also be able to follow along in the siddur during services because they will know all the Hebrew letters and vowels!

Explain that Hebrew is read from right to left, so the book opens the opposite way from English books. Direct students to open their books to page 4. Ask what they see on this page. (*a silver plate in 20 pieces*) Explain that as part of their study of Hebrew reading they will be going on a treasure hunt—a quest—using the digital application. When they complete a lesson on the computer they will write the key words and new letters and/or vowels on the corresponding piece of the plate, or color in the piece. Next, direct students to turn to page 8 and explain that at the end of each lesson they will solve a puzzle that will help them earn bonus points in the computer games.

With the approval of your education director, distribute candies, *alef-bet* sugar cookies, or some other sweet treat (you may want to have pretzels, fruit, or a sugar-free treat for students with dietary concerns). Tell students that there is a custom of eating a sweet treat on the first day of school, and especially on the first day of learning to read Hebrew. Ask students what they think the purpose of this custom is. (*study is sweet, learning to read Hebrew is a treat*) Together recite the Sheheḥeyanu, the blessing we say when we begin something new:

בָּרוּךְ אַתָּה, יְיָ אֱלֹהֵינוּ, מֶלֶךְ הָעוֹלָם,
שֶׁהֶחֱיָנוּ וְקִיְּמָנוּ וְהִגִּיעָנוּ לַזְּמַן הַזֶּה.

Blessed are You, Adonai our God, Ruler of the universe, who has kept us alive, sustained us, and enabled us to reach this season.

HOMEWORK

Review and practice at home will help students hone the Hebrew decoding skills and vocabulary they acquire in school. The digital application provides the ideal method for at-home practice. It extends Hebrew instructional time and allows parents to participate in their child's Hebrew studies. Students are likely to be captivated by the Hebrew computer games. It's homework they will want to do!

ASSESSMENT

Ongoing assessment will help you track student mastery of the material and plan remediation as necessary. You probably will not be able to assess every student on every lesson. Therefore, the assessments provided in Appendix C on page 123 are cumulative (Lessons 1–5, 6–10, 11–15, and 16–20). Students that are having difficulty should be evaluated more frequently, at least after every other lesson.

You can use the first assessment sheet in Appendix C, "Placement Test," to assess the skills of students who join the class mid-year or unexpectedly appear to be having trouble with certain letters and/or vowels. You can also use it toward the end of the year to assess the skills of the entire class or grade.

We recommend the following procedure for assessment:

- Provide students with a master copy of the assessment sheet. On a separate copy, one for each student, make notes about student errors. Ask each individual to read all ten items without stopping. Put a check next to each word that the student reads correctly. If the student makes mistakes on the first three items, or on five items total, stop the assessment and remediate. For example, allow the student to practice these items with a classroom aide or the resource room tutor. You can also review the material in the appropriate reading passages in the book ("Word Building" or "I Can Read Hebrew!").
- Mark a slash (/) through any item on which the student makes an error and write a phonetic equivalent of the mispronunciation above the slash; for example, *mal* instead of *tal*.
- If the student skips an item, put a slash (/) through it, but without a phonetic note.
- If the student adds a sound, such as an extra vowel at the end of a C-V-C syllable, draw a circle and write the addition inside it, for example: אֶחָ
- Do not let students see what you are writing. Accept self-corrections, but do not give feedback until the student has completed the evaluation.

Assessments can also reveal areas that the class should review as a whole. If you see that several students are having difficulty with the same item—for example, confusion of look-alike or sound-alike letters—a classroom or small group review may be beneficial.

See also "Tracking Students' Digital Activities" on page 13.

SCOPE AND SEQUENCE

PAGE IN STUDENT BOOK	VOWELS	LETTERS	KEY WORDS	LESSON
5	◌ָ ◌ַ ◌ֲ	שׁ מ ם	שַׁמָּשׁ שָׁם	1
9		א ע בּ	אַבָּא עַם	2
13	◌ֹ וֹ	ל ד	שָׁלוֹם אָדָם	3
17		ה י	יָד הַ־	4
21	◌ֶ ◌ֱ	ג	גֶשֶׁם שֶׁמֶשׁ	5
25	◌ִ ◌ִי ◌ָה	unvoiced ה & י	בִּימָה אִמָּא	6
30		צ ץ	מַצָּה מִיץ	7
35	◌ֵי	ר	רֶגֶל בֵּיצָה	8
40		ט תּ ת	טַלִּית תּוֹרָה	9
45	unvoiced ◌ְ	ב ו	הַבְדָּלָה מִצְוָה	10
50	◌ֵ	ס שׂ	סַבָּא סַבְתָּא יִשְׂרָאֵל	11
54	◌ֻ וּ	כּ ק	סֻכָּה קָדוֹשׁ	12
59	voiced ◌ְ	ז	מְזוּזָה הַלְלוּיָהּ	13
64	ךְ ךָ	ח כ ך	חַלָּה בְּרָכָה מֶלֶךְ	14
68	◌ַי	פּ	מִשְׁפָּחָה חַי	15
72	◌ֶיךָ	נ ן	נֵר יַיִן	16
78	◌חַ ◌ְוֹ		חַג שָׂמֵחַ מִצְוֹת	17
82	◌ָיו	פ ף	שׁוֹפָר אָלֶף	18
87	◌ֳ ◌ָ ◌שׁ שׂ◌		צָהֳרַיִם משֶׁה כָּל	19
92	וֹי וּי ◌ְ ◌ְ		אוֹי וַאֲבוֹי!	20

MULTI-SENSORY APPROACH TO HEBREW PHONICS

Students learn in different ways. The three primary modalities for learning are visual, auditory, and kinesthetic or tactile. The most effective way for the greatest number of students to master Hebrew phonetic decoding is for you to use a multi-sensory approach in which students see, hear, and physically form the letters and vowels.

The following steps demonstrate a multi-sensory approach to Hebrew phonics using as a model the letters and vowels in Lesson 1. The approach can be used to introduce all new Hebrew letters and vowels in *Alef Bet Quest.*

Lesson 1

Key Words: שָׁם שַׁמָּשׁ

New Letters: ם/מ שׁ

New Vowels: ֲ ַ ָ

1. Instruct students to repeat the key word שַׁמָּשׁ and ask, "What is the last sound that you hear in this word?" (*sh*) Hold up Phonics Flash Card #1 and say *sh*. Ask students to repeat the sound with you. You may wish to create a kinesthetic link with a hand motion by placing your index finger in front of your lips as if shushing them. Ask the class to repeat the movement. Post Phonics Flash Card #1 on the board with tape, Fun-Tak, or magnetized tape.
2. Ask students to draw the new letter in the air with their index fingers. Model this action for them first, with your back to the class, so they follow the correct directionality. Then ask the class to draw the letter as they say the sound.

   Make sure that students are following the proper direction.
3. Say the key word again, and ask what sound they hear at the beginning of the word. (*sha*) Hold up Phonics Flash Cards #1 and 5 and say *sha*. Ask students what vowel sound they hear in the key word. (*ah*) Show students Phonics Flash Card #5. Pass around one or more tongue depressors or Popsicle sticks and point out to students that it looks just like one of the Hebrew vowels with the *ah* sound (ַ). Show students Phonics Flash Cards # 4, 5, and 6, and tell students that all three of these vowels make the *ah* sound. Post two copies of #1 on the board, leaving a space between them. Post Phonics Flash Card #5 under the first שׁ.
4. Ask students to draw the two vowels ֲ and ָ in the air with their index fingers. Model this action for them and ask them to repeat it while saying *ah*.
5. Practice drilling the new letters and vowels. Write the combinations שַׁ and שָׁ on the board.

   Once students can easily blend these consonant-vowel (C-V) syllables, add a שׁ to the end of the syllables to create שַׁשׁ and שָׁשׁ.
6. Repeat the key word and ask the students what consonant sound they hear in the middle of the word. (*m*) Show the class Phonics Flash Card #2. Say the sound *m* and ask the class to repeat with you. You may wish to create a kinesthetic association by rubbing your stomach (as if enjoying something yummy) and saying *mmm*. Ask the class to repeat the sound and hand motion with you. Direct them to write the letter in the air as they say its sound.

   Make sure that students follow the proper direction.
7. Practice drilling the new letter מ with the vowels: מַ and מָ. Once most students can accurately decode these syllables, create combinations that include the שׁ: מַשׁ and מָשׁ.
8. Hold up Word Card #1 and ask the students to read the Hebrew word. (שַׁמָּשׁ) Ask a volunteer to point to the object that this word names, or to a picture.
9. Repeat this procedure for the second key word, שָׁם. Ask students what sound they hear at the end of the word. (*m*) Show the class Phonics Flash Card #3. Say the sound *m* and ask the class to repeat it with you. Again, you may wish to create a kinesthetic association by rubbing your stomach (as if enjoying something yummy) and saying *mmm*. Ask the students to identify the other symbol that makes the sound *m*. (Phonics Flash Card # 2)
10. Ask students to draw the new letter in the air with their index fingers. Model this action, then ask the class to draw the letter as they say the sound.

    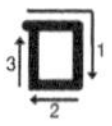

    Make sure that students follow the proper direction.

11. Practice drilling final *mem* with the other letters and vowels. Write the combinations מַם and שָׁם on the board and have students practice decoding it.
12. Hold up Word Card #2, and ask the students to read the Hebrew word. (שָׁם) Ask a volunteer to act out the meaning of this word by pointing "there."

The following is a brief outline of the steps above:

1. Ask students to repeat the key word and to identify a specific sound in the word.
2. Hold up the Phonics Flash Card that represents that sound.
3. Ask students to repeat the sound with you.
4. Create a kinesthetic link with the sound. Ask the class to repeat the sound with an associated motion.
5. Have students draw the new letter in the air with their index fingers as they say the sound.
6. Write on the board C-V and C-V-C combinations that include the new letters and vowels, and have students practice decoding them.

NOTE: You may wish to mark this section with a paper clip or bookmark so that you always have quick and easy access to these steps.

Phonics Flash Cards Master List

1. שׁ
2. מ
3. ם
4. ◌ָ
5. ◌ַ
6. ◌ֲ
7. א
8. ע
9. בּ
10. ל
11. ד
12. ◌ֹ
13. וֹ
14. ה
15. י
16. ג
17. ◌ֶ
18. ◌ֱ
19. ◌ִ
20. ◌ִי
21. צ
22. ץ
23. ר
24. ◌ֵי
25. ט
26. תּ
27. ת
28. ב
29. ו
30. ◌ְ
31. ס
32. שׂ
33. ◌ֵ
34. כּ
35. ק
36. ◌ֻ
37. וּ
38. ז
39. ח
40. כ
41. ך
42. פּ
43. ◌ַי
44. נ
45. ן
46. ◌ֶיךָ
47. ◌חַ
48. ◌ְוֹ
49. פ
50. ף
51. ◌ָיו
52. ◌ֳ
53. וֹי
54. וּי

Word Cards Master List

1. שַׁמָּשׁ
2. שָׁם
3. אַבָּא
4. עַם
5. שָׁלוֹם
6. אָדָם
7. יָד
8. הַ־
9. גֶּשֶׁם
10. שֶׁמֶשׁ
11. בִּימָה
12. אִמָּא
13. מַצָּה
14. מִיץ
15. רֶגֶל
16. בֵּיצָה
17. טַלִּית
18. תּוֹרָה
19. הַבְדָּלָה
20. מִצְוָה
21. סַבָּא
22. סַבְתָּא
23. יִשְׂרָאֵל
24. סֻכָּה
25. קִדּוּשׁ
26. מְזוּזָה
27. הַלְלוּיָהּ
28. חַלָּה
29. בְּרָכָה
30. מֶלֶךְ
31. מִשְׁפָּחָה
32. חַי
33. נֵר
34. יַיִן
35. חַג שָׂמֵחַ
36. מִצְוֹת
37. שׁוֹפָר
38. אָלֶף
39. צָהֳרַיִם
40. מֹשֶׁה
41. כָּל
42. אוֹי וַאֲבוֹי!

USING THE DIGITAL APPLICATION

Students will love playing the online games in the digital application, "The Quest for the Golden Kiddush Cup." The activities reinforce the reading concepts and vocabulary introduced in the book. The digital application also expands the amount of Hebrew instruction time and extends learning into the home. The computer becomes your teaching assistant! With the software, parents can help their children even if they cannot read Hebrew themselves.

When presenting the digital application to the students focus on the fun that they will have playing the computer games, and remind them that they will be able to score even more points by using the Hebrew they learn in class. When introducing the digital application to parents, emphasize the ways it can help their children, such as hearing Hebrew syllables, words, and sentences read aloud in American and Israeli accents, practicing their new decoding skills in online games, and taking a virtual trip through Israel. Tell parents their children can even e-mail their online scores directly to you!

Introducing the Digital Application

Ask students if they have ever gone on a treasure hunt or scavenger hunt. Ask what they did to find the "treasure," and discuss what made this activity fun. Ask students what the word "quest" means. (*a search or pursuit to find something, an adventurous expedition*) Tell them to turn to the back inside cover, and explain that this book comes with a built-in computer treasure hunt called "The Quest for the Golden Kiddush Cup." They will go on a virtual trip through Israel, collecting clues at every stop that will help them solve the mystery of the missing golden Kiddush Cup. After students complete a lesson in the book, they will play games on their computer to practice what they have learned in class.

Before you assign activities in the *Alef Bet Quest* digital application for the first time, tell students, and have them note, the class serial number. Or write the class's serial number on each CD wallet. Every student in the class will use the same serial number to become a member of the *Alef Bet Quest* digital database. You will use that serial number to track the class's progress online. After entering the class's serial number in their computer, students will be asked to register by creating their own user name and password. The students will then be members, and the database will automatically begin to track and store their results.

Make sure to record students' user names so you have a master list in case students forget. Send the class's serial number and the student's user name home to his or her parents. Students can keep their passwords private.

Tracking Students' Digital Activities

There are three ways to assess students' progress in the digital application:

1. Log on to www.behrmanhouse.com and click the blue "Assessment" button at the bottom left of the screen. Click on *Alef Bet Quest.* Put in your class's serial number. Review your students' results.
2. Students can print out a lesson summary when they have completed all the activities in a lesson and bring it in to class.
3. Students can e-mail the lesson summary directly to you. You may wish to set up a separate e-mail account to receive this information.

Inform your students how often you intend to assess their progress online. You may wish to check their progress each time you assign an activity or only after they complete a chapter in the book.

GAMES AND REVIEW ACTIVITIES

Games can add variety and energy to your classroom. They reinforce learning and capture students' attention through a fun, lively medium. As you plan to use the games below, or your own, keep the following in mind:

1. Choose games that contribute to improving specific skills and reading fluency—games that have pedagogic value.
2. Use games that move quickly. Don't spend more time on a game than it deserves.
3. Stop when students' interest begins to wane.
4. Choose age-appropriate games.
5. Use games that are easy to follow and organize. Explain rules clearly. Avoid complicated directions. You want students' attention focused on the skills being reinforced, not on rules.
6. Maintain control of the class.
7. Make sure that all students in the class are actively involved and can experience success.

Around the World

In this review game students sit in a circle facing inward. Choose one student to stand behind a seated student. Hold up a letter or vowel. Both students try to read the card first. The one who reads it first correctly continues "around the world" by standing behind the next student. The object of the game is for students to move, place by place, completely around the circle. You can also use this game to review vocabulary by showing a key-word picture and asking students to provide the correct key word, or by showing a written word that students must read.

Tic-Tac-Toe

Divide the class into two teams, X and O. Draw a tic-tac-toe grid on the chalkboard or whiteboard. Depending on what you want to review, in each square write a Hebrew letter and vowel, a syllable, or a word. In order to place an X or an O in a square, a student must read the item in the square correctly. You can create a permanent tic-tac-toe grid on a piece of oak tag and use Fun-Tak to post printed flash cards in the spaces, or you can use magnetic tape on a set of cards and post them on the board if it is magnetized.

Hint: Place the most difficult combinations, such as C-V-C syllables, in the four corners and the center of the game.

This game can also be used to review vocabulary by placing pictures in the squares and asking students to provide the Hebrew word, or by writing Hebrew words in the squares that students must read and translate.

Musical Words

Create a deck of ten or more Word Cards. Students sit or stand in a circle and pass the deck around while you play Jewish or Israeli music, such as *Z'man LaShir* and *Shiru Shalom Ivrit*. When the music stops, the student holding the deck must read and translate the top card. If that student cannot do so, the card goes to the next student. Once a student has correctly read and translated the word, he or she puts the card at the bottom of the deck and play continues.

Categories

Create a set of Word Cards with one card per student. Divide the words into categories with two to five words per category. Categories can include "people," "items in the synagogue," or "holiday objects." Categories can also be words that begin with (or contain) the same sound.

Distribute the cards at random, one per student. Tell the students to walk around the room and find everyone whose card is in the same category. You should tell the students what the categories are, especially the first few times you play this game. Once the students have found their groups, redistribute the cards and play again, noting how much more quickly they complete this activity in each successive round. Conclude the game by writing the categories on a set of envelopes and asking the students to place their cards in the correct one.

Beginning, Middle, End

In this game students identify the location of specific sounds within a word. This skill is known as auditory segmentation, and researchers have found that there is a strong correlation between a child's awareness of the sounds in words and later reading achievement.

Take three paper cups. Label one "Beginning," one "Middle," and one "End." Divide the class into two teams. You will also need tokens or plastic chips in two different colors, one for each team. Allow one team to go first. One at a time, students come up. Tell the team what sound they should listen for when you read a Hebrew word. The player must determine if the sound is at the beginning, in the middle, or at the end of the word. Read the word. The student has five or ten seconds to determine where the sound occurs and to place a token or chip in the correct cup. Feel free to repeat the word. If the student is correct, the chip remains in the cup. If the student is incorrect, remove the chip. Repeat until each member of the team has had a turn, then tally up their accumulated tokens or chips. Allow the second team to play in the same manner. You can also alternate turns between teams. The team with the highest score at the end of play wins.

Note: Begin with sounds that occur at the beginning of a word, then progress to those that fall at the end of a word, and only then ask students to determine sounds in the middle of the word. This is especially important the first time you play this game.

Letter Contest/Sound Contest

In this game students are asked to focus on one letter at a time as they hunt for a specific letter or sound inside a paragraph or other text passage.

Give each student a copy of the text passage. Select a letter, especially one that can be confused with other letters that look similar, for example, ר and ד or מ and ט. Ask students to look closely at each letter and circle as many examples of that letter as they can in one minute. When you call time, ask the students to write down the number of examples they found. In order to "win," each student must point out all the letters to you and the class. You can play multiple rounds of this game using different letters. Use a clean copy for each round. Alternatively, you can ask students to find all the examples of letters that make a certain sound, such as *s*, which can be made by ס and שׂ.

Phonics Bingo

For this game you will need to prepare a paper Bingo card for each student, divided into twenty-five squares in five rows and five columns. The center square is free—חָפְשִׁי (pronounced *ḥofshi*). The other twenty-four squares contain C-V and C-V-C syllables composed of letters and vowels that the students have learned. Be sure to write neatly and clearly. Each card may contain the same syllables, but they should be located in different squares. These syllables should also be written on index cards that you will read out to the students. Each student will need a small pile of beans, tokens, buttons, or squares of colored paper to use as Bingo markers.

Distribute Bingo cards and markers to the class. Select an index card and read the syllable written on it. Students should locate the syllable on their cards and place a marker on it. The first student who covers five squares in a row—either vertically, horizontally, or diagonally—calls out "Bingo." He or she must then read the syllables back to you. If the student is correct, he or she wins. This game can also be used to review vocabulary using pictures or written words in the squares on the Bingo cards.

Same or Different?

For this game you will need a pile of cards (or paper strips), each with a line drawn down the middle. Write two letters on a card, one on each side of the line. Some cards can have two of the same letter.

שׂ	שׂ

Other cards can have two different though similar-looking letters.

שׁ	שׂ

Divide the class into two teams. Each team chooses their first player. Hold up a card. The players call out "Same!" or "Different!" The student who calls out the correct answer first collects the card. At the end of play, the team with the most cards wins.

Begin with single letters, then move to two-letter and three-letter words:

שׁם	שׂם
גיר	גור

Note: Since the words contain no vowels, students are simply distinguishing visually between similar letters. They are not decoding the words.

Concentration

Prepare six to twelve pairs of cards. Pairs consist of two items that match, such as a Hebrew letter or vowel and its English sound equivalent, different Hebrew letters or vowels that make the same sound, or a Hebrew word and a picture that illustrates it. Make sure that all of the cards are the same size and color, and that students will not be able to see through them.

Place the cards face down in neat rows on the table. The first player turns two cards over. If they match, the player collects the set and takes another turn. If the cards do not match, the player turns them back over in the same spot, and the next player turns two cards over. Play continues until all the cards have been matched. The winner is the player who has collected the most matches.

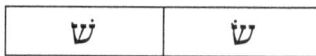

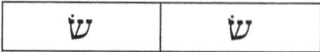

TECHNIQUES FOR STUDENTS WITH SPECIAL LEARNING NEEDS

Children learn and develop differently; no two students will acquire Hebrew decoding skills in exactly the same way. Although students with special learning needs can bring challenges to the classroom, you can serve your students best by recognizing each child's individual strengths. Consult with your religious school director to learn about each student's specific learning needs.

Alef Bet Quest provides a wide variety of learning activities, such as drawing, writing, and puzzles and games, as well as animated online activities and video games that are ideal for all students, including those with learning challenges.

The techniques and modifications listed below, while designed to benefit students with specific learning needs, will be useful for all students:

- Form a bond with your students. Reach out to students before the school year starts by sending home a letter or e-mail or by calling to introduce yourself. Begin the first class with a "get-to-know-you" game. Throughout the year, show a personal interest in students and their lives. Students will learn best in a setting where they feel safe, valued, and respected.
- Complete the review activity at the start of each chapter in *Alef Bet Quest*. This will help you determine if a student is having difficulty with the material from previous lessons. You will be able to catch problems such as students confusing look-alike letters and remediate appropriately through repetition and review.
- Model the correct pronunciation and phrasing for letters, vowels, words, phrases, and then sentences. Repeat several times, and do not assume that all of your students will be able to read the same items fluently and accurately when they see them again later. Repetition is essential for students with special learning needs.
- Use the "Multi-Sensory Approach to Hebrew Phonics" (see page 11) when introducing key words, letters, vowels, and their sounds. Activities that incorporate visual, auditory, and kinesthetic or tactile modes of learning give *all* students a pathway to success using the approach that is most comfortable and effective for them.
- Encourage students to consistently use the *Alef Bet Quest* digital application. These appealing activities provide essential review and practice at students' own pace. By assessing students' progress online, you will be able to see where they are having specific difficulties, enabling you to review the corresponding lesson in class. See "Using the Digital Application" on page 13 for more information.

For students with:

- **Attention problems:** Seat the student close to you. Repeat directions. Privately establish a refocusing system with the student, such as a gentle tap on the shoulder or moving closer to the student's desk. Assist students organizationally, for example, by sending home a sheet with the questions students should answer after completing a lesson on the computer.
- **Auditory processing issues:** Minimize noise and classroom distractions. Have the student repeat sounds and words back to you to ensure correct pronunciation.
- **Visual processing difficulty:** Read written directions aloud. For individual work, allow the student to work with an aide, a *madrich* or *madrichah*, or a classmate who can read directions or listen to the student read aloud. Have the student use an index card to track the line he or she is reading or cover the portion of the page not being worked on.
- **Emotional concerns, such as shyness or lack of self-esteem:** Allow the student to participate in choral reading so he or she does not feel singled out. Assess the student individually to build confidence. Provide matter-of-fact and low-key positive reinforcement to boost self-esteem.
- **Behavioral problems:** Set firm but reasonable expectations. Minimize transitions from one activity to another, and inform students of schedule changes. Maintain a positive relationship with parents through regular contact and open communication. Find out what types of discipline strategies work at home and in secular school and replicate wherever possible.

By providing your students with opportunities to succeed in a nurturing, safe environment, fostering tolerance, and creating a supportive atmosphere, you will help all of them to reach their highest learning potential.

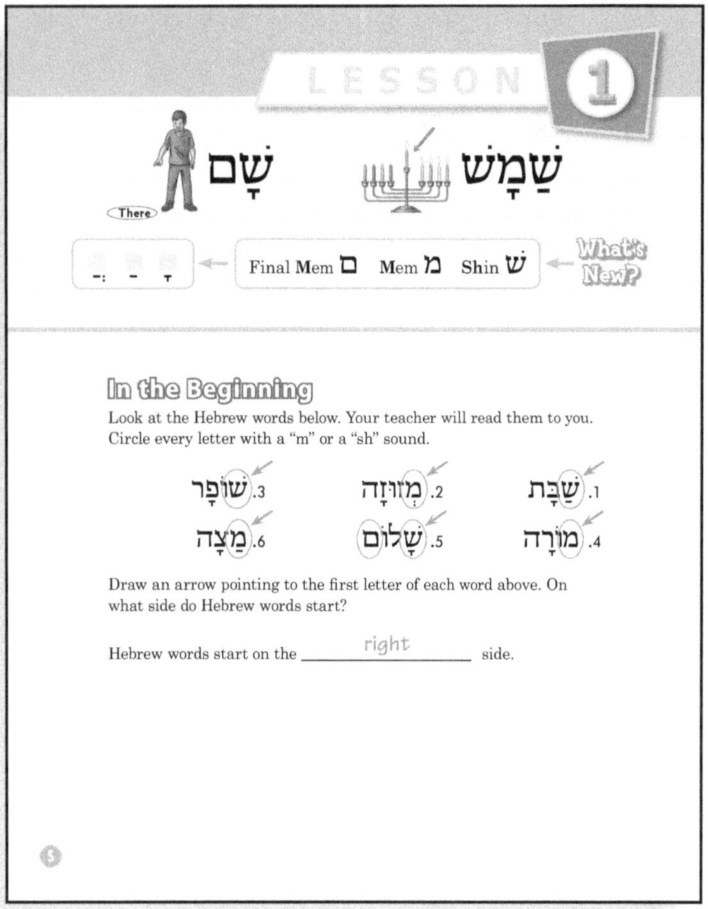
LESSON 1

שָׁם There

שַׁמָּשׁ

Final Mem ם Mem מ Shin שׁ ← What's New?

In the Beginning

Look at the Hebrew words below. Your teacher will read them to you. Circle every letter with a "m" or a "sh" sound.

.1 שַׁבָּת .2 מְזוּזָה .3 שׁוֹפָר

.4 מוֹרָה .5 שָׁלוֹם .6 מַצָּה

Draw an arrow pointing to the first letter of each word above. On what side do Hebrew words start?

Hebrew words start on the ___right___ side.

LESSON 1

Pages: 5–8

Key Words: שָׁם שַׁמָּשׁ

New Letters: ם/מ שׁ

New Vowels: ַ ָ ְ

Recommended Instructional Materials:
Phonics Flash Cards #1–6, Word Cards #1–2, a ḥanukkiyah with candles, several dreidels, tongue depressors or Popsicle sticks, crayons or colored pencils

Oral Language Lesson
(Optional)

If you are using the *Alef Bet Quest Companion Reader* or you want to enrich your program with oral Hebrew, begin the first class with the following lesson. Take attendance, asking student to respond in Hebrew when you call their names. Teach them the following words:

שְׁמִי ___________ שָׁלוֹם פֹּה לֹא פֹּה

If a student is absent, the class can respond:

___________ לֹא פֹּה

Set Induction

Ask students to name the Jewish holidays. When a student names Ḥanukkah, show the class the ḥanukkiyah and ask a volunteer to describe when and how we use it.

Introducing the Key Words and Deducing Their Sound-Symbol Associations

Point to the שַׁמָּשׁ and say: שַׁמָּשׁ. Ask the class to repeat the Hebrew word. Explain that the שַׁמָּשׁ is the "helper" candle because it helps to light all the other candles. Tell the students that both key words in this lesson are important at Ḥanukkah.

Introduce the new sounds, letters, and vowels in שַׁמָּשׁ using the "Multi-Sensory Approach to Hebrew Phonics" described on page 11.

Now introduce the second key word, שָׁם. Demonstrate the meaning of the word by pointing away from you and saying: "Not here, but שָׁם." If you have included the oral Hebrew language lesson, you can point at yourself and then away, saying:

"לֹא פֹּה. שָׁם!"

Hold up a dreidel. Explain that the letter שׁ on the dreidel stands for the Hebrew word שָׁם, because the Ḥanukkah miracle happened "there," in Israel. Pass the dreidels around the class, allowing students to trace the letter שׁ with their fingers.

Teach ם using the same multi-sensory approach described above.

Ask students to turn to page 5 in their textbooks and to point to the key words as you read each one aloud. Circulate to make sure that students identify the correct key word.

In the Beginning

Tell students to look at the two lines of words. Read the first line aloud, asking students to circle every letter that makes a *m* or a *sh* sound. Circulate to make sure that students are completing the task correctly. Write words #1–3 on the board. Ask volunteers to circle the letters on the board that they circled in their books. Repeat this procedure with the second

Letter Hint

There are five Hebrew letters that change shape at the end of a word. They are called "final letters."

The letter מ is one of the letters that has a final form. At the end of a word it looks like a marshmallow: ם

Circle every letter that we find only at the end of a Hebrew word.

ם מ ם שׁ מ ם שׁ מ ם

Word Building

Read these Hebrew syllables out loud.

1. שַׁ שָׁ שַׁ מָ מַ מָ
2. שַׁמָ שָׁשָׁ שַׁמַ מָשַׁ מַמָ מָמַ
3. שָׁם שַׁשׁ מָשׁ שָׁשׁ מַשׁ מַם
4. שַׁ-שָׁם שַׁשָׁם מַ-שָׁם מַשָׁם
5. מַ-מָשׁ מַמָשׁ שָׁ-מַם שָׁמַם
6. מָ-שַׁשׁ מָשַׁשׁ מָ-מַם מָמַם

6

line. Ask students on which side Hebrew words and sentences begin. (*the right*)

Letter Hint

Ask volunteers to read the first two paragraphs. Invite another student to summarize the information for the class.

Allow students to complete the activity. Circulate to make sure that students are completing the work correctly. Ask a volunteer to tell you how many letters they found that can only come at the end of a word. (*four*) As challenge questions, ask the class:

1. Which letter in the row can come anywhere in a word—the beginning, middle, or end? (שׁ)
2. How many examples of that letter did you find in this activity? (*two*)
3. Which letter could come at the beginning and middle, but not the end? (מ)
4. How many examples of that letter did you find in this activity? (*three*)

Word Building

Invite volunteers to read the first three lines. Then call on other students at random to take turns reading these Consonant-Vowel (C-V), Consonant-Vowel-Consonant (C-V-C), and Consonant-Vowel-Consonant-Vowel (C-V-C-V) syllables. Take note of any student who adds an extra vowel at the end of the second consonant of the C-V-C syllables. This is a fairly common problem for beginning Hebrew readers, but one that should be corrected immediately. If there are students in the class that have difficulty with this, ask them how line 2 differs from line 3 (*in line 2, there is a vowel after the second consonant, but in line 3 there is not*), and model the correct reading of these items for them. Repeat until students can successfully blend the second consonant to "close" the syllable.

Lines 4 through 6 contain pairs of words with two syllables. In the first example of each pair, the word is divided into its component syllables. In the second example, the syllables are blended together. Model reading the first pair on line 4, then have partners read lines 4–6 to one another. Ask volunteers to read one pair each. Call on other students until everyone in the class has had the opportunity to read.

I Can Read Hebrew!

Point out to the class that all of these are real Hebrew words and that they can already read two full sentences in Hebrew! *(Line 2: A shamash is there. Line 3: A shamash is really there.)* Highlight the fact that they have learned so much in only one lesson, and celebrate their accomplishment.

Note: Since the goal of *Alef Bet Quest* is decoding, students are not expected to translate the sentences in "I Can Read Hebrew!"

I Can Write Hebrew!

Ask students to trace the letters with their fingers then write the letters in pencil. Review the letter names and sounds as students write them. This provides auditory reinforcement for the visual and kinesthetic activity.

Ask students to write the key words for the lesson. For fun, students can write and illustrate the following sentence on a sheet of paper:

שַׁמָּשׁ שָׁם!

Over the course of several weeks, you can create an "art gallery" by displaying students' illustrations on a bulletin board. You can also invite students to write and illustrate sentences on the board. Students who prefer not to draw can simply write the sentences.

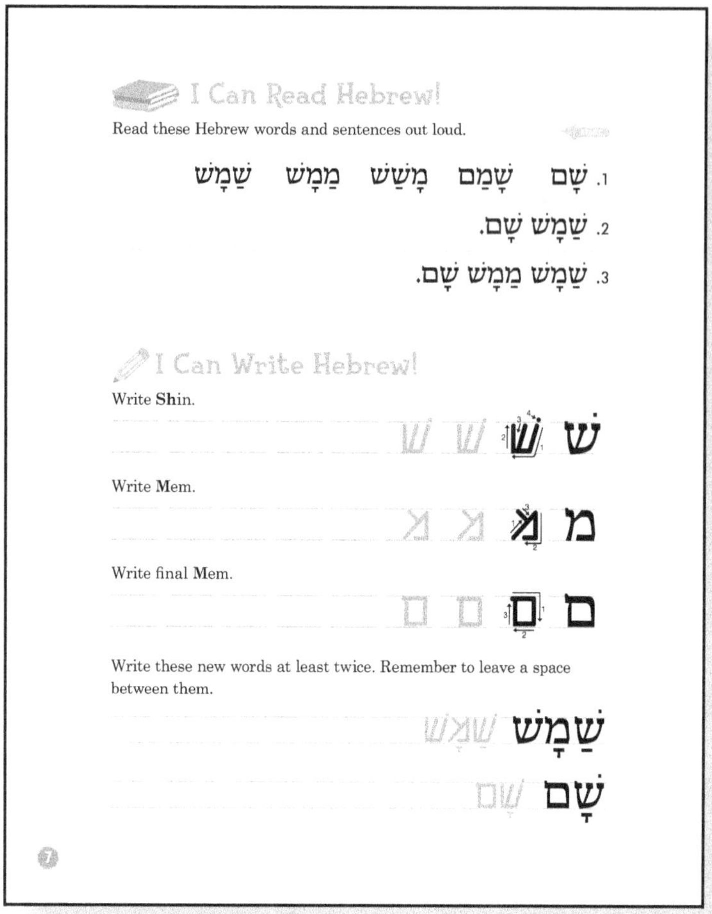
I Can Read Hebrew!

Read these Hebrew words and sentences out loud.

1. שָׁם שָׁמַם מְשַׁשׁ מַמָּשׁ שַׁמָּשׁ
2. שַׁמָּשׁ שָׁם.
3. שַׁמָּשׁ מַמָּשׁ שָׁם.

I Can Write Hebrew!

Write Shin.

שׁ

Write Mem.

מ

Write final Mem.

ם

Write these new words at least twice. Remember to leave a space between them.

שַׁמָּשׁ

שָׁם

7

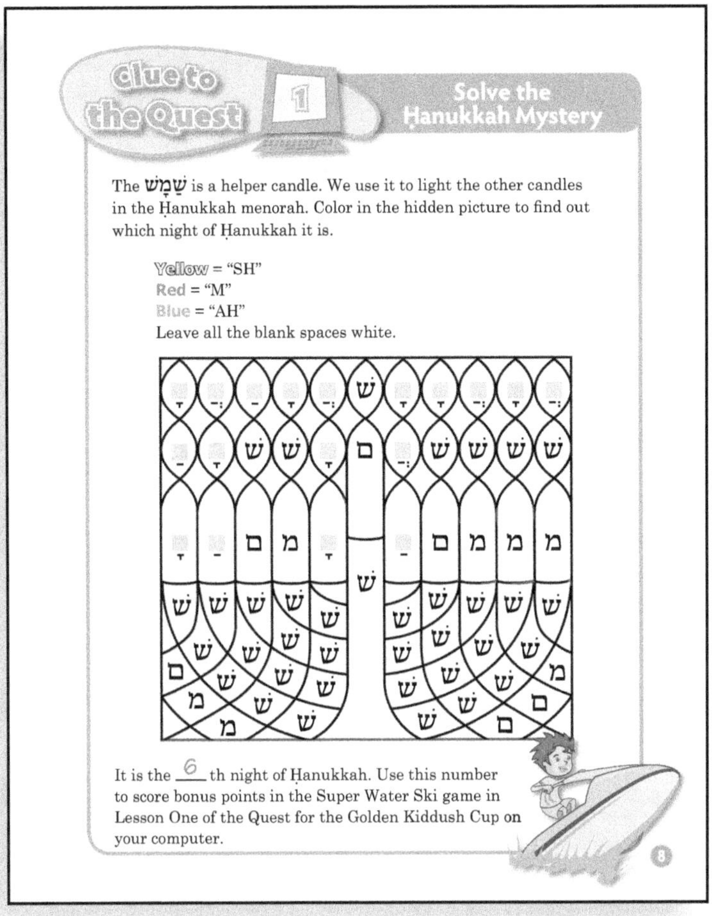
Clue to the Quest 1 Solve the Ḥanukkah Mystery

The שַׁמָּשׁ is a helper candle. We use it to light the other candles in the Ḥanukkah menorah. Color in the hidden picture to find out which night of Ḥanukkah it is.

Yellow = "SH"
Red = "M"
Blue = "AH"
Leave all the blank spaces white.

It is the 6 th night of Ḥanukkah. Use this number to score bonus points in the Super Water Ski game in Lesson One of the Quest for the Golden Kiddush Cup on your computer.

8

Quest for the Golden Kiddush Cup

When students complete this lesson in the digital application, and you have checked that they have done so, in the next class have them color piece #1 on the plate on page 4 of their book. They can also write in the key words and the new letters and vowels for this lesson on piece #1.

Assessment

For information on assessing students' progress, see page 9.

Clue to the Quest: Solve the Ḥanukkah Mystery

Read the directions together. Explain to students that the last page in every lesson contains a puzzle that will help them score bonus points in a game in the digital application. Allow students to color the puzzle in class. Once they have discovered what night of Ḥanukkah it is (6), tell them to look out for flags with that number when they play the Super Water Ski game in the digital application. By driving under those flags, they can score bonus points. Ask students to listen to the introduction and complete Lesson 1 in the digital application at home. You might ask students to print out or e-mail their lesson summaries to you when they have completed all the activities in a lesson.

Challenge students to come to class next time with the answers to the following questions. They can find the answers in the introduction and Lesson 1 of the digital application. Consider sending home a sheet with these questions—and the questions for each lesson in the digital application. Ask students to write the answers on the sheet and return it, with a parent's signature, at the next class.

1. Where do Ben and Batya's grandparents live? *(Jerusalem* or *Israel)*
2. What treasure did Ben and Batya's family once own? (*a golden Kiddush cup*)
3. Where were the clues to the treasure written down? (*on the back of a silver plate*)
4. What happened to the plate? (*it broke*)
5. How many pieces of the plate does the family still have? (*only one*)
6. What is the clue on the first piece of the plate? (*a dolphin*)
7. In what Israeli city do we find Dolphin Reef? *(Eilat)*

LESSON 2

עַם אַבָּא

What's New?

Bet בּ Ayin ע Alef א

Vowels You Know

Letters You Know

מ/ם שׁ

Letter Hint

The letters א and ע do not make any sound of their own. When an א or an ע has a vowel under or next to it, it makes only the sound of the vowel.

9

Oral Language Lesson (Optional)

Review the previous lesson's oral language lesson by saying: אַבָּא פֹּה.

Walk across the room, point to the "father" actor, and say: אַבָּא שָׁם.

Wave to him and say: שָׁלוֹם אַבָּא.

Letter Hint

Invite a volunteer to read the English explanation.

LESSON 2

Pages: 9–12

Key Words: אַבָּא עַם

New Letters: א ע בּ

Recommended Instructional Materials:
Phonics Flash Cards #3–5 and 7–9, Word Cards #1–4, a baby doll, a necktie

Review Activity

Play Tic-Tac-Toe (see page 14 for instructions) using letter and vowel combinations that the students learned in Lesson 1. Place the most difficult combinations, such as C-V-C syllables, in the four corners and the center of the game. Ask students to answer the questions you posed about the digital application at the end of Lesson 1 (see page 20).

Set Induction

Ask students to look at the picture of the man and woman at the bottom of page 9 in their books and to interpret the drawing—without reading the explanation above it. Can students suggest a better way of depicting letters that make no sound? Invite volunteers to draw or act out their suggestions.

Introducing the Key Words and Deducing Their Sound-Symbol Associations

Ask for a boy volunteer. Place the knotted necktie loosely around his neck and ask him to hold the doll as if it were a baby. Present your actor to the class, and say: אַבָּא. Ask students to repeat after you. Point to the picture of the father and say: אַבָּא. Again, have students repeat.

Introduce the new letters using the "Multi-Sensory Approach to Hebrew Phonics" described on page 11.

Next, introduce the second key word, עַם. Ask the students what they see in the picture. (*ancient tribe or people standing at a mountain*)
Help students imagine the mountain as Mount Sinai and the people as the Israelites—the Jewish nation or people.

Super Reading Secret #1

Every syllable has a consonant (letter) and one vowel: בַּ
Some syllables have two consonants and a vowel: עַם
Some words have more than one syllable: אַבָּא

Blend letters and vowels into smooth syllables. Then blend syllables into smooth words. Practice reading these syllables out loud. Circle every syllable in each word:

שַׁמָּשׁ = שַׁ מָּשׁ

1. אָשַׁ אַשׁ אָשַׁם
2. שָׁמַ שָׁם שָׁמַע

Word Building

Read these Hebrew syllables out loud.

1. אַ מָ עַ שָׁ בַּ אָ
2. אַם מָם עַם שָׁם בַּם אָם
3. שָׁ-מַם שָׁמַם שַׁ-שָׁם שַׁשָׁם מַ-בָּם מַבָּם
4. שַׁ-עָשׁ שַׁעָשׁ שַׁ-בָּע שַׁבָּע שָׁ-מַע שָׁמַע
5. שַׁעְם מַעְם עְמַם אְשַׁם בָּאַם מַשָּׁם

10

Word Building

Call on students to read these C-V and C-V-C syllables. Take note of any student who has difficulty blending the second consonant of the C-V-C syllables and provide remediation as necessary.

Once every student has had the opportunity to read the lines, for variety ask students to read the words in each *column*.

Super Reading Secret #1

The ability to separate complex words into their component syllables is known as "syllable segmentation." This "word-attack" skill enables students to break a new, unknown word into its individual components in order to systematically sound it out. Even students who can read C-V and C-V-C syllables with ease often have trouble decoding multi-syllabic words because they cannot break the word down into syllables.

Visual segmentation, in which students break printed words into their component syllables, is a more difficult skill than *auditory* segmentation, in which students analyze spoken words.

Although researchers have not found a definitive reason for this, some speculate that auditory segmentation may involve neurological processes that do not automatically transfer to the analysis of written language. For this reason, you may wish to begin by asking students to clap out the syllables in a variety of words:

מַעְם שַׁבָּע שַׁעְם מַבָּם עַם שָׁם בַּם בָּא

As students clap out the words, ask them to identify the number of syllables contained in each. This activity creates a bridge between auditory and visual segmentation.

Next, display word cards 2 and 4, then 1 and 3 on the chalkboard or whiteboard ledge. Ask students to clap out the syllables for עַם and שָׁם then שַׁמָּשׁ and אַבָּא. Ask students, How many syllables are in the words עַם and שָׁם? (*one*) How many syllables are in the words שַׁמָּשׁ and אַבָּא? (*two*) Next, ask them how many vowels are in the words עַם and שָׁם (*one*), and how many are in the words שַׁמָּשׁ and אַבָּא (*two*). Help students recognize that the emphasis in אַבָּא is on the first syllable and the emphasis in שַׁמָּשׁ is on the second syllable.

Ask a volunteer to read the English explanation. Have students read each Hebrew line quietly to themselves while they circle the syllables in each word. Review as a class.

I Can Read Hebrew!

Point out to the class that all of these are real Hebrew words and that they can now read three more sentences in Hebrew! (*Line 4: Father/Dad is there. Father/Dad heard. Line 5: Father/Dad came.*) Ask students to identify words they know. (אַבָּא, שָׁם) Highlight the fact that they have learned so much, and celebrate their accomplishment.

I Can Write Hebrew!

Ask students to trace the letters with their fingers then write the letters in pencil. Review the letter names and sounds as students write them. This provides auditory reinforcement for the visual and kinesthetic activity.

Ask students to write the key words for the lesson. Students can also write and/or illustrate the following sentences:

אַבָּא שָׁם!

עַם שָׁם!

I Can Read Hebrew!

Read these Hebrew words and sentences out loud.

1. בָּא בָּם עַם שָׁם עָשׁ שַׁמָּשׁ
2. אָשַׁם שָׁמַם עָמַם אָשַׁם עַמָּא עָמַם
3. עַמָּם עָשַׁשׁ שַׁעַם מַבָּע בָּאַשׁ מַבַּע
4. אַבָּא שָׁם. אַבָּא שָׁמַע.
5. אַבָּא בָּא.

I Can Write Hebrew!

Write Alef.

א

Write Ayin.

ע

Write Bet.

בּ

Write these new words at least twice. Remember to leave a space between them.

אַבָּא

עַם

11

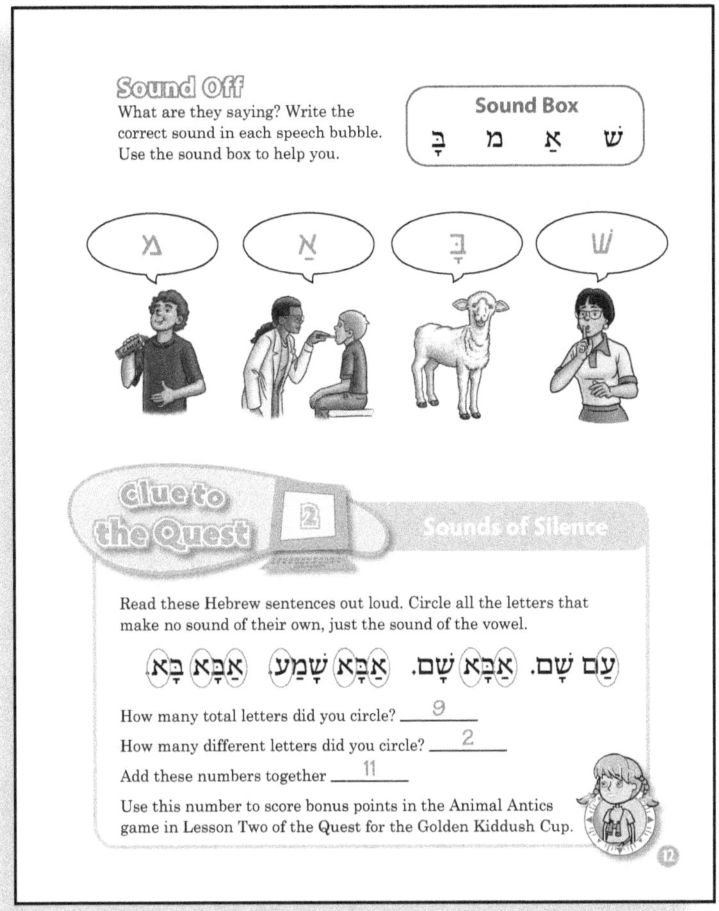

Sound Off

What are they saying? Write the correct sound in each speech bubble. Use the sound box to help you.

Sound Box

שׁ אַ מ בָּ

Clue to the Quest 2 Sounds of Silence

Read these Hebrew sentences out loud. Circle all the letters that make no sound of their own, just the sound of the vowel.

עַם שָׁם. אַבָּא שָׁם. אַבָּא שָׁמַע. אַבָּא בָּא.

How many total letters did you circle? 9

How many different letters did you circle? 2

Add these numbers together 11

Use this number to score bonus points in the Animal Antics game in Lesson Two of the Quest for the Golden Kiddush Cup.

12

Sound Off

Identifying the relationship between a sound and its written symbol (letter and/or vowel) is the most important skill in phonetic decoding. "Sound Off" helps students review the sound-symbol relationships they have learned so far. Circulate among students as they complete this activity individually.

Clue to the Quest: Sounds of Silence

Ask a volunteer to read the directions. Allow students to circle the letters individually then discuss their answers as a class to make sure that each student has the correct total number. (*11*) Ask students to complete Lesson 2 in the digital application at home. You might ask students to print out or e-mail their lesson summaries when they have completed all the activities in the lesson.

In the game for this lesson, Animal Antics, students win points for shooting words that contain the new letters in this lesson. Encourage students to have fun with this fast-paced game that trains them to distinguish specific Hebrew letters.

Challenge students to come to class next time with the answers to the following questions. They can find the answers in Lesson 2 of the digital application.

1. In what desert is Timna Valley Park located? (*the Negev*)
2. What animal did Ben, Batya, and Rachel find there? (*a camel*)

Quest for the Golden Kiddush Cup

When students complete this lesson in their digital application, have them color piece #2 on the plate on page 4 of their book. They can also write in the key words and the new letters for this lesson.

Assessment

For information on assessing students' progress, see page 9.

LESSON 3

שָׁלוֹם אָדֹם

What's New? Lamed ל Dalet ד ← וֹ

Vowels You Know

Letters You Know

א בּ מ/ם ע שׁ

I Can Read Hebrew!

Read these Hebrew words out loud.

1.	עַם	דָם	שָׁם	עַמָם	לָמַד	עָמַד
2.	בַּד	מַד	שָׁדַד	מָדַד	לָעַד	עַד
3.	אַל	דַל	שָׁל	מָל	בַּל	עַל
4.	עָלַל	דָלַל	שָׁאַל	מָעַל	בָּעַל	עַמָל
5.	עֲלַע	בָּלַם	שָׁלַם	בָּלַע	בַּלָשׁ	עָלַם
6.	לָעַד	אָדָם	בַּעַד	בָּדַד	בָּדָל	מָעַד

13

I Can Read Hebrew!

Ask volunteers to read three words on each of the lines. Once students have all had a chance to read, ask students to read whole lines. For variety ask students to read the words in each column.

Oral Language Lesson (Optional)

In this and future lessons, have students use the words פֹּה and לֹא פֹּה when you take attendance. Introduce the word !בּוֹא Whenever possible, use pictures or pantomime to indicate the meaning of the Hebrew, rather than English translation, as this is the most effective way for children to learn a new language. Teach the command !בּוֹא by calling one of the boys up to the front of the room and using a gesture to indicate "come here." Tell students that they have not yet learned all the letters and vowels in the feminine form of !בּוֹא. (!בּוֹאִי)

Introduce the words עוֹלָם and -בַּ/-בָּ. You can show a world map, a picture of the earth, or a globe to introduce the word עוֹלָם. You can put coins or a pencil in a box or cup to teach the prefix -בַּ/-בָּ. Show a picture of people shaking hands or getting along and say: שָׁלוֹם בָּעוֹלָם.

LESSON 3

Pages: 13–16

Key Words: שָׁלוֹם אָדֹם

New Letters: ל ד

New Vowels: וֹ

Recommended Instructional Materials:
Phonics Flash Cards #1–13, Word Cards #5–6, a peace symbol, red crayons, red items such as red paper or a red book, a small paper bag

Set Induction

As students enter the room, greet each one by saying שָׁלוֹם. Ask students if they have ever experienced a day when everything seemed to go well. Invite one or two volunteers to describe their day. Tell students that the word שָׁלוֹם—a key word for today's lesson—is the Hebrew word that describes that sense of wholeness, harmony, and well-being. שָׁלוֹם is so important that we use it as a greeting and as a farewell. When we wish each other שָׁלוֹם, we are wishing one another peace and harmony.

Review Activity

Place Phonics Flash Cards #1–9 in a paper bag. Ask individual students to pull a card from the bag and read the sound printed on it. You may also ask students to name the letters. Ask students to answer the question(s) you posed at the end of Lesson 2 (see page 24).

Introducing the Key Words and Deducing Their Sound-Symbol Associations

Point to the picture of the dove, and say: שָׁלוֹם. Ask the class to repeat the word. Introduce the new letters and vowel using the "Multi-Sensory Approach to Hebrew Phonics" described on page 11. Next, introduce the second key word, אָדֹם. Hold up the red-colored items, saying אָדֹם each time. Ask students to guess the meaning of אָדֹם. Introduce the new sounds, letters, and vowel using the same multi-sensory approach.

Vowel Hint

Here's a good way to remember the sound of the new vowels: וֹ ◌ֹ

When you see a Hebrew vowel that is Over a letter, remember to say "Oh."

I Can Read Hebrew!

Read these Hebrew words and sentences out loud.

1. אוֹ בּוֹ לֹא לָמוֹ עַמוֹ דָמוֹ
2. מוֹל בּוֹשׁ עֹל לוֹד אֹם עוֹד
3. מָלוֹא שָׁלוֹשׁ שָׁלוֹם לָמוֹד עֲמוֹד אָדֹם
4. מֹעַל שׁוֹלַל עוֹלַל מוֹלָד מוֹדָע עוֹלָם
5. אַבָּא שָׁם. אָדָם לֹא שָׁם. שָׁלוֹם אַבָּא.
6. אַבָּא שָׁמַע. אַבָּא בָּא. שָׁלוֹם אָדָם.

14

Vowel Hint

Ask students where they will find the *ah* vowels in Hebrew. (*under the letters*) Tell students that most Hebrew vowels can be found under the letters. The new vowel is different.

Ask a volunteer to read the English passage.

I Can Read Hebrew!

Using the first four lines of "I Can Read Hebrew," ask the class to read just the vowels, without the consonants. Tell them to raise their hands over their heads whenever they read an *oh* vowel. This activity helps train students in the unique directionality of Hebrew reading, which not only requires them to read from right to left, but up and down as well.

This second "I Can Read Hebrew" exercise provides practice with the new vowels in this lesson. Ask volunteers to read three words on each of the first four lines. Once students have all had a chance to read, ask students to read whole lines. For lines five and six, ask them to read full sentences as smoothly and fluently as possible.

Point out to the class that all of these are real Hebrew words, as were those on the previous page, and that they can also read three more sentences in Hebrew! As always, celebrate their accomplishment. *(Line 5: Father/Dad is there. Adam is not there. Shalom Father/Dad. Line 6: Father/Dad heard. Father/Dad came. Shalom Adam.)*

I Can Write Hebrew!

Ask students to trace the letters with their fingers then write the letters in pencil. Review the letter names and sounds as students write them.

Ask students to write the key words for the lesson. Students can also write and/or illustrate the following sentences:

שַׁמָּשׁ אָדָם שָׁם.
שָׁלוֹם אַבָּא!

The "Write" Word

This activity reviews previous vocabulary and provides additional opportunities for students to practice writing. Encourage students to say the letter names (as well as the words) as they write them. This provides auditory reinforcement to the visual information and students' kinesthetic action. Circulate to make sure that students are writing the letters correctly and in the right direction. Make note of any student who is writing from left to right, remind him or her of the direction in which we write Hebrew, and remediate as necessary. For example, you can have students draw an arrow on the right side of the word or use a colored pencil to trace the Hebrew letters from right to left.

I Can Write Hebrew!

Write Lamed.

ל ל ל ל

Write Dalet.

ד ד ד ד

Write these new words at least twice.

שָׁלוֹם שָׁלוֹם

אָדָם אָדָם

The "Write" Word

Write the correct word on the line under each picture.

Word Bank

עַם שַׁמָּשׁ שָׁלוֹם אַבָּא

אַבָּא

שָׁלוֹם

עַם

שַׁמָּשׁ

15

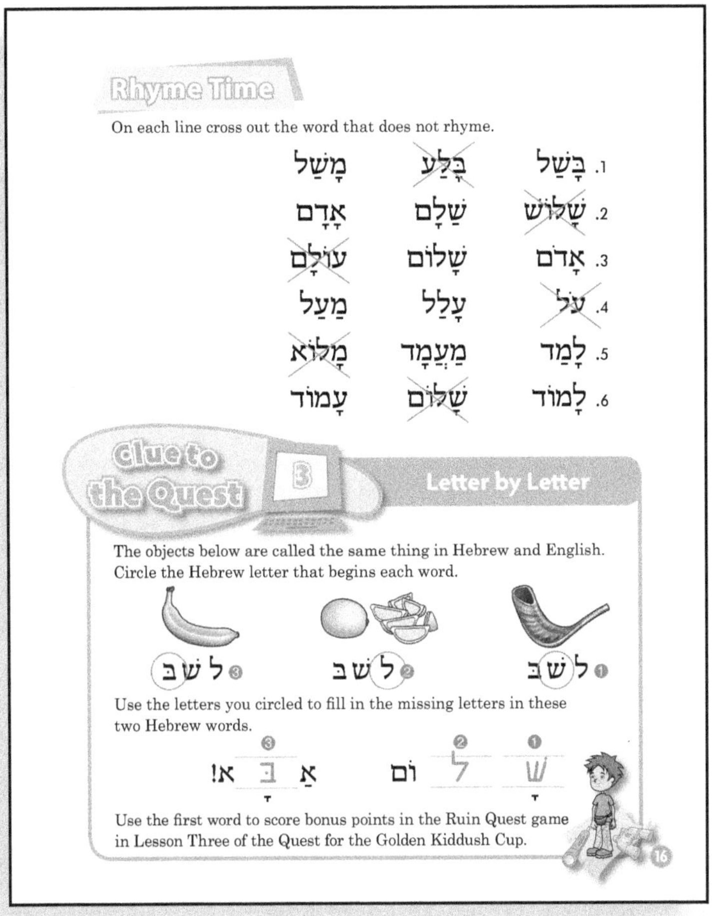

Challenge students to come to class next time with the answers to the following questions. They can find the answers in Lesson 3 of the digital application.

1. What is another name for Lake Kinneret? (*the Sea of Galilee*)
2. What town lies on the shore of Lake Kinneret? (*Tiveria or Tiberias*)

If students print out or e-mail their lesson summary, remind them to do so when they have completed all the activities in this lesson.

Quest for the Golden Kiddush Cup

When students complete this lesson in the digital application, have them color piece #3 on the plate on page 4 of their book. They can also write in the key words and new letters and vowels for this lesson.

Assessment

For information on assessing students' progress, see page 9.

Rhyme Time

Phonological awareness is the sensitivity to and understanding of the sound structure of language. Phonemic awareness, the most sophisticated level of phonological awareness, is the ability to recognize, identify, and manipulate those sounds as they are represented by written symbols. Phonemic awareness is necessary for successfully learning to read any alphabetic language. The positive impact of phonological and phonemic awareness on a child's reading and spelling achievement will endure throughout a child's school years. The ability to hear and identify words that rhyme is one important aspect of phonological awareness because rhyming is the ability to identify words that have identical final sound segments.

Ask a volunteer to read the instructions. Tell the class to listen carefully and ask a second volunteer to read line 1. Ask which two words rhyme. (בָּשַׁל and מָשַׁל) Tell students to cross out the other word (בָּלַע) on line 1 and to work with a partner to complete the remaining lines.

Have students take turns reading the words to their partners and discuss their choices together.

Clue to the Quest: Letter by Letter

Another important aspect of phonemic awareness is the ability to isolate sounds within a word and match those sounds to the letters that represent them. "Letter by Letter" provides practice in this important area.

Ask a volunteer to read the directions. Allow students to circle the letters individually and write their answers in the correct spaces. Ask what Hebrew sentence they wrote. (שָׁלוֹם אַבָּא!)

Ask students to complete Lesson 3 in the digital application at home. In the Ruin Quest game students win points for recognizing and capturing words that contain the new letters for this lesson. They score bonus points for capturing the word שָׁלוֹם.

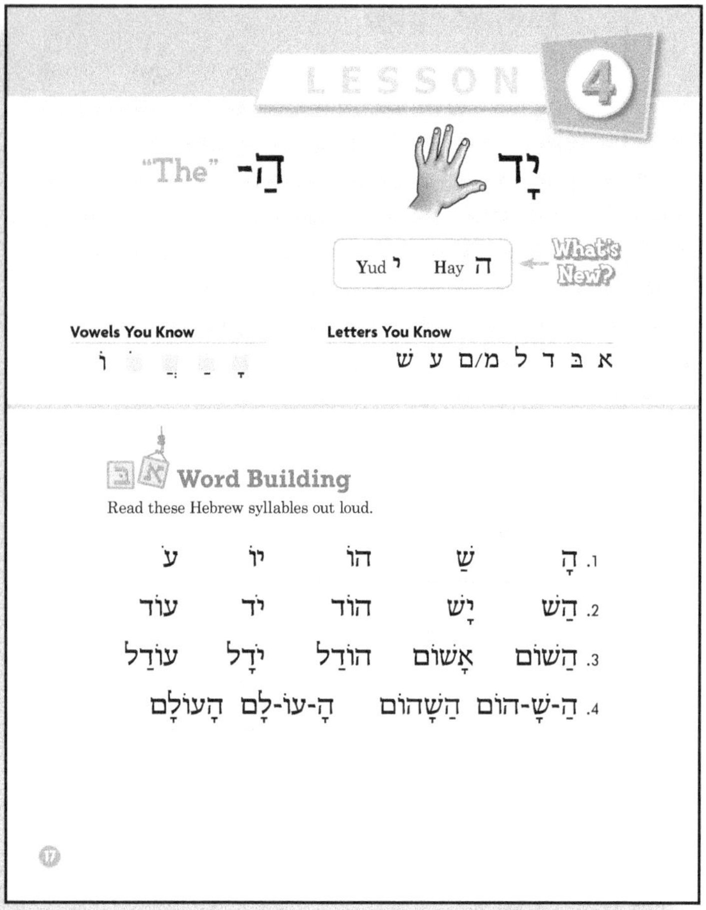

LESSON 4

"The" הַ-

יָד

Yud י Hay ה ← What's New?

Vowels You Know

ָ ַ ֵ ֶ ִ וֹ

Letters You Know

א בּ ד ל מ/ם ע שׁ

Word Building

Read these Hebrew syllables out loud.

1. הָ שַׁ הוֹ יוֹ עֹ
2. הַשׁ יָשׁ הוֹד יָד עוֹד
3. הַשּׁוֹם אָשׁוֹם הוֹדַל יָדַל עוֹדַל
4. הַ-שָׁ-הוֹם הַשָּׁהוֹם הָ-עוֹ-לָם הָעוֹלָם

17

Word Building

Some students have difficulty discriminating between similar sounds such as *ya*, *ha*, and *ah*. This reading drill provides practice in this area.

Ask volunteers to read the first three lines. Repeat until all students have had a turn. Then call on students to read down the columns. Line 4 contains three-syllable words that are segmented, then combined. Ask volunteers to read syllable by syllable and then to blend them smoothly.

Oral Language Lesson (Optional)

Introduce the word עַל by using objects to mime or demonstrate its meaning. Hold up a Ḥanukkah candle and say: שַׁמָּשׁ. Place the candle on top of your open hand. Say: שַׁמָּשׁ עַל הַיָּד, emphasizing the word עַל. Repeat with: הַשַּׁמָּשׁ עַל הַיָּד.

Place your hand on top of the candle. Say: הַיָּד עַל הַשַּׁמָּשׁ. Have students repeat the activity. Introduce the word דָּג by showing a picture of a fish or drawing one on the board.

LESSON 4

Pages: 17–20

Key Words: יָד הַ-

New Letters: י ה (Voiced)

Recommended Instructional Materials:
Phonics Flash Cards #4–5, 11, and 14–15; Word Cards #1–8; a Torah pointer (יָד)

Review Activity

Place Word Cards # 1–6 randomly on the chalkboard or whiteboard ledge.

1. Point to the words and pronounce them one at a time with the class repeating. Repeat with all the words.
2. Next, ask a volunteer to come up, point to a word, and read it. If the student is correct, the class should repeat it. If the class is silent, the student should try to self-correct. Repeat until every student has had at least one turn.

Set Induction

Hold up your hand and say: יָד. The class should repeat the word. Invite students to hold up a hand and say: יָד. Repeat several times until you are confident that the students understand the word. Next, show them a Torah pointer. Explain that to avoid smudging the writing in a Torah scroll, we do not touch it directly with our fingers. Instead we point to the words with a special pointer called a יָד. Ask students how they think the Torah pointer got its name. (*it is shaped like a hand; it takes the place of your hand*) Pass the pointer around the class and allow students to feel its shape.

Introducing the Key Words and Deducing Their Sound-Symbol Associations

Introduce the new sounds and letters using the "Multi-Sensory Approach to Hebrew Phonics" described on page 11. Tell students that the key word הַ- means "the," and it is always attached to the beginning of the word it is specifying.

Same Sound

Circle the syllable in each line below that makes the same sound as the syllable on the right.

1. הַ	אָ	הֹ	אֹ	עֹ	עַ	הָא
2. עַ	אֹ	הַ	יֹ	אֲ	הֹ	עֹ
3. הֹ	אָ	הֹ	אֹ	עֹ	יֹ	יָ

I Can Read Hebrew!

Read these Hebrew words and sentences out loud.

1. יָם יוֹם יוֹמָם יָד יָדוֹ יַעֲמֹד
2. הָלַם הֲדֹם הֲלוֹם הוֹד הֲלֹא הוֹדוֹ
3. בֹּהַל שֹׁהַם מָהוֹד הֲדוֹם לַהֲמֹם יַהֲלוֹם
4. הַיָם יַעַל הַיוֹם הָאָדָם הָעוֹלָם הַשָׁלוֹם
5. הַיָד עַל הַשַׁמָשׁ.
6. שָׁלוֹם עַל הָעוֹלָם.

18

Same Sound

This activity provides students with additional practice in differentiating between similar sounds. Allow students to complete it individually. Suggest that they read each syllable aloud but quietly. Have students check one another's work.

I Can Read Hebrew!

Ask volunteers to read three words on each of the first four lines. Once students have all had a chance to read, ask them to read whole lines. If you are also completing the oral language lesson, students will be able to understand the sentences in lines 5 and 6. (*Line 5: The hand is on the shamash/helper candle. Line 6: Peace is on the world.*)

I Can Write Hebrew!

Ask students to trace the letters with their fingers then write the letters in pencil. Review the letter names and sounds as students write them.

Ask students to write the key words for the lesson. Students can also write and/or illustrate the following sentences:

הַשַּׁמָּשׁ עַל הַיָּד.
שָׁלוֹם עַל הָעוֹלָם!

Sound Check

The ability to hear and identify homonyms (words that sound the same) is an important aspect of phonemic awareness because it demonstrates the reader's ability to associate sounds with all of the symbols that can represent them. This activity asks students to identify and match Hebrew homonyms.

Allow students to work with partners in completing this activity. You may choose to assign stronger readers to work with weaker readers. Ask the first partner to read the first word in the right-hand column aloud. The second student should scan the words in the left-hand column and identify the match, point to it, and read it aloud. If both partners agree, they should connect the words. If they do not, they should work together to find the correct answer. They should repeat this procedure with the second word, switching roles, and continue, alternating, until the activity is complete. Circulate to see if anyone needs assistance.

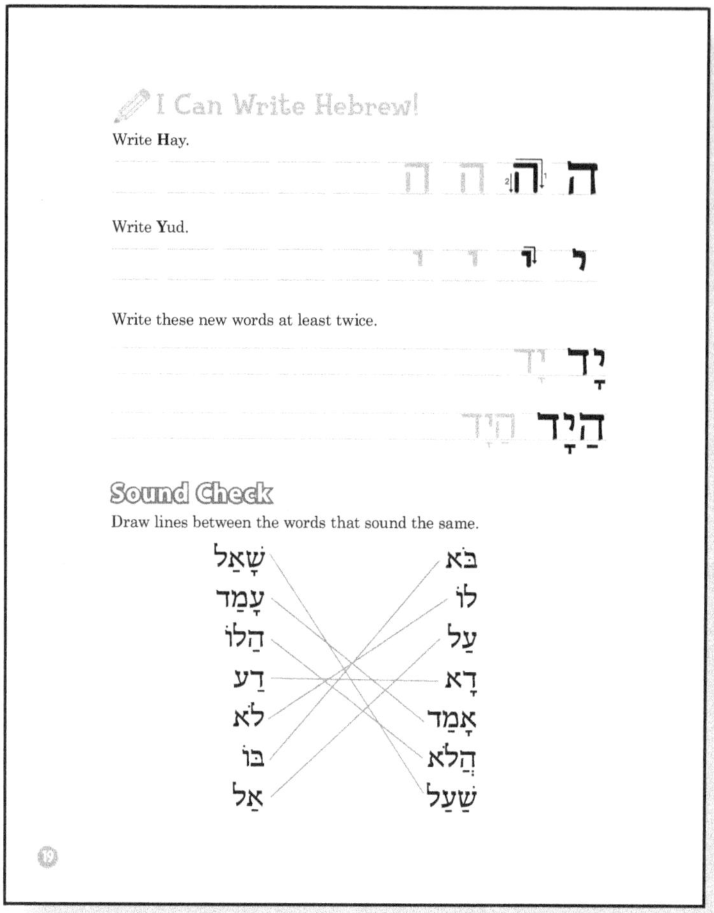
I Can Write Hebrew!

Write Hay.

ה ה ה ה

Write Yud.

י י י י

Write these new words at least twice.

יָד יָד

הַיָּד הַיָּד

Sound Check

Draw lines between the words that sound the same.

שָׁאַל	בָּא
עָמַד	לוֹ
הֲלוֹ	עַל
דַע	דָא
לֹא	אָמַד
בּוֹ	הֲלֹא
אַל	שַׁעַל

19

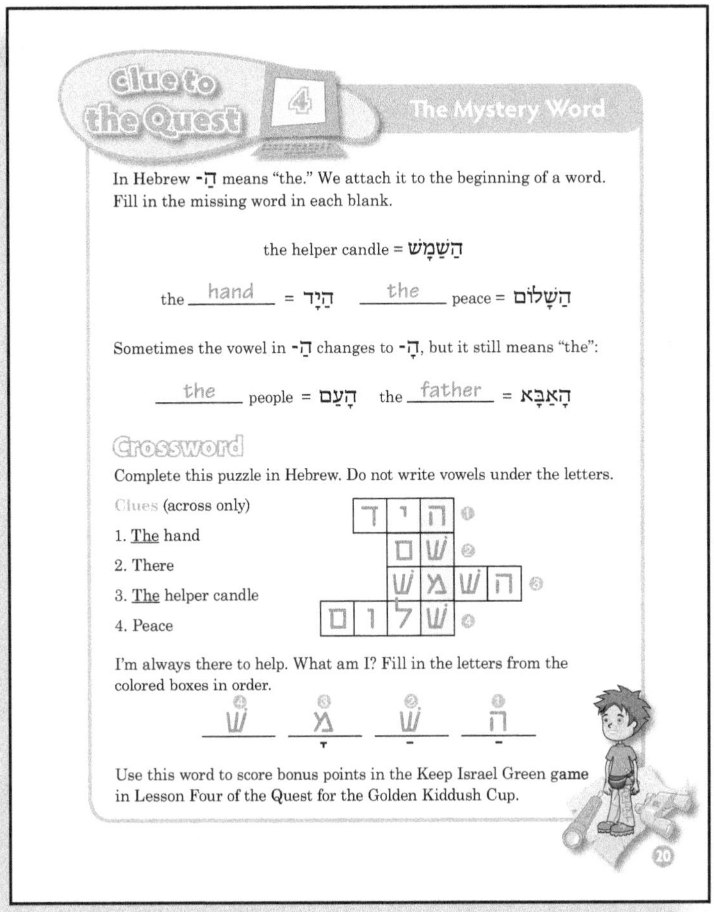

Clue to the Quest 4 The Mystery Word

In Hebrew -הַ means "the." We attach it to the beginning of a word. Fill in the missing word in each blank.

the helper candle = הַשַּׁמָּשׁ

the hand = הַיָּד the peace = הַשָּׁלוֹם

Sometimes the vowel in -הַ changes to -הָ, but it still means "the":

the people = הָעָם the father = הָאַבָּא

Crossword

Complete this puzzle in Hebrew. Do not write vowels under the letters.

Clues (across only)

1. The hand
2. There
3. The helper candle
4. Peace

1. הַיד
2. שם
3. השמש
4. שלום

I'm always there to help. What am I? Fill in the letters from the colored boxes in order.

הַשַּׁמָּשׁ

Use this word to score bonus points in the Keep Israel Green game in Lesson Four of the Quest for the Golden Kiddush Cup.

20

Clue to the Quest: The Mystery Word

The crossword puzzle reviews several key words from the previous lessons and gives students practice in using the Hebrew definite article, -הַ. When the prefix is added to a word that begins with an א or an ע, the vowel changes and it becomes -הָ, but it still sounds the same, and it still means "the."

Ask a volunteer to read the directions, then fill in the blanks as a class. Allow students to work independently to complete the crossword puzzle. Circulate to provide assistance as needed and to make sure that students are completing the puzzle correctly. Students can use the answer word (הַשַּׁמָּשׁ) to score bonus points in the "Keep Israel Green" game in Lesson 4 on the digital application.

Challenge students to come to class next time with the answers to the following questions. They can find the answers in Lesson 4 of the digital application.

1. What is the name of Israel's largest waterfall? (*the Gamla*)
2. In what region of Israel is it found? (*the Golan Heights*)

If students print out or e-mail their lesson summaries, remind them to do so when they have completed all the activities in this lesson.

Quest for the Golden Kiddush Cup

When students complete this lesson in their digital application, have them color piece #4 on the plate on page 4 of their book. They can also write in the key words and the new letters for this lesson.

Assessment

For information on assessing students' progress, see page 9.

LESSON 5

שֶׁמֶשׁ גֶשֶׁם

What's New? Gimel ג ◌ֱ ◌ֶ

Vowels You Know

Letters You Know
א ב ד ה י ל מ/ם ע ש

Vowel Hint

A triangle of three dots under a Hebrew letter makes the sound of "Eh." This vowel looks like three little Eggs in a nest!

A set of five dots under a Hebrew letter also makes the sound of "Eh." This vowel looks like five little Eggs in a nest!

21

Oral Language Lesson (Optional)

Draw a snowman and snow on the board and a boy and introduce the words שֶׁלֶג (snow) and יֶלֶד (boy). Incorporate the words into sentences such as:

אָדָם יֶלֶד. הַיֶלֶד בַּשֶׁלֶג. אָדָם בַּשֶׁלֶג.
שֶׁלֶג בַּיָד.

Introduce the word שֶׁל ("of" or "belonging to"). You can incorporate this word into phrases such as: הַדָג שֶׁל אָדָם אַבָּא שֶׁל אָדָם.

You can also remind students of blessing phrases that contain the word שֶׁל:

נֵר שֶׁל שַׁבָּת נֵר שֶׁל חֲנֻכָּה
נֵר שֶׁל יוֹם טוֹב

LESSON 5

Pages: 21–24

Key Words: גֶשֶׁם שֶׁמֶשׁ

New Letter: ג

New Vowels: ◌ֱ ◌ֶ

Recommended Instructional Materials: Phonics Flash Cards #1–18, Word Cards #9–10, paper napkins, a bag of jelly beans or candy buttons or grapes

Review Activity

To review the letters and vowels that students have learned so far, play "Around the World" using Phonics Flash Cards #1–15. (See page 14 for complete directions.)

Set Induction

Draw a sun on one end of the board and a cloud with raindrops on the other end. Use your drawings to introduce the key words (גֶשֶׁם, שֶׁמֶשׁ). Allow students to take turns being "weather forecasters" describing the weather using the new key words.

Introducing the Key Words and Deducing Their Sound-Symbol Associations

Introduce the new sounds, letter, and vowels using the "Multi-Sensory Approach to Hebrew Phonics" described on page 11.

Vowel Hint

Distribute paper napkins to the students and ask them to crumple them into the shape of a nest.

Distribute the candy buttons, jellybeans, or grapes, and ask students to arrange three of them into a triangle that points down (◌ֶ).

Ask a volunteer to read the explanation in the book. Allow the students to eat the candy or grapes, saying *eh* before they eat each piece. Repeat to create the other vowel (◌ֱ). Remind students that both vowels make the same sound (*eh*).

I Can Read Hebrew!

Read each of these Hebrew words out loud.

1. גַג דָג לֹג עָג גוֹד עוֹג
2. שָׁגַג דַאָג גָדֹל לָעַג דָגוֹ עָגֹל
3. גַם גָמָל גַל גָד אָגַד עָגַל
4. גָלַם לָגַם גָלַל לַהַג גָלַד גָאַל
5. אֲגַם דָגַל הַגָדוֹל בָּגַד גָמַד גָדוֹל

Sound Advice

The objects below have the same name in Hebrew and English. Cross out all the objects that do not begin with the new letter ג.

22

I Can Read Hebrew!

The first reading selection in this chapter focuses on the new letter, ג. Ask volunteers to read three examples in a row on each line. Once every student has had the opportunity to read, ask them to read full lines, then full columns. Since one of the goals of the Hebrew reading program is for students to read whole passages, encourage students to read multiple words each time they read in class.

Sound Advice

The ability to separate words into their component speech sounds (or phonemes) is known as phonemic segmentation. Reading researchers have found that there is a strong correlation between a child's awareness of the sounds in words and later reading achievement. In fact, this skill is one of the best predictors of reading success.

This activity provides students with practice in segmenting the initial phoneme of several words using cognates (words that are the same in both Hebrew and English). Because it is easier to isolate the initial sound of a word, this first activity focuses on initial phonemes. At the same time, some students have difficulty making fine auditory distinctions. The sounds *g* and *k* are similar, and some students confuse them. This activity provides students with practice in making this fine auditory distinction. If a student struggles with this activity, it may indicate that he or she has difficulty making fine auditory distinctions and may need additional practice in this area.

Have students complete the activity individually, then review together.

I Can Read Hebrew!

This second reading passage focuses on the *eh* vowel. In lines 1–4, the third and sixth words rhyme. Ask volunteers to read three words at a time then full lines.

Lines 5–8 are all real sentences *(Line 5: Adam is a big boy. Line 6: A big fish is in the ocean. Line 7: Snow is in Adam's hand. Line 8: A big flag is in father's hand.)* Challenge students to read these lines smoothly and fluently. If you are also completing the oral language lesson, students will be able to understand many of the words in these sentences.

I Can Write Hebrew!

Ask students to trace the letters with their fingers then write the letters in pencil. Review the letter names and sounds as students write them.

Ask students to write the key words for the lesson. Students can also write and/or illustrate the following sentences:

הַשֶּׁמֶשׁ עַל הָעוֹלָם.

גֶשֶׁם שָׁם.

I Can Read Hebrew!

Read these Hebrew words and sentences out loud.

1. דֶגֶל שֶׁלֶג בֶּגֶד גֶלֶם שֶׁמֶשׁ אֶגֶד
2. מֶגֶד דֶגֶם יֶלֶד גֶשֶׁם אֶמֶשׁ שֶׁלֶד
3. אֹהֶל גֹדֶל גֹלֶם גֹדֶשׁ גֹמֶד אֹדֶם
4. אֶל אֶלָּא שֶׁלֹא אֱיָל אֱיָלוֹ שֶׁלוֹ
5. אָדָם יֶלֶד גָדוֹל.
6. דָג גָדוֹל בַּיָם.
7. שֶׁלֶג בַּיָד שֶׁל אָדָם.
8. דֶגֶל גָדוֹל בַּיָד שֶׁל אַבָּא.

I Can Write Hebrew!

Write Gimel.

ג ג

Write these new words.

גֶשֶׁם

שֶׁמֶשׁ

23

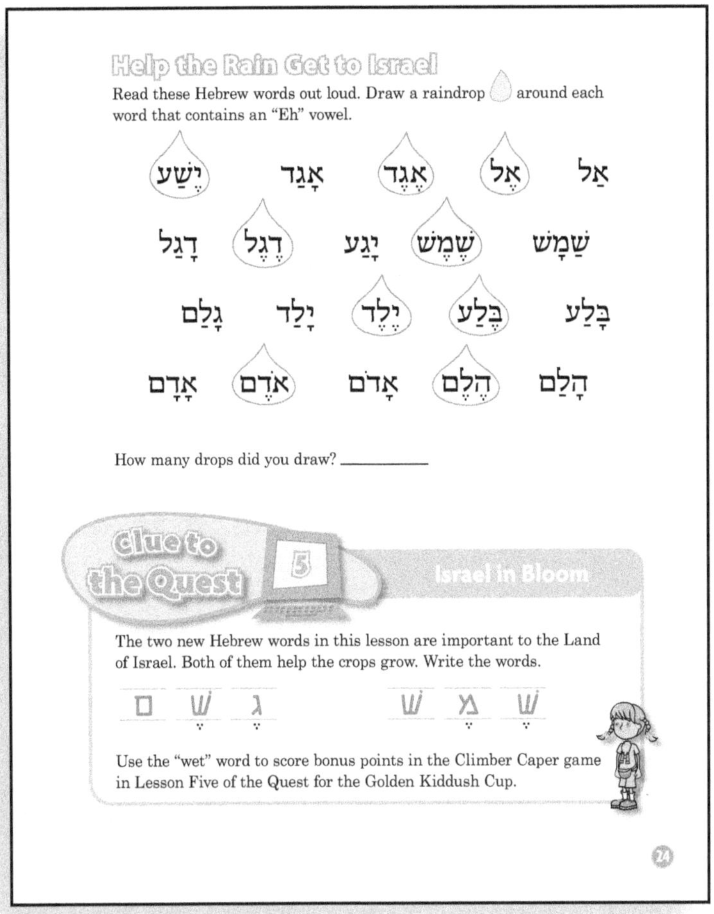
Help the Rain Get to Israel

Read these Hebrew words out loud. Draw a raindrop around each word that contains an "Eh" vowel.

אַל אֶל אֶגֶד אָגַד יֶשַׁע

שַׁמָּשׁ שֶׁמֶשׁ יָגַע דֶּגֶל דָּגַל

בָּלַע בֶּלַע יֶלֶד יָלַד גָּלַם

הָלַם הֶלֶם אָדֹם אֹדֶם אָדָם

How many drops did you draw? ________

Clue to the Quest 5 Israel in Bloom

The two new Hebrew words in this lesson are important to the Land of Israel. Both of them help the crops grow. Write the words.

ג ש ם   ש מ ש

Use the "wet" word to score bonus points in the Climber Caper game in Lesson Five of the Quest for the Golden Kiddush Cup.

24

Assessment

For information on assessing students' progress, see page 9.

Help the Rain Get to Israel

This activity requires students to focus on minor visual distinctions (ֶ ָ). It also gives them practice in identifying the sound of the new vowel (*eh*). Ask a volunteer to read the directions.

Have students complete the activity with a partner, taking turns reading the words aloud to one another.

Clue to the Quest: Israel in Bloom

In this activity students review the key words from this lesson, as well as their meanings. Ask a volunteer to read the instructions. Students can complete this activity individually or with a partner.

Ask students to complete Lesson 5 in the digital application at home. In the "Climber Caper" game that accompanies this lesson, students win points for recognizing and capturing words that contain the new vowels. This provides additional practice in making fine visual distinctions.

They score bonus points by using the clue word. (גֶשֶׁם)

Challenge students to come to class next time with the answers to the following questions. They can find the answers in Lesson 5 of the digital application.

1. What temple is located in Haifa? (*the Bahai Temple*)
2. In what city can you find the "best falafel" in Israel? (*Haifa*)

If students print out or e-mail their lesson summaries, remind them to do so when they have completed all the activities in this lesson.

Quest for the Golden Kiddush Cup

When students complete this lesson in their digital application, have them color piece #5 on the plate on page 4 of their book. They can also write in the key words and the new letter and vowels for this lesson.

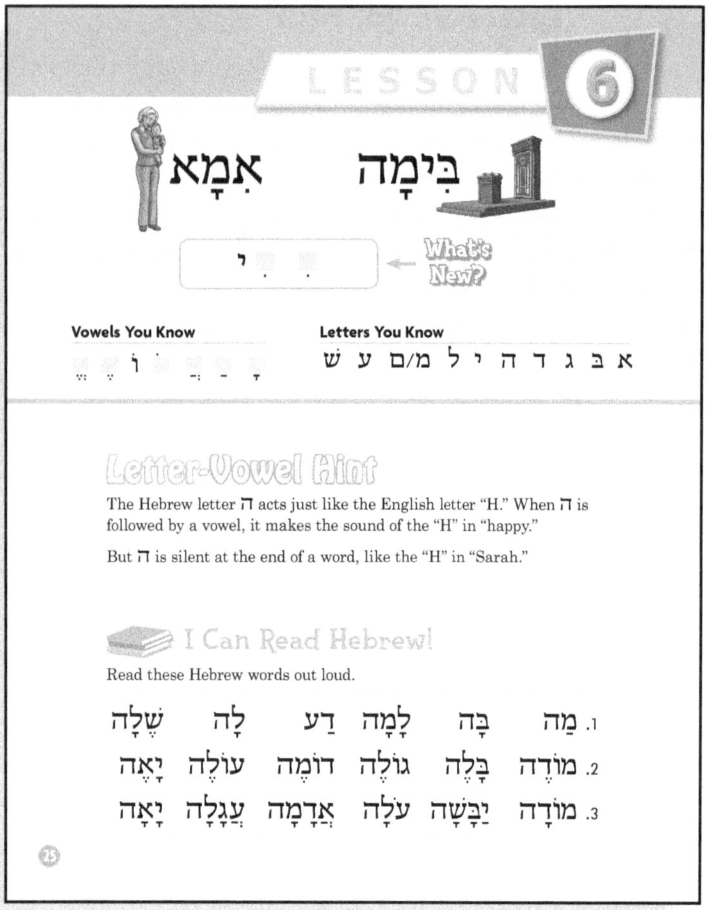
LESSON 6

אִמָּא בִּימָה

What's New?

◌ִ ◌ִי

Vowels You Know

◌ָ ◌ַ ◌ֲ ◌ֶ ◌ֱ וֹ ◌ֹ ◌ֵ ◌ֶ

Letters You Know

א ב ג ד ה י ל מ/ם ע שׁ

Letter-Vowel Hint

The Hebrew letter ה acts just like the English letter "H." When ה is followed by a vowel, it makes the sound of the "H" in "happy."

But ה is silent at the end of a word, like the "H" in "Sarah."

I Can Read Hebrew!

Read these Hebrew words out loud.

1. מַה בָּה לָמָּה דַע לָה שֶׁלָּה
2. מוֹדֶה בָּלֶה גוֹלֶה דוֹמֶה עוֹלֶה יָאֶה
3. מוֹדָה יַבָּשָׁה עֹלָה אֲדָמָה עֲגָלָה יָאָה

25

LESSON 6

Pages: 25–29

Key Words: בִּימָה אִמָּא

New Vowels: ◌ִ ◌ִי

Recommended Instructional Materials: Several sets of cards containing מ ◌ֶ ◌ֱ וֹ א ע ◌ָ ◌ַ ◌ֲ ם, Phonics Flash Cards #2, 4, 7, 9, 14, and 19–20, Word Cards #11–12, a cardigan sweater, a baby doll, a tie

Review Activity

Play "Concentration" (see page 15 for instructions). Divide the class into groups of up to four students. Distribute cards with ◌ָ ◌ַ ◌ֲ ם מ ◌ֶ ◌ֱ וֹ א ע

Set Induction

Write the following English words on the board: *happy, oh, honey, Sarah.* Call on a volunteer to read the words. Ask the class to tell you if the letter *h* in each is sounded out as a consonant or if it is sounded as part of the vowel. Next, write these words on the board: *yes, playmate, yarn, key, you, journey.* Ask the class to tell you if the letter *y* in each is sounded out as a consonant or if it is sounded as part of the vowel. Tell students that, just like English, Hebrew has two letters that act just like *h* and *y* in these examples.

Introducing the Key Words and Deducing Their Sound-Symbol Associations

Consider taking students to the sanctuary to stand on the *bimah.* Introduce the key word בִּימָה and use it to introduce the new vowel using the "Multi-Sensory Approach to Hebrew Phonics" described on page 11.

Next, introduce the second key word, אִמָּא. Ask for a girl to volunteer. Drape the cardigan sweater over her shoulders and ask her to hold the doll as if it were her own baby. Present your actor to the class and say: אִמָּא. Have students repeat the word.

Letter-Vowel Hint

Allow students to read the information silently, then ask volunteers to explain it in their own words.

I Can Read Hebrew!

Invite students to read three words at a time and then to read the columns of words. Line 2 highlights the fact that ה can help any vowel, not just ◌ָ.

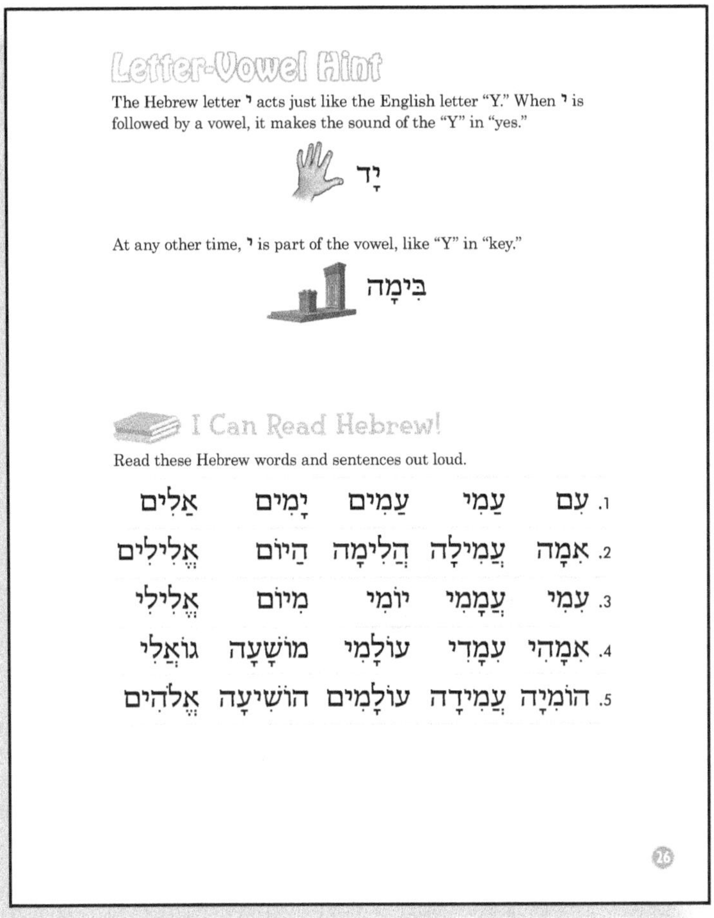

Letter-Vowel Hint

The Hebrew letter י acts just like the English letter "Y." When י is followed by a vowel, it makes the sound of the "Y" in "yes."

יָד

At any other time, י is part of the vowel, like "Y" in "key."

בִימָה

I Can Read Hebrew!

Read these Hebrew words and sentences out loud.

1. עִם עַמִי עַמִים יָמִים אַלִים
2. אִמָה עֲמִילָה הֲלִימָה הַיוֹם אֱלִילִים
3. עִמִי עֲמָמִי יוֹמִי מִיוֹם אֱלִילִי
4. אִמָהִי עִמָדִי עוֹלָמִי מוֹשָׁעָה גוֹאֲלִי
5. הוֹמִיָה עֲמִידָה עוֹלָמִים הוֹשִׁיעָה אֱלֹהִים

26

Letter-Vowel Hint

Allow students to read the information silently, then ask volunteers to explain it in their own words.

Ask students to create statements about how they can tell when ה and י are sounded consonants and when they help the vowels. For example, students may say: ה or י is a sounded consonant when it is immediately followed by a vowel. When ה or י is not followed by a vowel, it helps the vowel.

I Can Read Hebrew!

This second reading selection focuses on the letter י as a consonant or as part of a vowel. Ask students to read individual words then whole lines. For variety, you can also ask students to read whole columns of words.

Note that all of lines 4 and 5, as well as part of lines 2 and 3, contain three-syllable words. By this point, most of the class should be able to read these longer words. Take note of students who are having difficulty with multi-syllable words and provide additional practice as necessary.

Sound Bite

It can be difficult for early readers to determine when the letters ה and י are acting as sounded consonants or are helping the vowel. The "Sound Bite" activity provides students with practice in this important skill.

Ask students to complete this activity independently. Circulate around the room to provide assistance as needed and to make sure that students are completing this activity correctly.

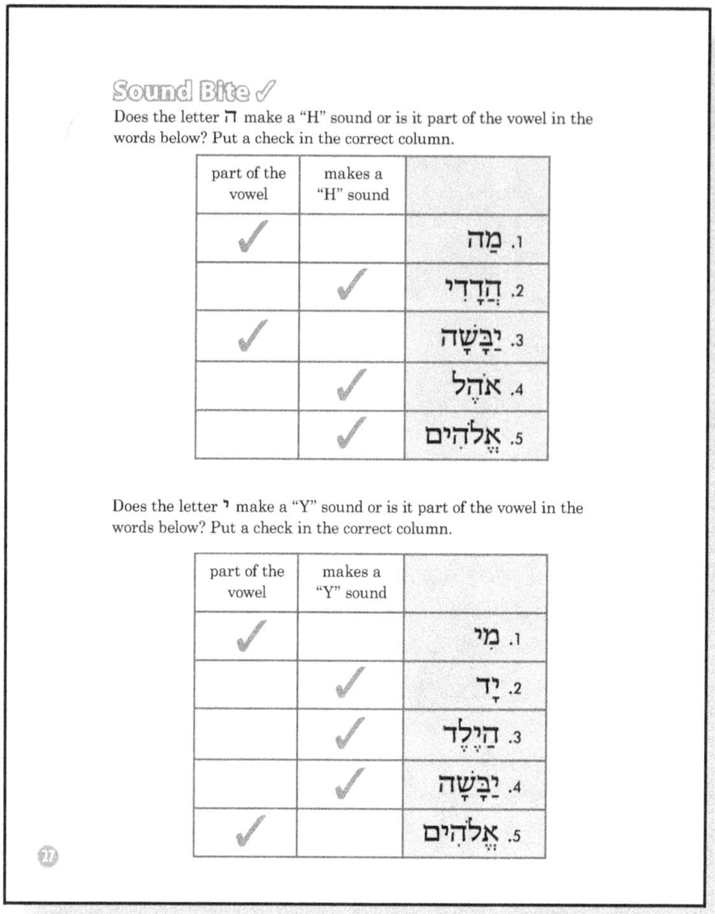

Sound Bite ✓

Does the letter ה make a "H" sound or is it part of the vowel in the words below? Put a check in the correct column.

part of the vowel	makes a "H" sound	
✓		1. מַה
	✓	2. הֲדָרִי
✓		3. יַבָּשָׁה
	✓	4. אֹהֶל
	✓	5. אֱלֹהִים

Does the letter י make a "Y" sound or is it part of the vowel in the words below? Put a check in the correct column.

part of the vowel	makes a "Y" sound	
✓		1. מִי
	✓	2. יָד
	✓	3. הַיֶּלֶד
	✓	4. יַבָּשָׁה
✓		5. אֱלֹהִים

27

Oral Language Lesson
(Optional)

Introduce the question word מִי and the third person feminine pronoun הִיא.

Point to various girls in the class and say: הִיא, followed by the student's name (הִיא דִינָה; הִיא סוּזָן; הִיא גֶ'ן).

Then ask: מִי הִיא?

You may need to provide the answer at first, but encourage the students to respond.

Invite volunteers to take the roles of אִמָּא and אַבָּא. Use the props associated with אִמָּא and אַבָּא (necktie, sweater, and doll) to indicate their roles.

Point to אִמָּא and say:

מִי הִיא? הִיא אִמָּא.

Point to אַבָּא and say:

מִי זֶה? זֶה אַבָּא.

Although students have not learned ז, teach them זֶה orally.

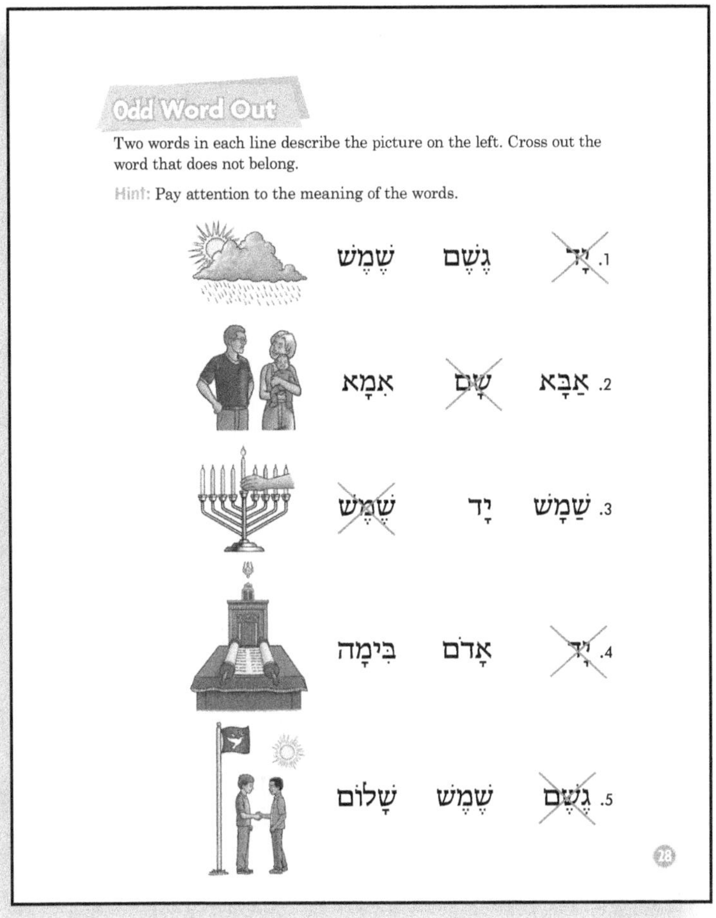
Odd Word Out

Two words in each line describe the picture on the left. Cross out the word that does not belong.

Hint: Pay attention to the meaning of the words.

1. יָד גֶּשֶׁם שֶׁמֶשׁ
2. אַבָּא שָׁם אִמָּא
3. שַׁמָּשׁ יָד שֶׁמֶשׁ
4. יָד אָדָם בִּימָה
5. גֶּשֶׁם שֶׁמֶשׁ שָׁלוֹם

28

Odd Word Out

This activity reviews ten of the twelve key words that students have learned so far. Allow students to work with a partner to complete the activity. One partner should read the three words out loud. The other should point to the two things found in the picture and name them in Hebrew. The first partner should then read the word for the item that was not found, and both should cross out that item. Repeat, with students alternating roles for each line.

Circulate around the room to provide assistance as needed.

Just for Fun

Ask students to write and illustrate one of the following sentences on a sheet of paper:

1. אִמָּא שָׁם.
2. אִמָּא עַל הַבִּימָה.
3. אַבָּא עַל הַבִּימָה.

Add the drawings to your bulletin board.

Clue to the Quest: Going Up to the Bimah

Ask a volunteer to read the instructions. Tell the class to listen carefully and ask a second volunteer to read line 1 (on the bottom step). Ask which word does not rhyme with the others. (מִיָד) Tell students to cross out that word. Allow students to work with a partner to complete the remaining lines. Students should take turns reading the words to their partners and can discuss their choices together. Circulate to provide assistance as needed and to make sure that students are completing the page correctly.

When all the pairs have completed the page, ask what number they got. (*18*) Tell them that with this number they will score bonus points in the "Super Water Ski" game when they ski under the banner that has the number 18 on it. They score regular points by skiing under the banners that contain the Hebrew letter י.

Challenge students to come to class next time with the answers to the following questions. They can find the answers in Lesson 6 of the digital application.

1. Which biblical prophet hid in a cave in Haifa? (*Elijah*)
2. About how many years ago did Elijah live? (*three thousand*)

If students print out or e-mail their lesson summaries, remind them to do so when they have completed all the activities in this lesson.

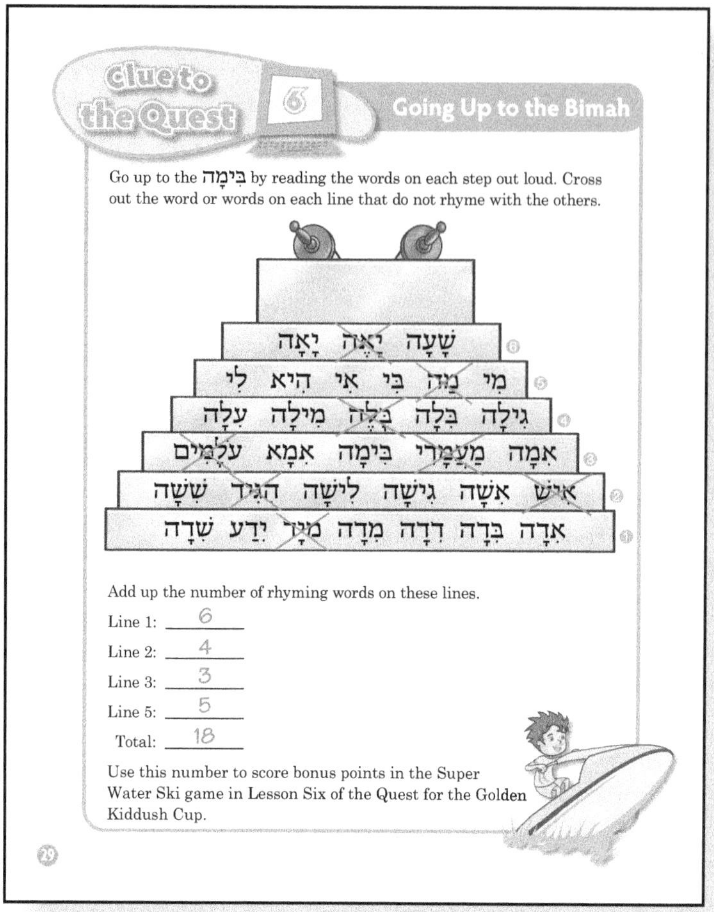
Clue to the Quest 6 Going Up to the Bimah

Go up to the בִּימָה by reading the words on each step out loud. Cross out the word or words on each line that do not rhyme with the others.

6 שָׁעָה יָאֶה יָאָה
5 מִי מַדּוּ בִּי אִי הִיא לִי
4 גִילָה בִּלָה בְּלֵה מִילָה עָלָה
3 אִמָּה מַעֲמָרִי בִּימָה אִמָּא עֹלָמִים
2 אִישׁ אִשָּׁה גִישָׁה לִישָׁה הִגִּיד שִׁשָּׁה
1 אִדָה בְּדָה דִדָה מִדָה מִיָד יַדַע שִׂדָה

Add up the number of rhyming words on these lines.

Line 1: 6
Line 2: 4
Line 3: 3
Line 5: 5
Total: 18

Use this number to score bonus points in the Super Water Ski game in Lesson Six of the Quest for the Golden Kiddush Cup.

29

Quest for the Golden Kiddush Cup

When students complete this lesson in their digital application, have them color piece #6 on the plate on page 4 of their book. They can also write in the key words and the new vowels for this lesson.

Assessment

For information on assessing students' progress, see page 9.

LESSON 7

מַצָה מִיץ

Final TZadi ץ TZadi צ ← What's New?

Vowels You Know

Letters You Know

א בּ ג ד ה י ל מ/ם ע שׁ

I Can Read Hebrew!

Read these Hebrew words out loud.

1. צַד מִצַד צֶדַע צִידָה בָּצַע יָצָא
2. צַעַד מָצָא צֶמֶד דִיצָה בָּצָל יוֹצִיא
3. צָם מוֹצָא יָצָא צִדִי בֹּץ הוֹצָאָה
4. צָמָא יָמָה צַמָה צִבַּע בִּצָה הִצִילָה
5. צוֹם הַיוֹם עֲצוֹם צָעוֹד מָצוֹא צָלוֹל

30

I Can Read Hebrew!

This reading selection drills the new letter צ in the initial and medial positions within a word, using all of the vowels that students have learned so far. Ask volunteers to read the words in each line, two at a time. Once students have had a few turns at reading individual words, ask them to read full lines, then full columns.

LESSON 7

Pages: 30–34

Key Words: מַצָה מִיץ

New Letters: ץ צ

Recommended Instructional Materials:
Phonics Flash Cards #2, 4–5, 14, and 20–22, Word Cards #1–14, a box of matzah, a container of juice and cups for the class

Review Activity

Play "Musical Words" (see page 14 for instructions) using Word Cards #1–12. Ask students to read and translate the words.

Set Induction

Ask students to tell the class what they know about Passover. (*Answers may include: it celebrates our freedom from slavery in Egypt, we have a seder, we eat matzah instead of bread.*) If the students do not mention Passover foods, ask them to describe the special foods we eat and drink at the seder. (*matzah, parsley, bitter herbs, four cups of wine or juice*) Tell students that the key words for this lesson are two things we eat and drink at the seder.

Introducing the Key Words and Deducing Their Sound-Symbol Associations

Introduce the key word מַצָה by holding up a piece of matzah and saying the word. Have students repeat after you. Encourage the proper pronunciation (*mah-tzah*). Once every student can identify the word, distribute and allow students to eat a small piece of matzah.
Introduce the key word מִיץ in the same way, providing cups of juice to students as they ask for it in Hebrew. Teach students to say: מִיץ, בְּבַקָשָׁה (*juice, please*). Introduce the new sounds and letters using the "Multi-Sensory Approach to Hebrew Phonics" described on page 11.

I Can Read Hebrew!

This reading selection reviews צ in the initial and medial positions of a word as well as in the final position (ץ). Ask the students to read lines 1–3 three words at a time. Once they have all had turns, ask them to read complete lines, and include line 4 as well.

Lines 5 and 6 contain complete sentences. Ask students to read these sentences as smoothly and fluently as possible. (*Line 5: Adam is in the play. Gila is in the play. Line 6: The play is on the stage.*)

I Can Write Hebrew!

Ask students to trace the letters with their fingers, then to write the letters in pencil. Review the letter names and sounds as students write them.

Ask students to write the key words for the lesson. Students can also write and/or illustrate the following sentences:

הַמִּיץ אָדֹם!

הַמַּצָּה שָׁם!

Oral Language Lesson

(Optional)

Introduce the question word מַה?.

Point to various objects (or pictures of objects) that the students have learned in Hebrew, and ask:

מַה זֶה?

Students answer, for example:

זֶה מִיץ. זֶה שׁוֹפָר. זֶה שַׁמָּשׁ.

Be sure to ask the question so that only masculine nouns are required in the answer.

Once students are completely comfortable with the word מַה?, review the question word מִי?.

Use these two question words to review all of the nouns that students have learned so far.

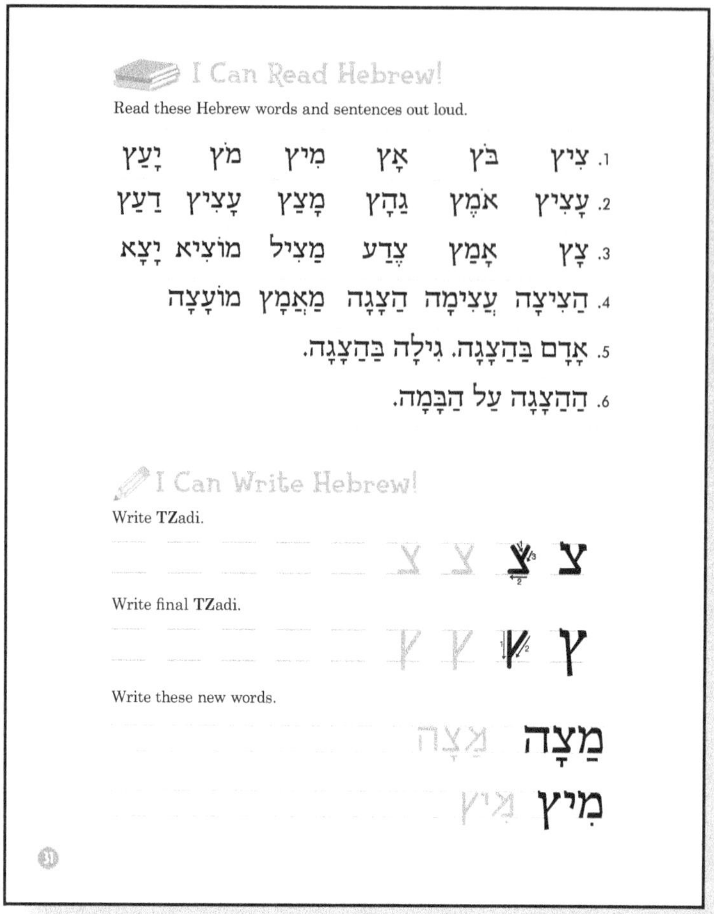

I Can Read Hebrew!

Read these Hebrew words and sentences out loud.

1. צִיץ בֹּץ אָץ מִיץ מֹץ יָעַץ
2. עָצִיץ אֹמֶץ גַּהָץ מָצַץ עָצִיץ דַּעַץ
3. צָץ אָמַץ צֶדַע מַצִּיל מוֹצִיא יָצָא
4. הַצִּיצָה עֲצִימָה הַצָּגָה מַאֲמָץ מוֹעָצָה
5. אָדָם בַּהַצָּגָה. גִּילָה בַּהַצָּגָה.
6. הַהַצָּגָה עַל הַבָּמָה.

I Can Write Hebrew!

Write TZadi.

צ

Write final TZadi.

ץ

Write these new words.

מַצָּה

מִיץ

31

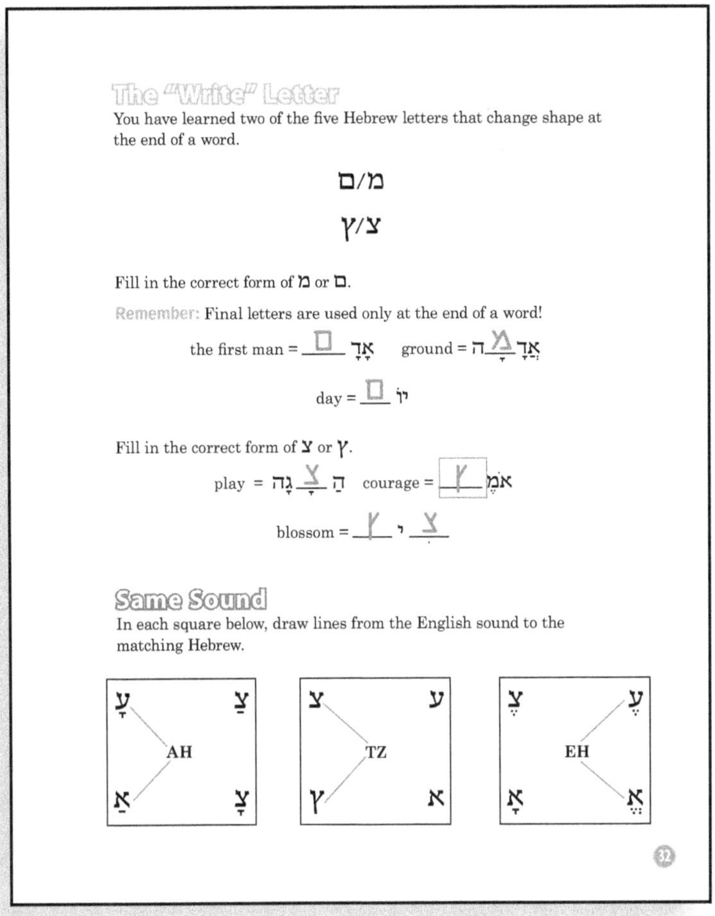

The "Write" Letter

You have learned two of the five Hebrew letters that change shape at the end of a word.

מ/ם

צ/ץ

Fill in the correct form of מ or ם.

Remember: Final letters are used only at the end of a word!

the first man = אָדָם   ground = אֲדָמָה

day = יוֹם

Fill in the correct form of צ or ץ.

play = הַצָּגָה   courage = אֹמֶץ

blossom = צִיץ

Same Sound

In each square below, draw lines from the English sound to the matching Hebrew.

The "Write" Letter

In this activity students practice writing the regular and final forms of two letters they have learned. Writing provides kinesthetic reinforcement for visual information, so practicing the dual forms in isolation should help students remember them.

Ask a volunteer to read the information at the top of the page. Complete the ם/מ section together as a class. Then ask students to complete the ץ/צ individually. Circulate among students to provide assistance as needed.

Same Sound

The center square reviews the new letters for this lesson. The other two squares review vowel pairs that represent identical sounds. All three squares challenge students to make fine visual distinctions between the צ and the ע.

Have students complete the activity individually. Review together.

Sound Check

This activity asks students to identify and match Hebrew homonyms. In keeping with the Passover theme of this lesson, one version of each pair can be found in the Kiddush cup, while the other is in one of the drops spilled while reciting the Ten Plagues.

Allow students to work with partners in completing this activity. You may choose to assign stronger readers to work with weaker readers. Ask the first partner to read aloud from the words in the Kiddush cup, beginning with the first word in the right-hand column (הִיא). The second student should scan the words in the drops on the right side of the cup and identify the match, point to it, and read it aloud. If both partners agree, they should draw a line to connect the words.

If they do not, they should work together to find the correct answer. They should repeat this procedure with the second word, switching roles, and continue, alternating, until they complete the activity.

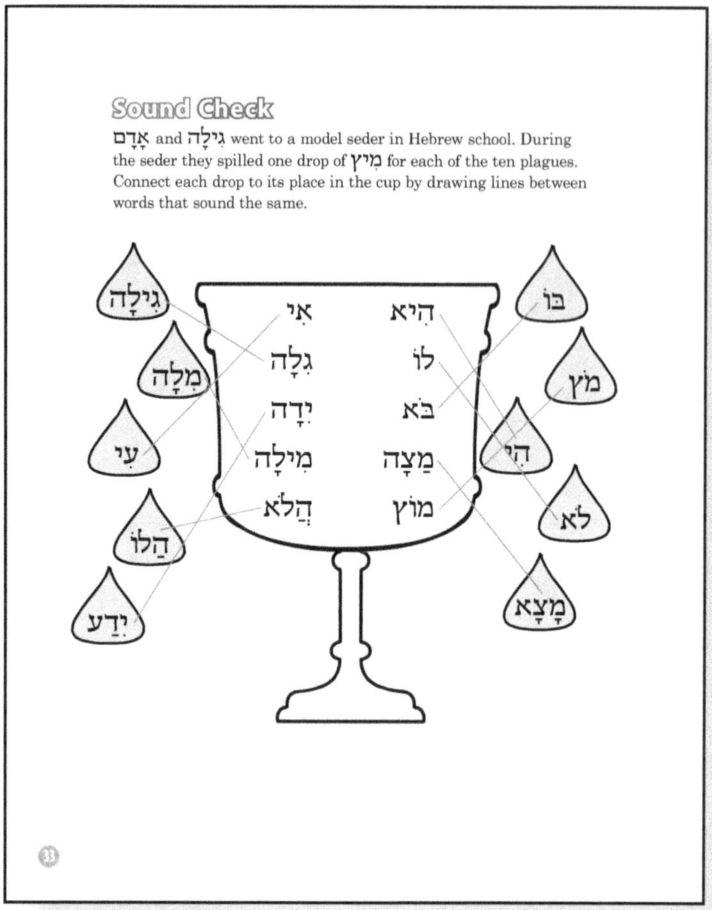

Assessment

For information on assessing students' progress, see page 9.

If students have difficulty pronouncing the צ in the initial position, for example, if they substitute either a *z* or *s* sound, have them read the following English words, noting the differences between the *ts*, *z*, and *s* sounds.

since	cats	blintz	sits
visits	bar Mitzvah	bat Mitzvah	sheets
picks	Bessie	Betsy	bass
zoo	pizza	buzz	blaze
itsy bitsy	Mitsubishi	tsunami	tsetse fly

Clue to the Quest: Reading Riddle

"Reading Riddle" allows students to review key words and to use individual letters from those words to create a new word. That new word provides an answer to a riddle. Since the theme of this lesson is Passover, the Reading Riddle here also centers on the Passover seder. Students are asked to name the book that everyone reads at the table. (הַגָּדָה)

Ask a volunteer to read the instructions at the top of the page. Allow students to work individually or with a partner to complete the page. Circulate to provide assistance as necessary. Students can use the answer to score bonus points in the "Animal Antics" game in the digital application.

Challenge students to come to class next time with the answers to the following questions. They can find the answers in Lesson 7 of the digital application.

1. Which desert city do Ben, Batya, and Rachel visit? (*Be'ersheva*)
2. What kind of מִיץ does Ben like best? (*orange*)
3. What kind of מִיץ does Batya like best? (*cranberry*)

If students print out or e-mail their lesson summaries, remind them to do so when they have completed all the activities in this lesson.

Quest for the Golden Kiddush Cup

When students complete this lesson in their digital application, have them color piece #7 on the plate on page 4 of their book. They can also write in the key words and the new letters for this lesson.

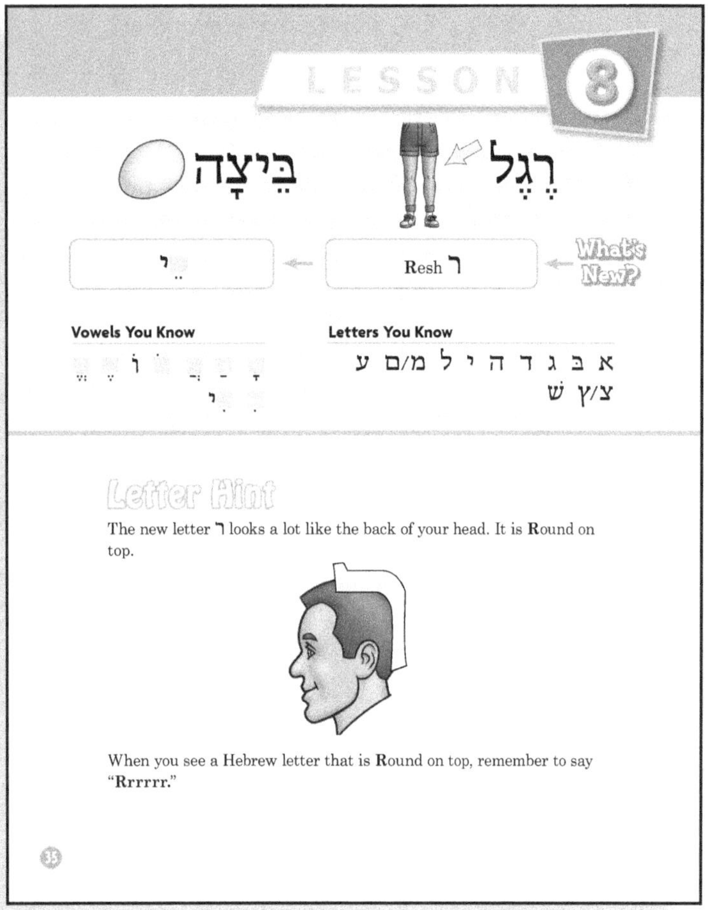

Introducing the Key Words and Deducing Their Sound-Symbol Associations

Have students stand on one leg. Introduce the key word רֶגֶל and use it to introduce the new letter using the "Multi-Sensory Approach to Hebrew Phonics" described on page 11.

Next, have students turn back to the illustration of the nests and eggs on page 21. Introduce the key word בֵּיצָה and use it to introduce the new vowel using the same approach.

Letter Hint

Like the Vowel Hint in Lesson 5, this Letter Hint provides students with a mnemonic. Mnemonics are especially helpful for students who are good auditory learners, as the auditory information helps them to remember the visual cue, which is more difficult for them to process.

Ask a volunteer to read the information. You can add a nice tactile or kinesthetic association by allowing students to feel the round shape of the backs of their own heads.

LESSON 8

Pages: 35–39

Key Words: רֶגֶל בֵּיצָה

New Letter: ר

New Vowel: ֵי

Recommended Instructional Materials: **Phonics** Flash Cards #4, 9–10, 14, 16–17, 21, and 23–24, Word Cards #1–16, three paper cups (one labeled "Beginning," one "Middle," and one "End"), tokens or plastic chips in two different colors

Review Activity

Play "Beginning, Middle, End" (see page 14 for instructions). Tell students to pay attention to where the target sound falls within each word. Use the following words for each target sound.

צ: צְדָקָה מַצָּה מִיץ צֶדֶק בֵּיצָה פִּיצָה

מ: שָׁם מַצָּה שֶׁמֶשׁ מְזוּזָה אִמָּא תַּלְמִיד

ג: גֶשֶׁם שֶׁלֶג הַגָּדָה גְלִידָה רֶגֶל דָג גוֹרִילָה

ר: גִּיר רֶגֶל עֶרֶב בֹּקֶר יִשְׂרָאֵל שׁוֹפָר רַבָּה

Set Induction

Write or display the following letters on the board: א בּ ג ד ה י ל מ ע שׁ ם צ ץ Ask students if they have ever looked at the clouds and thought that they looked like recognizable shapes. Ask students to look at these letters the same way. Allow a minute of concentrated silence, then ask volunteers what shapes they see in these Hebrew letters. For example: מ looks like a mountain; ד looks like a door. Encourage students to associate the letter with a word beginning with the same sound (a mnemonic or "aid to memory").

I Can Read Hebrew!

Read each of these Hebrew words out loud.

1. צַבָּר גָּהַר שָׁמַר יָשַׁר עֲצוֹר אֲדָר
2. רַבָּה רֹאשׁ רָמָה רַעַל רֶגֶל גּוֹרָל
3. בּוֹר אוֹר מֹר שׁוֹר צוֹר דוֹר
4. גִּבּוֹר מָאוֹר שָׁמוֹר מִשּׁוֹר לִיצוֹר מִדּוֹר
5. בָּרֹד אֶרֶץ מָרוֹם שֶׁרֶץ מֶרֶץ דָּרוֹם
6. מָהִיר אֲשֶׁר שָׁמִיר שַׁעַר הָדָר אַדִּיר

What's in a Name?

The Hebrew *alef bet* comes from the first alphabet ever invented. These first letters were pictures of everyday items. The letters got their names from the words they pictured. For example, the letter י comes from the Hebrew word יָד. The letter ר comes from רֹאשׁ. The letter מ comes from מַיִם.

Finish the picture. Make the ר into a person's head.

ר

36

Oral Language Lesson (Optional)

Introduce three classroom words מוֹרֶה מוֹרָה גִּיר and the command בּוֹאִי!

Teach the command בּוֹאִי! by calling one of the girls up to the front of the room and using a gesture to indicate "come here." Alternate by calling boys up with the command בּוֹא!

You should also review the question words introduced in the previous two lessons, using questions and answers such as:

מִי מוֹרֶה? אַבָּא מוֹרֶה. מִי הִיא? הִיא מוֹרָה.

מַה זֶה? זֶה גִּיר.

You can also review previous vocabulary (such as שֶׁל עַל בַּ־ הַ־):

הַגִּיר בַּיָּד. אַבָּא שֶׁל אָדָם מוֹרֶה.

I Can Read Hebrew!

In this first reading selection students practice the new letter ר. Lines 1, 3, 4, and 6 provide practice with the new letter in the final position of the word. With the exception of the last word, line 2 provides exposure to the new letter in the first position, and also requires students to differentiate between the sounds *r* and *l*, sounds with which some students have difficulty. Line 5 provides practice with ר in the middle of a word, the most difficult position from which to extrapolate and analyze speech sounds.

Ask students to take turns reading individual words, then groups of three words, then full lines.

What's in a Name?

This activity refers to the historical development of the Hebrew alphabet. Examples of the original Semitic alphabet, from which many alphabets derive, were discovered in the Sinai desert and in Israel. The inscriptions date to about 1500 BCE. The letter symbols were highly pictographic and were derived from Egyptian hieroglyphic signs—with one important difference.

In the Egyptian system of hieroglyphics, each individual symbol stood for either a full word or a syllable. In the Semitic system, each symbol stood for a single consonant sound, and that sound was the first one in the name of the object pictured. The ר, for example, was drawn as a person's head and stood for the sound *r*, the first in the Hebrew word רֹאשׁ. Similarly, the letter ב was a picture of a house, and it stood for the sound *b*, which is the first sound in the Hebrew word for house, בַּיִת.

Ask a volunteer to read the information, then discuss the examples, and ask students to complete the drawing activity individually.

I Can Read Hebrew!

This second reading passage focuses on the new vowel taught in this chapter. Lines 1 and 2 focus on the use of the vowel in the final position of the word, while lines 3 and 4 focus on its use in the initial or medial vowel positions, which are more difficult. Ask volunteers to read three words at a time then full lines.

Lines 5 and 6 contain actual sentences, two per line, and should be read as full sentences. Challenge students to read them as smoothly as possible. (*Line 5: Rami lives in the city. Rami lives in the apartment. Line 6: Shira is a teacher. She lives in the apartment.*)

I Can Write Hebrew!

Ask students to trace the letters with their fingers then write the letters in pencil. Review the letter names and sounds as students write them.

Ask students to write the key words for the lesson. Students can also write and/or illustrate the following sentences:

יָד עַל רֶגֶל.
בֵּיצָה עַל מַצָּה.

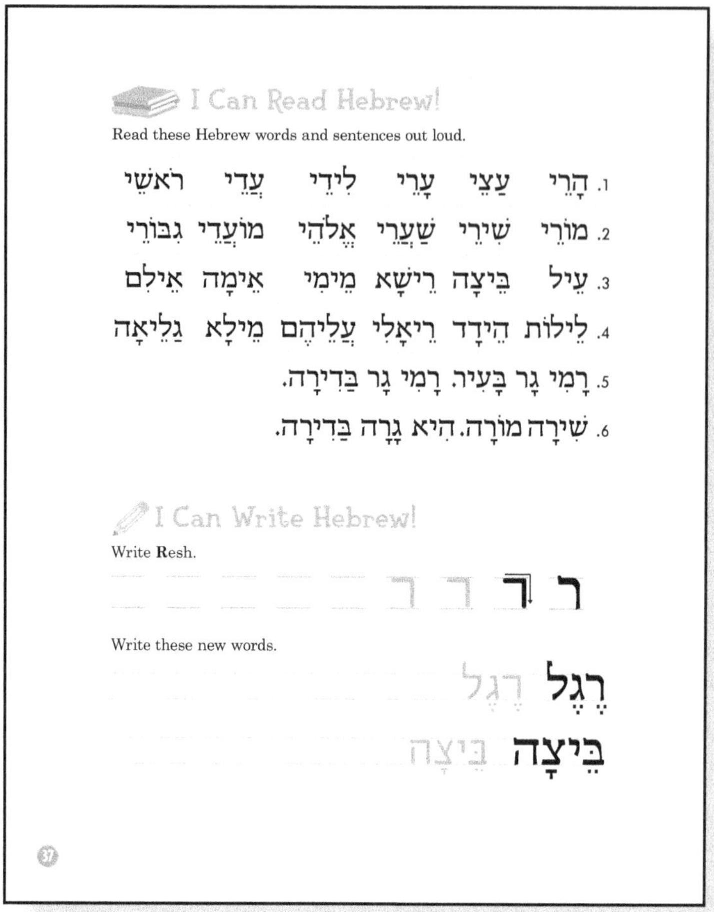

I Can Read Hebrew!

Read these Hebrew words and sentences out loud.

1. הָרֵי עַצֵי עָרֵי לִידֵי עֲדֵי רֹאשֵׁי
2. מוֹרֵי שִׁירֵי שַׁעֲרֵי אֱלֹהֵי מוֹעֲדֵי גִּבּוֹרֵי
3. עֵיל בֵּיצָה רֵישָׁא מֵימִי אֵימָה אֵילִם
4. לֵילוֹת הֵידָד רֵיאָלִי עֲלֵיהֶם מֵילָא גַּלֵיאָה
5. רָמִי גָּר בָּעִיר. רָמִי גָּר בַּדִּירָה.
6. שִׁירָה מוֹרָה. הִיא גָּרָה בַּדִּירָה.

I Can Write Hebrew!

Write Resh.

ר ר ר ר

Write these new words.

רֶגֶל רֶגֶל

בֵּיצָה בֵּיצָה

37

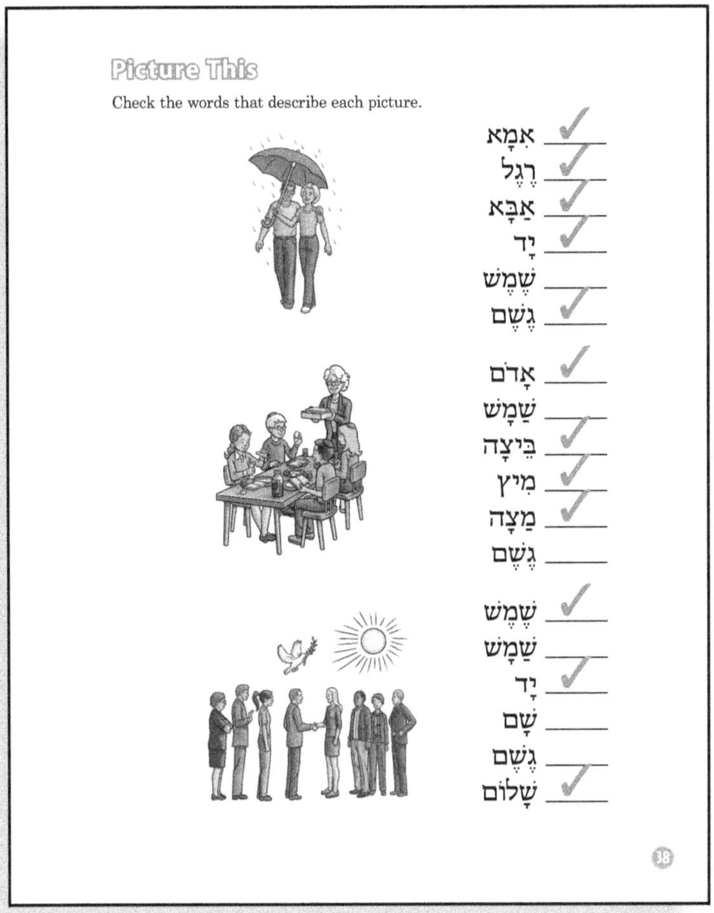

Picture This

Here students review the key words they have learned by putting a check next to each word that describes the picture.

Before students complete the page, you may want to do a full review of the key words they have learned so far. Using four to six cards at a time, display Word Cards #1–16 on the chalkboard or whiteboard ledge or on a bulletin board. Call on students one at a time, and read one of the words. The student must then point to the word and read it. If he or she is correct, the class should repeat the word. If the student's choice is incorrect, ask him or her to self-correct.

You can also ask the student to find a word according to its meaning. For example, display the following words:

גֶּשֶׁם רֶגֶל שֶׁמֶשׁ שַׁמָּשׁ שָׁלוֹם

Ask a student to find the word that means "sun" (שֶׁמֶשׁ), that means "rain" (גֶּשֶׁם), that means "leg" (רֶגֶל), etc. The student should point to the word and read it. If he or she is correct, the class should repeat the word. If the student's choice is incorrect, ask him or her to self-correct.

For variety, you or a student can draw pictures of the words, and students can then identify the matching words.

If you prefer, you can use this group word-identification activity as a test of mastery *after* the students complete page 38.

Complete the first part of the activity together as a class, then allow students to complete the other two individually or with a partner. Circulate around the room to provide assistance as needed.

Odd Letter Out

Researchers in Israel have discovered that Hebrew reading places a greater demand on the learner's visual processing system than reading European languages, like English, because Hebrew requires the reader to pay close attention to tiny visual differences. Therefore Hebrew reading instruction should incorporate activities that train the eye to make fine visual distinctions. This activity provides students with such practice. At the same time, it provides a review of those letter and vowel combinations that represent identical sounds, such as אַ and עֲ.

In line 1, students are asked to identify the combinations that make the same sound (בִּ and בִּי), and to discriminate between בִּי and בֵּי. In line 2, they are asked to associate עַ/עֲ with אַ/אָ, and to differentiate between עָ and צָ. Line 3 reviews the new letter ר, and contrasts it with ה. These answers provide the clues for the reading riddle, "Passover Preparations," that follows.

Have students complete the activity with a partner.

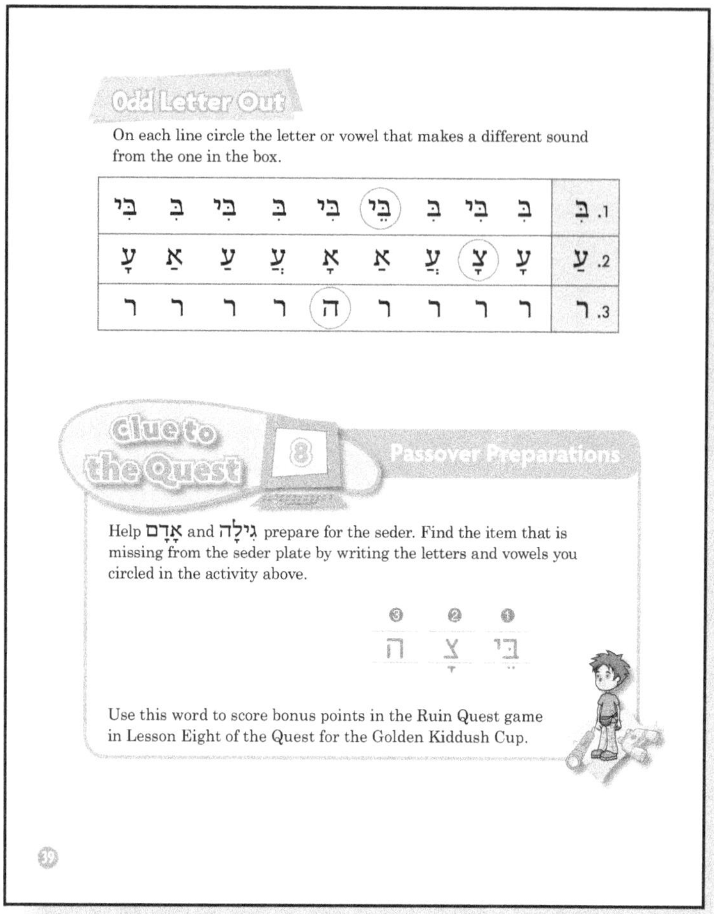

Odd Letter Out

On each line circle the letter or vowel that makes a different sound from the one in the box.

בִּי	בִּ	בִּי	בִּ	בִּי	בֵּי	בִּ	בִּי	בִּ	בִּ .1
עָ	אַ	עַ	עֲ	אָ	אַ	עֲ	צָ	עָ	עַ .2
ר	ר	ר	ר	ה	ר	ר	ר	ר	ר .3

Clue to the Quest 8 Passover Preparations

Help אָדָם and גִּילָה prepare for the seder. Find the item that is missing from the seder plate by writing the letters and vowels you circled in the activity above.

❸ ה ❷ צָ ❶ בֵּי

Use this word to score bonus points in the Ruin Quest game in Lesson Eight of the Quest for the Golden Kiddush Cup.

39

Clue to the Quest: Passover Preparations

Ask a volunteer to read the instructions. Allow students to work individually or with a partner to complete the activity. Circulate to provide assistance as necessary. Students can use the answer word (בֵּיצָה) to score bonus points in the "Ruin Quest" game in Lesson 8 of the digital application.

Challenge students to come to class next time with the answers to the following questions. They can find the answers in Lesson 8 of the digital application.

1. What do you find in Tzippori? (*mosaic art*)
2. What kind of egg did Ben think he found? (*a dinosaur egg*)

If students print out or e-mail their lesson summaries, remind them to do so when they have completed all the activities in this lesson.

Quest for the Golden Kiddush Cup

When students complete this lesson in their digital application, have them color piece #8 on the plate on page 4 of their book. They can also write in the key words and the new letter and vowel for this lesson.

Assessment

For information on assessing students' progress, see page 9.

Letter Hint

Ask a volunteer to read the information in the Letter Hint. Invite students to try to create their own mnemonic for these letters based on an English word that begins with the same sound as the new letters. For example, students may say, "*Tet* looks like an upside-down **t**ent, open on the **t**op."

Oral Language Lesson (Optional)

Review the word יֶלֶד and introduce יַלְדָּה and the second-person pronouns אַתָּה and אַתְּ.

Point to individual students in the class and say: אַתָּה יֶלֶד or אַתְּ יַלְדָּה.

You can also review the following words with these second-person pronouns, allowing students to play the roles: אַבָּא אִמָּא מוֹרֶה מוֹרָה

LESSON 9

Pages: 40–44

Key Words: טַלִּית תּוֹרָה

New Letters: ט תּ/ת

Recommended Instructional Materials:
Phonics Flash Cards #4–5, 10, 13–14, 20, 23, and 25–27; Word Cards #1, 3, 7, 9–10, and 12–18; a tallit and a small toy Torah; a small poster with Hebrew phrases (you can enlarge the phrases at the bottom of page 42 in the student edition); crayons or colored pencils

Review Activity

Play "Categories" (see page 14 for instructions) using Word Cards #1, 3, 7, 9–10, and 12–16. Tell the class the categories they should look for: Body Parts (רֶגֶל, יָד), Weather (שֶׁמֶשׁ, גֶּשֶׁם), Holidays Items (שַׁמָּשׁ, מַצָּה), People (אִמָּא, אַבָּא), "What's for Breakfast?" (בֵּיצָה, מִיץ).

Set Induction

Tell the students that the two key words for this lesson also fit into a category. Introduce the key words by showing the class a tallit and a small Torah. Pass them around the class and teach the words טַלִּית and תּוֹרָה. Ask students what category or categories these items fit into. (*ritual objects, synagogue, prayer, holy objects*)

Introducing the Key Words and Deducing Their Sound-Symbol Associations

Point to the picture of the tallit and say: טַלִּית. Ask the class to repeat the Hebrew word.

Introduce the new letter, *Tet*, ט, and its sound using the "Multi-Sensory Approach to Hebrew Phonics" described on page 11.

Next, introduce the second key word, תּוֹרָה. Highlight the other new letter, *Tav* (תּ, ת), stressing that these are the same letter. Point out that this letter and ט make the same sound (*t*).

I Can Read Hebrew!

This reading selection drills the new letters in all three positions within a word (beginning, middle, and end). Lines 2, 3, and 5 contain three-syllable words.

Ask volunteers to read the words in each line in groups of three words then two. Once students have had a few turns at reading individual words, ask them to read full lines then full columns.

I Can Write Hebrew!

Ask students to trace the letters with their fingers then write the letters in pencil. Review the letter names and sounds as students write them. This provides auditory reinforcement for the visual and kinesthetic activity.

Ask students to write the key words for the lesson. Students can also write and/or illustrate the following sentences:

הַטַלִּית שֶׁל אַבָּא.
תּוֹרָה שָׁם.

In preparation for the activity on the next page, ask students to close their books.

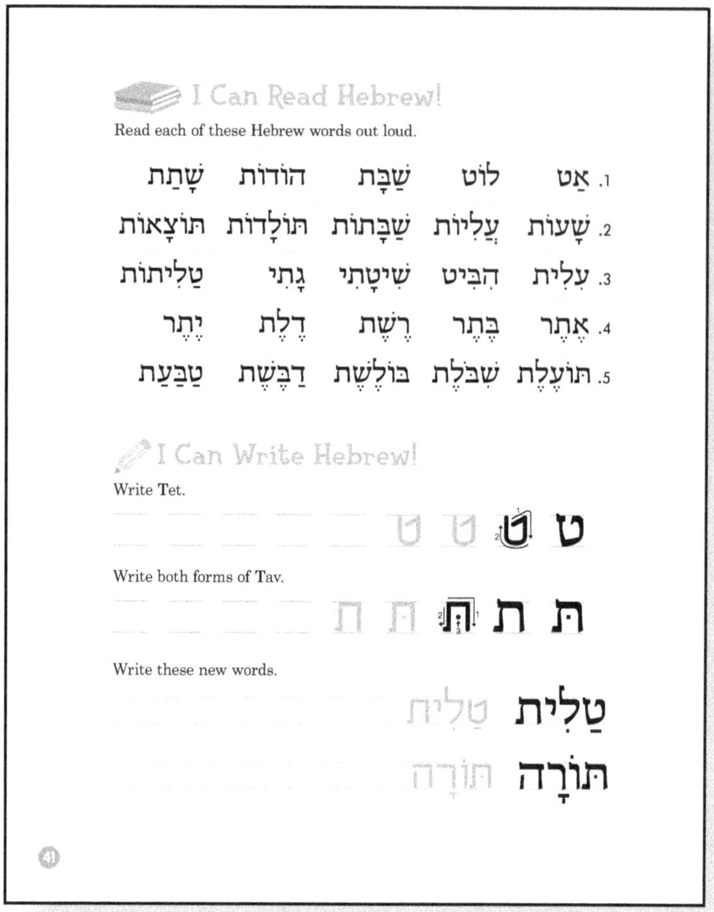
I Can Read Hebrew!

Read each of these Hebrew words out loud.

1. אַט לוֹט שַׁבָּת הוֹדוֹת שָׁתַת
2. שָׁעוֹת עֲלִיּוֹת שַׁבָּתוֹת תּוֹלָדוֹת תּוֹצָאוֹת
3. עִלִּית הִבִּיט שִׁיטָתִי גָּתִי טַלִּיתוֹת
4. אֶתֶר בֶּתֶר רֶשֶׁת דֶּלֶת יֶתֶר
5. תּוֹעֶלֶת שִׁבֹּלֶת בּוֹלֶשֶׁת דַּבֶּשֶׁת טַבַּעַת

I Can Write Hebrew!

Write Tet.

ט

Write both forms of Tav.

תּ ת

Write these new words.

טַלִּית

תּוֹרָה

41

Super Reading Secret #2

Blend words into smooth phrases and sentences.

Read these words out loud.

1. טַל דוֹרוֹת תָּמָר עֹלַת מַעֲלוֹת
2. בֵּיתִי עִתּוֹ תּוֹרָתִי אֱמוֹרִי תּוֹרָתוֹ
3. אַתָּה בָּרָאתָ עָתִיד תָּמִיד רָצִיתָ
4. טֶרֶם שַׁבָּתוֹת עֲטֶרֶת בַּצִיצִית הוֹדָאוֹת

Blend these words into smooth phrases.

הַיָּד + עַל + הַתּוֹרָה = הַיָּד עַל הַתּוֹרָה.

צִיצִית + עַל + הַטַּלִּית = צִיצִית עַל הַטַּלִּית

Now read these phrases smoothly.

1. הַיָּד עַל הַטַּלִּית
2. הַטַּלִּית עַל הַתּוֹרָה
3. הַטַּבַּעַת שֶׁל אִמָּא
4. הַטַּלִּית שֶׁל אַבָּא

42

Then ask students to open their books to page 42 and read the directions to them. Invite volunteers to read the individual words in lines 1–4 at the top. Then allow students to read the phrases in the middle and at the bottom of the page, first as a group and then as individuals.

Super Reading Secret #2

In Super Reading Secret #1 (Lesson 2, page 10 in the student edition) students learned about syllable segmentation, both auditory and visual. This critical word-attack skill allows students to break complex words into their individual syllables so that they can be sounded out with ease. Then they smoothly blend syllables into whole words.

Here students learn to blend individual words into whole phrases. Display the poster with large Hebrew phrases.

The first step will be to create an auditory-visual-kinesthetic association. Students will hear the phrase while looking at it (auditory-visual). They will then say the phrase while looking at it and drawing an arc in the air with their arms from right to left in a smooth motion (auditory-visual-kinesthetic).

Hold a pointer or ruler under the first phrase on the poster and read it fluidly (not one word at a time) while drawing an arc in the air from right to left. The class repeats the phrase while also drawing an arc in the air from right to left. The direction of this arc is important as it reinforces the directionality of Hebrew reading. Take note of any student who has difficulty with the direction and provide immediate remediation, such as repeating the correct movement.

Repeat this procedure several times with the class as a whole, then ask individual students to lead the class. Give a volunteer the pointer and read one of the phrases. The student should hold the pointer under the phrase and read it while drawing an arc through the air from right to left. If the student has read the correct phrase, the class should repeat the phrase while also drawing an arc through the air. If the student is incorrect, ask him or her to self-correct. Repeat this step, allowing all students to participate.

Colors Galore

This activity reviews all of the vowels that students have studied so far. Distribute crayons or colored pencils to the class, and ask a volunteer to read the directions at the top of the page. Tell students to read each word aloud quietly and to color each box according to the code. You may want to complete the top line together as a class to make sure that students understand what they need to do. Circulate to provide assistance as necessary.

Once students have completed the coloring, ask them what they think the object might be. (*a* טַלִּית) Invite a volunteer to write the word טַלִּית on the board. Tell students that they can add the צִיצִית (fringes) at the corners to complete the drawing.

Colors Galore!

Color in blue all of the words that have the "ay" vowel.
Red = "eh"
Green = "ee"
Orange = "oh"
Leave white all of the words that have the "ah" vowel.

אוֹת	אַתָּה	אֱמֶת	עֵיל	לֵית	עֵיט	עִלִי	בָּה	בֵּי
מֹר	מָטָר	מֶתֶג	מָעַל	עַם	שַׁבָּת	בִּישׁ	בַּת	בֵּית
הוֹד	בָּלַט	תֶּלֶם	תַּעַר	תָּמָר	מָר	מִי	מַה	מֵי
יוֹם	הָמַם	יֶתֶר	יָתַר	מָעַט	טָעַם	הִיא	תָּם	הֵי
בֹּץ	יָעַץ	אֶרֶץ	אֲדָר	טָרַד	טַל	טִיל	אֲגַם	אֵיד
דוֹר	דָּגַר	דֶּרֶשׁ	דָּרַשׁ	תָּלַשׁ	לָטַשׁ	מִיץ	מָט	טֵית
צוֹם	צַלָּם	צֶלֶם	עָטָה	שָׁמַט	צָמָא	צִדִּי	בַּעַת	בֵּיצֵי

Bonus question: Can you tell what this object is?
Write the word in Hebrew. טַלִית
Hint: It is a key word in this chapter.

43

Rhyme Time

Circle the two words on each line that rhyme.

1. אָטוֹם אוֹתָם יָתוֹם טָעִים
2. טַלִּית שֶׁלֶט תָּמִיד שַׁלִּיט
3. דֶּגֶל דֶּלֶת תֶּלֶם מֶלֶט
4. מַעֲטֶה מַטָּרָה עֲתִידָה עֲטָרָה

Clue to the Quest 9 Reading Riddle

Fill in the letters for each word.

I come with some strings attached. They remind you of the 613 commandments in the Torah. What am I? Write the circled letters in the numbered spaces below to solve the riddle. Do not include vowels or dots!

ט ל י ת

Use this word to score bonus points in the Keep Israel Green game in Lesson Nine of the Quest for the Golden Kiddush Cup.

44

Quest for the Golden Kiddush Cup

When students complete this lesson in their digital application, have them color piece #9 on the plate on page 4 of their book. They can also write in the key words and the new letters for this lesson.

Assessment

For information on assessing students' progress, see page 9.

Rhyme Time

The ability to hear and identify words that rhyme is an important aspect of phonological awareness.

Ask a volunteer to read the instructions. Tell the class to listen carefully and ask a second volunteer to read line 1. Ask which two words rhyme. (יָתוֹם and אָטוֹם) Tell students to circle these two words. They can complete the activity individually or in pairs. Circulate to provide assistance as necessary.

Clue to the Quest: Reading Riddle

Read the instructions at the top of the page and allow students to work individually or with a partner to complete the activity. Circulate to provide assistance as necessary. When students have filled in the Hebrew for the key words, ask a volunteer to read the riddle, and allow students to fill in the answer. (טַלִּית)

Students can use the answer word to score bonus points in the "Keep Israel Green" game in Lesson 9 on the digital application. This game asks students to collect tokens for points while avoiding heavy objects that waste game time. They can also collect words that contain specific letters for additional points.

Challenge students to come to class next time with the answers to the following questions. They can find the answers in Lesson 9 of the digital application.

1. Where can you ski and snowboard in Israel? (*Mount Hermon*)
2. What do you find on that mountain in the summer? (*wildflowers*)

If students print out or e-mail their lesson summaries, remind them to do so when they have completed all the activities in this lesson.

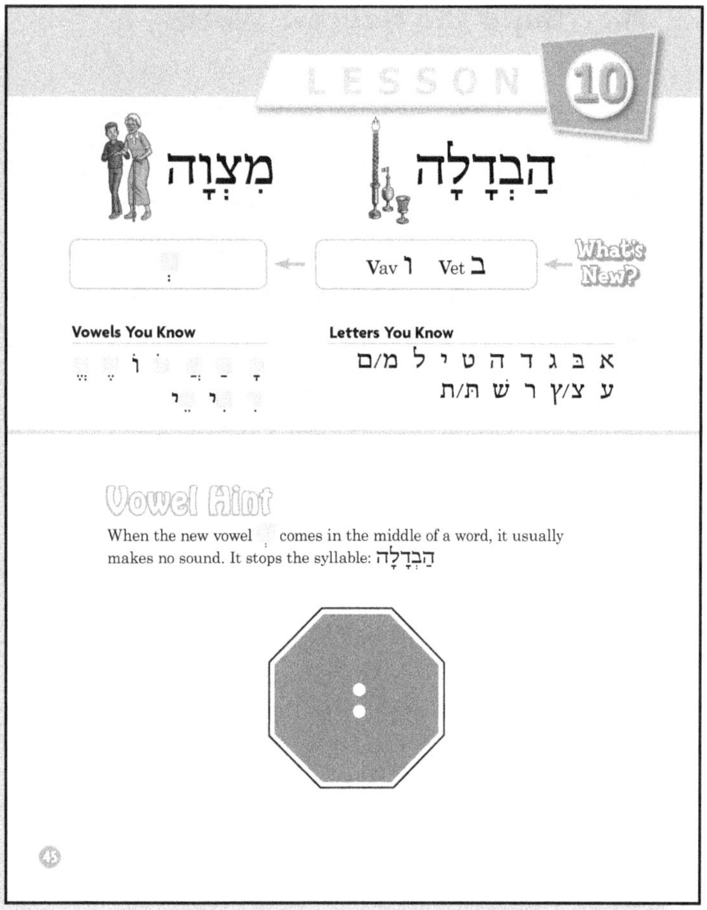

LESSON 10

מִצְוָה הַבְדָּלָה

Vav ו Vet ב What's New?

Vowels You Know

Letters You Know

א ב ג ד ה ט י ל מ/ם
ע צ/ץ ר ש ת/ת

Vowel Hint

When the new vowel ְ comes in the middle of a word, it usually makes no sound. It stops the syllable: הַבְדָּלָה

45

LESSON 10

Pages: 45–49

Key Words: הַבְדָּלָה מִצְוָה

New Letters: ב ו

New Vowel: ְ (unvoiced)

Recommended Instructional Materials: Phonics Flash Cards #2, 4–5, 10–11, 14, 19, 21, and 28–30; Word Cards #19–20; teacher-made Bingo cards composed of the letters and vowels learned to this point; a Havdalah set including a braided candle and a spice box filled with sweet spices; fine- or medium-tip black markers, glue, Popsicle or art sticks, and red construction-paper octagons (enough for the class)

Review Activity

Play "Phonics Bingo" (see page 15 for instructions).

Set Induction

Ask students: How do you know when you should stop an activity? (*Answers may include: you come to a red light, you see a stop sign, a bell rings, your parent calls you to dinner.*) Ask: How do we know when Shabbat ends? (*Answers may include: when Saturday night comes, when we see three stars in the sky, there's a calendar that tells you the times.*) Tell students about the short Havdalah ceremony at the end of Shabbat, and allow them to smell the sweet spices and feel the braided candle. Tell them that this lesson is all about knowing when and how to "stop" in Hebrew reading.

Introducing the Key Words and Deducing Their Sound-Symbol Associations

Point to the picture of the Havdalah set in the book and say: הַבְדָּלָה. Ask the class to repeat the word. Introduce the new letter ב, its sound, and the unvoiced ְ using the "Multi-Sensory Approach to Hebrew Phonics" described on page 11.

Next, introduce the second key word, מִצְוָה. Ask students why they think this art was chosen. (*boy helping old lady; mitzvah means "commandment," and commandments in the Torah include helping others*) Highlight the fact that both new letters (ב and ו) make the same sound.

Vowel Hint

Ask a volunteer to read the information in the Vowel Hint. Have students make their own "*Sh'va* Stop Signs" using octagons cut from red construction paper, black markers, and Popsicle or art sticks. Have students write their names on the back of their stick and save for later lessons.

Oral Language Lesson (Optional)

Introduce the words תַּלְמִיד תַּלְמִידָה רַב using sentences such as:

רַב עַל הַבִּימָה.
אַתָּה תַּלְמִיד. אַתְּ תַּלְמִידָה.

Build the Hebrew Words

Each of these lines contains one Hebrew word written three ways. Read each line to learn how the ְ works.

.1	אֶת רוֹג	אֶתרוֹג	אֶתְרוֹג
.2	אַשׁ רֵי	אַשׁרֵי	אַשְׁרֵי
.3	תַּל מִיד	תַּלמִיד	תַּלְמִיד
.4	שַׁל וָה	שַׁלוָה	שַׁלְוָה
.5	עִב רִית	עִברִית	עִבְרִית
.6	תּוֹל דוֹת	תּוֹלדוֹת	תּוֹלְדוֹת
.7	מִצ וָה	מִצוָה	מִצְוָה
.8	הַב דָלָה	הַבדָלָה	הַבְדָלָה

Super Reading Secret #3

The Hebrew "stop sign" shows where some syllables end. Circle the syllables in the words below.

Remember: Hebrew syllables can have only one vowel that makes a sound!

מִדְרָשׁ מִדְרָשָׁה מֶמְשָׁלָה מֶמְשַׁלְתִּי אַמְבַּטְיָה

46

Super Reading Secret #3

Ask a volunteer to read the directions. Ask students to clap out the syllables before they circle them.

As a bonus question, ask students how many times the unsounded *sh'va* appears in each word. (*once in each of the first three words, twice in the last two words*)

Build the Hebrew Words

Here students practice decoding words that contain the unvoiced *sh'va*. In each of the eight lines, a word is written in three different ways. In the first column on the right, the word has been split into its two component syllables, separated by a space (as if they were two single-syllable words). In the middle column, the syllables have been combined, but with no marking to show that the first syllable is a C-V-C syllable. The third example shows the word written correctly with the *sh'va*. You can use this word building activity in the following ways:

1. Alternate reading the syllables with the students. You read the first syllable and the class reads the second. On line 1 for example, read אֶת and the students read רוֹג. Repeat for all three examples on the line. When you and the class have read all eight lines in this way, reverse roles so that the students read the first syllable.
2. Read the first syllable and the students read the rest of the word, then together blend the whole word.
3. Divide the class into two groups. The first group reads the initial syllable and the second group completes the word. After the class has read all the words in this manner, switch so that the second group reads the first syllable and the first group completes the word.
4. Have a student volunteer read the first syllable and the class complete the word.

5 Ask each student in turn to complete the word after you read the first part. Then randomly call on individuals to read the whole word.

I Can Read Hebrew!

This reading selection drills the new letters ב and ו in all three positions within a word (beginning, middle, and end). One word on line 4 and three on line 5 are three-syllable words. Line 6 is composed of three short sentences. (*David is a boy. David is a student. You are a student [female].*)

Ask volunteers to read the words in each line, in groups of three words then two. Once students have had a few turns reading individual words, ask them to read full lines, then columns of five words. Line 6 should be read as full, smoothly blended sentences. If necessary, review the process for fluent phrase reading that was described on page 54.

I Can Write Hebrew!

Ask students to trace the letters with their fingers then write the letters in pencil. Review the letter names and sounds as students write them.

Ask students to write the key words for the lesson.

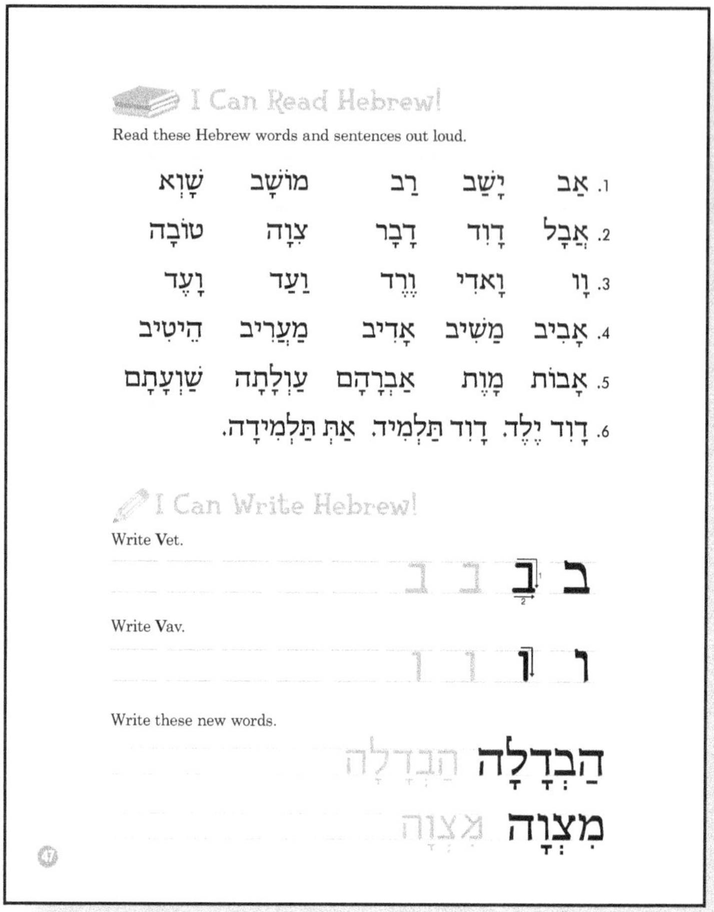
I Can Read Hebrew!

Read these Hebrew words and sentences out loud.

1. אַב יָשַׁב רַב מוֹשָׁב שָׁוְא
2. אֲבָל דָוִד דָבָר צִוָה טוֹבָה
3. וָו וָאדִי וֶרֶד וַעַד וָעֶד
4. אָבִיב מַשִׁיב אָדִיב מַעֲרִיב הֵיטִיב
5. אָבוֹת מָוֶת אַבְרָהָם עוֹלָתָה שַׁוְעָתָם
6. דָוִד יֶלֶד. דָוִד תַּלְמִיד. אַתְּ תַּלְמִידָה.

I Can Write Hebrew!

Write Vet.

ב בּ ב ב

Write Vav.

ו ו ו ו

Write these new words.

הַבְדָלָה הַבְדָלָה

מִצְוָה מִצְוָה

47

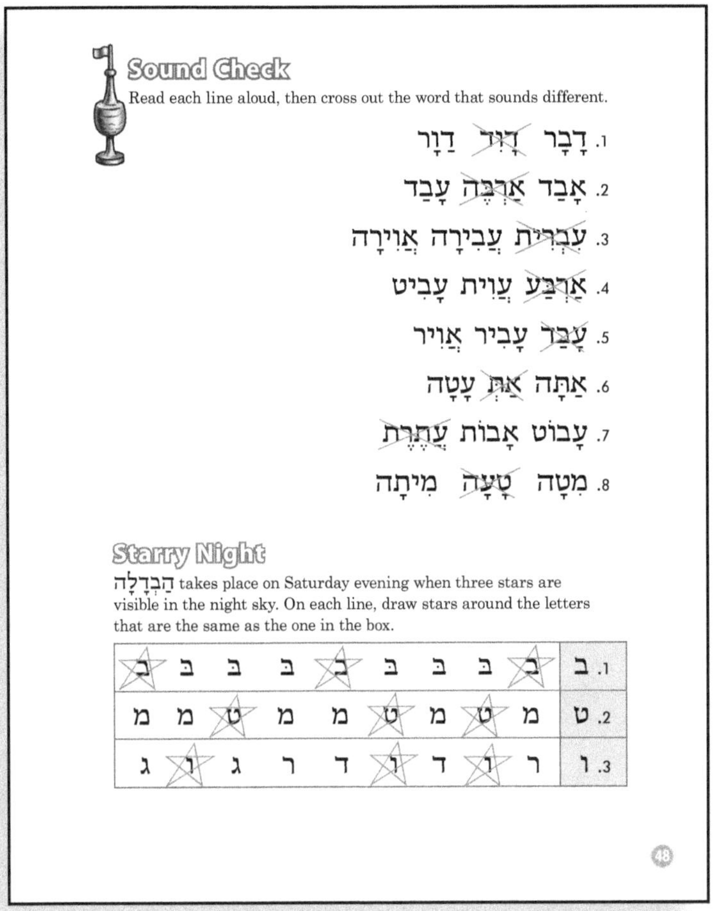

Sound Check

Read each line aloud, then cross out the word that sounds different.

1. דָבָר דָוִד דַוָר
2. אָבַד אַרְבֶּה עָבַד
3. עִבְרִית עֲבִירָה אֲוִירָה
4. אַרְבַּע עֲוִית עָבִיט
5. עָבַד עָבִיר אֲוִיר
6. אַתָּה אַתְּ עָטָה
7. עָבוֹט אָבוֹת עֲתֶרֶת
8. מִטָּה טָעָה מִיתָה

Starry Night

הַבְדָלָה takes place on Saturday evening when three stars are visible in the night sky. On each line, draw stars around the letters that are the same as the one in the box.

ב	בּ	בּ	בּ	ב	בּ	בּ	בּ	ב	ב .1
מ	מ	ט	מ	מ	ט	מ	ט	מ	ט .2
ג	ו	ג	ר	ד	ו	ד	ו	ר	ו .3

48

Sound Check

This activity asks students to identify Hebrew homonyms and to exclude the word on each line that sounds different.

Allow students to work with partners in completing this activity. You may choose to assign stronger readers to work with weaker readers. Ask the first partner to read the first line aloud. The second student should scan the words on the line, identify the word that is different, point to it, and read it aloud. If both partners agree, they should cross out the word identified. If they do not, they should work together to find the correct answer. They should repeat this procedure with the second line, switching roles, and continue, alternating, until they complete the activity.

Starry Night

This activity provides students with practice in fine visual discrimination.

In line 1, students are asked to differentiate between ב and בּ. Line 2 provides visual discrimination between ט and מ, and line 3 challenges students to distinguish between ו, ר, ד, and ג.

Allow students to work on this activity individually. Circulate to provide assistance as necessary.

Ask students how many stars they drew on each line. (*three*) Ask students why they think the activity required that they draw three stars. (*three stars traditionally signify the time when Shabbat is over and the* הַבְדָלָה *ceremony begins*)

Braid the Havdalah Candle

Complete this activity as a class. Ask a volunteer to read the instructions. Explain to the students that all of the words in this activity are cognates (words that are similar in Hebrew and English). The first word starts at the top of the column on the right. Tell the students to find the second half of this word in the column on the left. Help them complete the activity by providing the following hints:

- This is where you put your photographs.
- This is a special fruit that accompanies the lulav on the holiday of Sukkot.
- This is a way to listen to the news in the car.
- He was the first of our ancestors.

Ask students to connect the words as you give them the hints. Circulate to provide help as needed.

Clue to the Quest: Reading Riddle

Read the instructions and allow students to work individually or with a partner to complete the activity. Circulate to provide assistance as necessary. When students have filled in the Hebrew for the key words, ask a volunteer to read the riddle, and allow students to fill in their answers.

Students can use the answer, מַצָּה, to score bonus points in the "Climber Caper" game in Lesson 10 on the digital application.

Challenge students to come to class next time with the answers to the following questions. They can find the answers in Lesson 10 of the digital application.

1. What is the largest city in Israel? (*Tel Aviv*)
2. What is *Shuk HaCarmel*? (*an outdoor market*)

If students print out or e-mail their lesson summaries, remind them to do so when they have completed all the activities in this lesson.

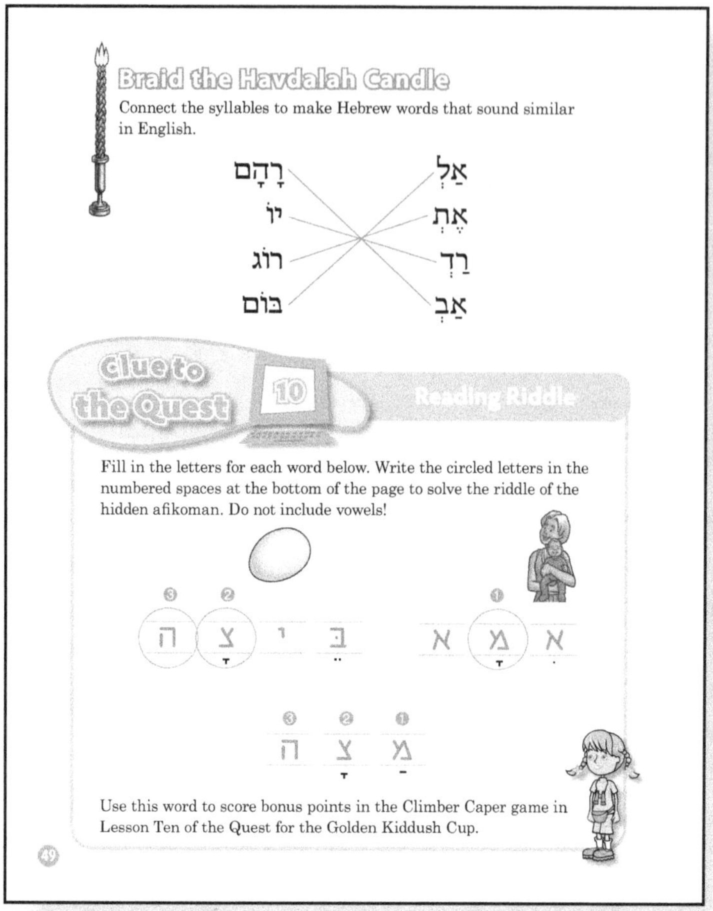
Braid the Havdalah Candle

Connect the syllables to make Hebrew words that sound similar in English.

רָהָם — אַל
יוֹ — אֶתְ
רוֹג — רַד
בּוֹם — אַבְ

Clue to the Quest 10 Reading Riddle

Fill in the letters for each word below. Write the circled letters in the numbered spaces at the bottom of the page to solve the riddle of the hidden afikoman. Do not include vowels!

Use this word to score bonus points in the Climber Caper game in Lesson Ten of the Quest for the Golden Kiddush Cup.

49

Quest for the Golden Kiddush Cup

When students complete this lesson in their digital application, have them color piece #10 on the plate on page 4 of their book. They can also write in the key words and the new letters and vowel for this lesson.

Assessment

For information on assessing students' progress, see page 9.

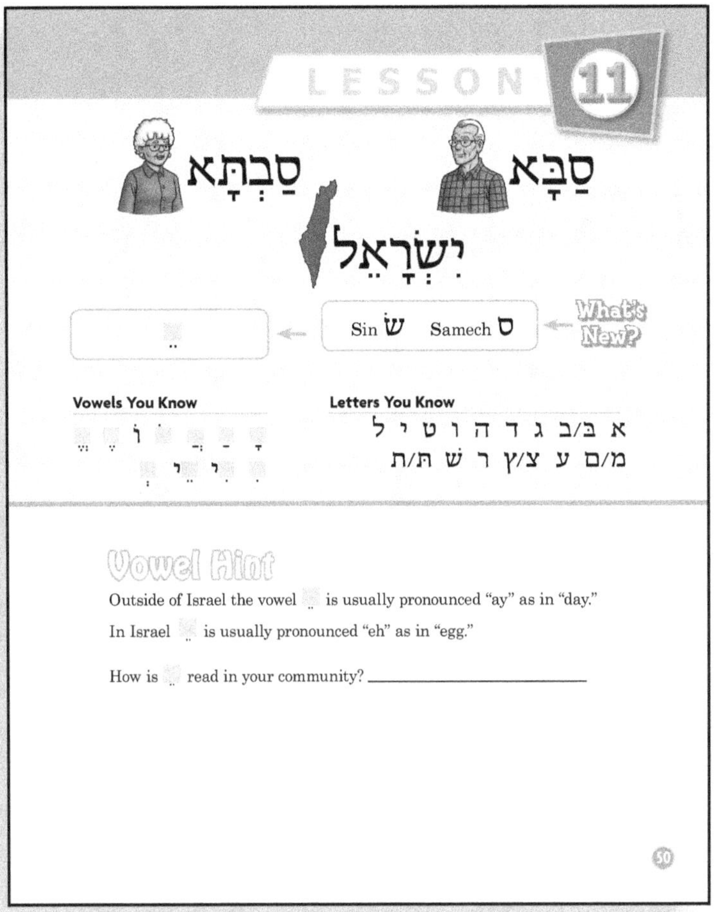

Next, show students a map of Israel, introduce the key word יִשְׂרָאֵל, and use it to introduce the new letter שׂ and the new vowel ◌ֵ, using the same multi-sensory approach.

Vowel Hint

Ask a volunteer to read the information in the Vowel Hint at the bottom of page 50. Explain that pronunciations vary from one place to another. Discuss how the new vowel ◌ֵ is pronounced in your congregation or community (*ay* or *eh*).

Oral Language Lesson (Optional)

Review the words: רַב יַלְדָּה אַתְּ אַתָּה תַּלְמִיד תַּלְמִידָה

You can also review the following sentences:

אַתָּה יֶלֶד. אַתְּ יַלְדָּה.

אַתָּה תַּלְמִיד. אַתְּ תַּלְמִידָה.

Introduce the words: לוֹמֵד/לוֹמֶדֶת and עִבְרִית

Practice the words using the following sentences:

אַתָּה תַּלְמִיד. אַתָּה לוֹמֵד עִבְרִית.

LESSON 11

Pages: 50–53

Key Words: סַבָּא סַבְתָּא יִשְׂרָאֵל

New Letters: ס שׂ

New Vowel: ◌ֵ

Recommended Instructional Materials:
Phonics Flash Cards #4–5, 7, 9–10, 15, 19, 23, 26, 28, and 30–33; Word Cards #1–23

Review Activity

Distribute Word Cards #1–20 among students, giving each student one to four Word Cards. Ask all students who have cards with a specific sound, such as *sha*, to stand up. (שַׁמָּשׁ, שָׁלוֹם) Call on one of those students to read aloud the word and, if possible, to explain its meaning. Continue asking for words with specific sounds until all students have had a turn.

Set Induction

Write the following English words on the board:

sit city cent sent center simple seed
cell sell cymbal symbol

Ask students what they notice about these words. (*they all contain the s sound; the s sound is made by two different English letters*) Tell students that there are also two Hebrew letters that stand for the *s* sound, and they will learn the sound in the lesson.

Introducing the Key Words and Deducing Their Sound-Symbol Associations

Introduce the key words סַבָּא and סַבְתָּא. Invite three girls to the front of the room. Ask one to be יַלְדָּה, one to be אִמָּא, and one to be סַבְתָּא. Consider having these students hold up cards with their labels. Prompt יַלְדָּה to turn to אִמָּא and say, שָׁלוֹם אִמָּא. Then have אִמָּא turn to סַבְתָּא and say, שָׁלוֹם אִמָּא. Then have יַלְדָּה turn to סַבְתָּא and say, שָׁלוֹם סַבְתָּא. Repeat, having three boys playing יֶלֶד, אַבָּא, and סַבָּא. Use the words to introduce the new letter ס, applying the "Multi-Sensory Approach to Hebrew Phonics" described on page 11.

אַתְּ תַּלְמִידָה. אַתְּ לוֹמֶדֶת עִבְרִית.

I Can Read Hebrew!

Line 1 drills the new vowel ֵ in the first syllable, while lines 2 and 3 focus on the use of the vowel in the second syllable. Ask volunteers to read three words at a time, then full lines.

Lines 4, 5, and 6 contain actual sentences and should be read as full sentences. (*Line 4: Adam learns Hebrew. Gila learns Hebrew. Line 5: They like to learn Hebrew. Line 6: Grandfather says: "Gila is a good girl, and Adam is a good boy."*) If you are including the optional oral language component, students should be able to understand some of these words.

The "Write" Letter

This activity assists in developing visual discrimination skills.

Have students complete the activity individually.

I Can Read Hebrew!

Read these Hebrew words and sentences out loud.

1. לֵב לֵוִי עֵץ עֵצִי שֵׁם שֵׁמִי
2. יוֹבֵל מִלֵּל עָצֵל גּוֹלֵל אָשֵׁם שׁוֹמֵם
3. צִלְצֵל מִלְמֵל צִמְצֵם גִּרְגֵּר רִשְׁרֵשׁ מִשְׁמֵשׁ
4. אָדָם לוֹמֵד עִבְרִית. גִּילָה לוֹמֶדֶת עִבְרִית.
5. הֵם אוֹהֲבִים לִלְמוֹד עִבְרִית.
6. סַבָּא אוֹמֵר: "גִּילָה יַלְדָּה טוֹבָה, וְאָדָם יֶלֶד טוֹב."

The "Write" Letter

The objects below are called the same thing in Hebrew and English. Write the Hebrew letter that begins each word.

Letter Box

ר י ו ד

ו ר ד י

51

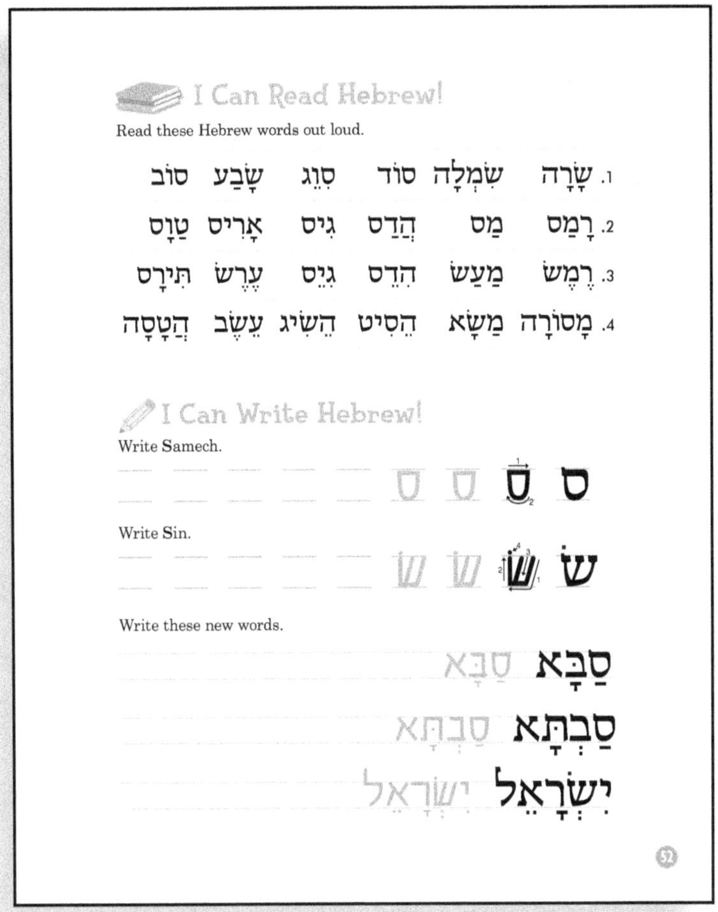

I Can Read Hebrew!

Read these Hebrew words out loud.

1. שָׂרָה שִׂמְלָה סוֹד סִוֵג שָׂבַע סוֹב
2. רָמַס מַס הֲדַס גִיס אָרִיס טַוָס
3. רֶמֶשׂ מַעַשׂ הֵדֵס גֵיס עֶרֶשׂ תִּירָס
4. מָסוֹרָה מַשָּׂא הֵסִיט הֵשִׂיג עֵשֶׂב הֲטָסָה

I Can Write Hebrew!

Write Samech.

ס ס

Write Sin.

שׂ שׂ

Write these new words.

סַבָּא סַבָּא

סַבְתָּא סַבְתָּא

יִשְׂרָאֵל יִשְׂרָאֵל

52

I Can Read Hebrew!

This reading selection drills the new letters שׂ and ס in all three positions within a word (beginning, middle, and end). It is easiest for students to hear sounds in the initial position of a word, therefore line 1 contains the new letters in the initial position. It is next easiest for students to hear sounds at the ends of words, therefore lines 2 and 3 provide practice with the new letters at the ends of words. Line 4 contains words that have the new sound in the middle.

Ask volunteers to read the words in each line, in groups of three words. Once students have had a few turns at reading individual words, ask them to read full lines, then columns of four words.

I Can Write Hebrew!

Ask students to trace the letters with their fingers then write the letters in pencil. Review the letter names and sounds as students write them.

Ask students to write the key words for the lesson. Students can also write and/or illustrate the following sentences:

סַבָּא עַל הַבִּימָה.
טַלִּית עַל סַבְתָּא.
יִשְׂרָאֵל שָׁם.

Clue to the Quest: Help with the Harvest

This exercise reviews the two letters that represent the *v* sound, introduced in the previous lesson. At the same time, students are required to distinguish between בּ and ב, and to identify when ו is acting as a consonant rather than the vowel וֹ.

Ask students to complete this activity individually. Circulate to provide assistance as needed. Once students finish, they should count the number of circled oranges and enter that number on the line provided (*10*). They will use that number to score bonus points in the "Super Water Ski" game in Lesson 11 of the digital application.

Challenge students to come to class next time with the answers to the following questions. They can find the answers in Lesson 11 of the digital application.

1. Why is the Dead Sea called a "dead sea"? (*because it is so salty that nothing can live in it*)
2. Why do some people take Dead Sea mud baths? (*because it is good for the skin*)

If students print out or e-mail their lesson summaries, remind them to do so when they have completed all the activities in this lesson.

Quest for the Golden Kiddush Cup

When students complete this lesson in their digital application, have them color piece #11 on the plate on page 4 of their book. They can also write in the key words and the new letters and vowel for this lesson.

Assessment

For information on assessing students' progress, see page 9.

LESSON 12

קִדּוּשׁ סֻכָּה

What's New? Kaf כּ Koof ק — וּ ֻ

Vowels You Know

Letters You Know

א בּ/ב ג ד ה ו ט י ל

מ/ם ס ע צ/ץ ר שׁ/שׂ תּ/ת

Hidden Picture

Color in blue all the letters that make the sound "S." Leave white all the letters that make any other sound.

ס	מ	שׁ	ם	מ	ם	מ	ם	מ	ם	שׁ	ם
שׁ	שׂ	מ	ס	שׁ	שׂ	שׁ	ס	שׂ	ס	שׂ	ס
ם	ס	ם	שׂ	שׁ	שׂ	ם	שׁ	שׂ	שׁ	שׁ	שׂ
שׁ	שׂ	שׁ	ס	מ	ס	שׁ	ם	ס	ם	ם	ס
מ	שׂ	ס	שׂ	ס	שׂ	ם	שׁ	שׁ	שׂ	ס	ם

Which two Hebrew letters make the "S" sound? שׂ and ס

54

LESSON 12

Pages: 54–58

Key Words: סֻכָּה קִדּוּשׁ

New Letters: כּ ק

New Vowels: וּ ֻ

Recommended Instructional Materials:
Phonics Flash Cards #1, 4, 11, 14, 19, 31, and 34–37; Word Cards #24–25; copies of the Hebrew text of Ecclesiastes 3:1–8 for the class; a Kiddush cup

Review Activity

Play "Letter Contest/Sound Contest" (see page 14 for instructions) using the text of Ecclesiastes 3:1–8. Pay particular attention to those letters that have been introduced in the past few lessons, such as ר, שׂ, ס, ו, ב, ט, and תּ/ת.

Set Induction

Write the following English words on the board:

cat kangaroo cake key cot koala cut kung fu cocoa kite

Ask students what they notice about these words. (*they all start with the k sound; the k sound is made by two different English letters*) Tell students that there are also two Hebrew letters that stand for the *k* sound, and they will learn the sound in this lesson.

Introducing the Key Words and Deducing Their Sound-Symbol Associations

Show students a picture of a סֻכָּה (found in any holiday book). Introduce the key word סֻכָּה, and use it to introduce the new letter כּ and the new vowel ֻ, using the "Multi-Sensory Approach to Hebrew Phonics" described on page 11.

Next, hold up the Kiddush cup, introduce the key word קִדּוּשׁ, and use it to introduce ק and וּ using the same approach.

Hidden Picture

This activity provides students with practice in fine visual discrimination between ס and ם, as well as between שׁ and שׂ. At the same time, it reinforces the idea that ס and שׂ both make the sound *s*.

Ask a volunteer to read the instructions, then allow students to work on this activity individually.

Circulate to provide assistance as necessary. The hidden picture is שׂ ס.

Oral Language Lesson (Optional)

Introduce the words: קוֹרֵא/קוֹרֵאת
כִּתָּה מוּסִיקָה הוּא כּוֹתֵב/כּוֹתֶבֶת

Practice the words using the following sentences:

אָדָם לוֹמֵד עִבְרִית בַּכִּתָּה. גִּילָה לוֹמֶדֶת עִבְרִית בַּכִּתָּה.
אָדָם כּוֹתֵב עִבְרִית. גִּילָה כּוֹתֶבֶת עִבְרִית.
הוּא קוֹרֵא עִבְרִית. הִיא קוֹרֵאת עִבְרִית.
אָדָם לוֹמֵד מוּסִיקָה. גִּילָה לוֹמֶדֶת מוּסִיקָה.

I Can Read Hebrew!

This activity drills the new letters כּ and ק in all three positions within a word (beginning, middle, and end). The first line presents the sound at the end of the word (ק only). Lines 2 and 3 provide practice with both letters in the initial position, while lines 4 and 5 consist of words with the *k* sound in the middle. The last three words of line 5 are three-syllable words.

Ask volunteers to read the words in lines 1–4, in groups of three, and line 5 one word at a time. Once students have had a few turns reading individual words, ask them to read full lines, then columns of five words. Finally, challenge each student to read line 5.

Sound Check

In this activity students identify homonyms. Allow students to work with partners in completing this activity. You may choose to assign stronger readers to work with weaker readers. Ask the first partner to read the first word in the right-hand column aloud. The second student should scan the words in the left-hand column and identify the match, point to it, and read it aloud. If both partners agree, they should connect the words. If they do not, they should work together to find the correct answer. They should repeat this procedure with the second word, switching roles, and continue, alternating, until the activity is complete.

I Can Read Hebrew!

Read these Hebrew words out loud.

1. וָתִיק סֶלֶק צֶדֶק שׁוּק דַּבֵּק מָרָק
2. קֶרֶב כִּסֵּא קֶצֶב כָּשֵׁר קֹדֶשׁ קֶרֶם
3. כָּרוֹת כִּסְלֵו כָּבוֹד כַּאֲשֶׁר קָדוֹשׁ קָרוֹב
4. בֹּקֶר מִקְרָא צִדְקוֹ שֶׁקֶר מִקְדָּשׁ מָקוֹם
5. תִּקְוָה לִקְרַאת צַדִּיקִים יִתְקַדֵּשׁ מַקְדִּישִׁים

Sound Check

Draw lines between the words that sound the same.

שַׂר	עָדַר
אֲדָר	קַד
עֶרֶשׂ	אֶרֶס
כַּד	סָר
סַגִּי	הַכֹּל
הַקּוֹל	שַׂגִּיא

Vowel Hint

Here's a good way to remember the sound of the new vowels.

The end of a train is called a cabOOse. When you see a Hebrew vowel that looks like a little train, remember to say "OO".

I Can Read Hebrew!

Read these Hebrew words and sentences out loud.

1. עָשׂוּ הוֹדוּ רֵעֵהוּ אִמְרוּ תָּמוּ
2. יָמוּשׁ דִּבּוּר עֲבוּר אָהוּב כָּתוּב
3. סֻלָּם דֻּבָּה גֻּלָּה מֻשָּׂא כֻּלָּה
4. מֻשְׁלָם דֻּגְמָה אֲגֻדָּה מֻסְוָה סֻכָּה
5. אָסוּר הִדְלִיקוּ גִּלּוּל הָאֲמוּרָה יִקְרָאֻהוּ
6. אָדָם וְגִילָה לוֹמְדִים בַּכִּתָּה.
7. אָדָם קוֹרֵא עִבְרִית. גִּילָה קוֹרֵאת עִבְרִית.

56

Vowel Hint

Like several previous Letter and Vowel Hints, this Vowel Hint provides students with a mnemonic, or "aid to memory."

Ask a volunteer to read the information. Invite students to draw ֻ on the board. You can add a tactile or kinesthetic association by asking students to imitate the motion that a train engineer makes when pulling the train's whistle chain. Students should make this motion when they pronounce each of the new vowels.

Help students create a mnemonic for וּ, for example, *"ooh,* I have a stomach ache."

I Can Read Hebrew!

Here students practice the new vowels. Line 1 presents וּ at the end of the word. Line 2 presents this vowel embedded within the second syllable of the word. Lines 3 and 4 focus on ֻ in the initial syllable, and line 5 presents both vowels in various medial and terminal positions. Ask volunteers to read individual words then full lines. They can also read columns of five words.

Lines 6 and 7 contain full sentences. Challenge students to read them as smoothly and rhythmically as possible. (*Line 6: Adam and Gila learn in the classroom. Line 7: Adam reads Hebrew. Gila reads Hebrew.*)

I Can Write Hebrew!

Ask students to trace the letters with their fingers then write the letters in pencil. Review the letter names and sounds as students write them. This provides auditory reinforcement for the visual and kinesthetic activity.

Ask students to write the key words for the lesson. Students can also write and/or illustrate the following sentences:

גֶשֶׁם עַל הַסֻּכָּה.

קִדּוּשׁ שָׁם.

Decorate the Sukkah

This activity reviews several pairs of letters that represent single sounds. Ask a volunteer to read the directions, and allow students to complete the activity individually. Circulate to provide assistance as needed.

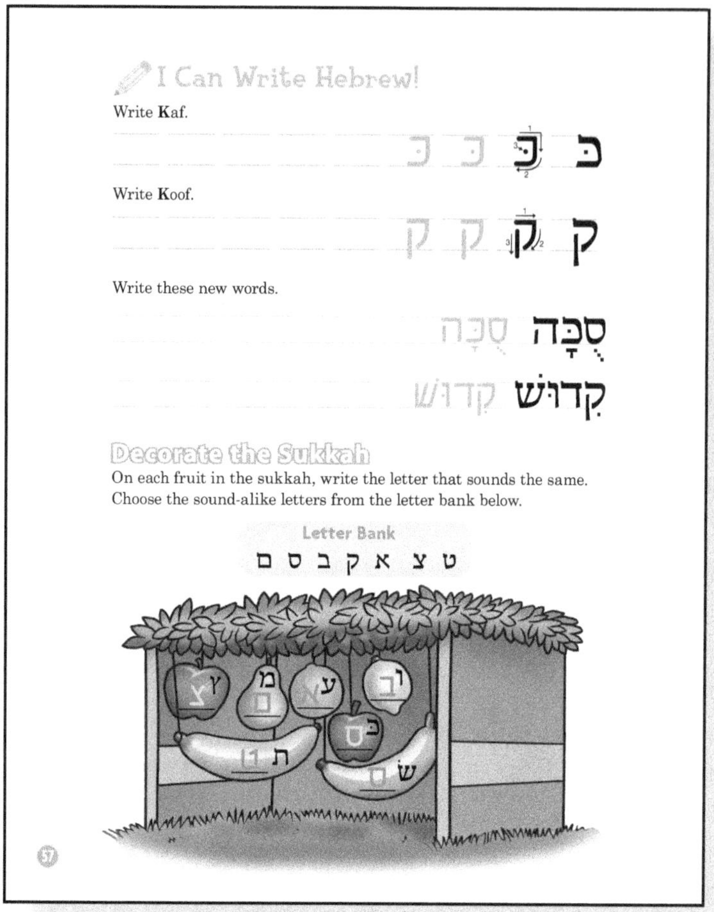

I Can Write Hebrew!

Write **K**af.

כ

Write **K**oof.

ק

Write these new words.

סֻכָּה

קִדּוּשׁ

Decorate the Sukkah

On each fruit in the sukkah, write the letter that sounds the same. Choose the sound-alike letters from the letter bank below.

Letter Bank

ט צ א ק ב ס ם

57

Odd Letter Out

On each line, circle the letter that does not make the sound of the letter in the box.

ת	ת	ט	ט	ת	**ה**	ת	ט	ת	T .1
ו	ב	ו	**י**	ו	ו	ו	ב	ו	V .2
ר	ר	ר	ר	ר	ר	ר	**ד**	ר	R .3
הַ	אָ	הָ	עָ	עָ	אַ	אָ	עַ	הָ	AH .4
ד	ד	ד	**ר**	ד	ד	ד	ד	ד	D .5
וּ	עֻ	אֻ	וּ	וּ	**א**	אֻ	עֻ	וּ	OO .6
ס	שׂ	**שׁ**	שׂ	ס	שׂ	שׂ	ס	ס	S .7

Clue to the Quest 12 Reading Riddle

Write the circled letters in the numbered spaces. Do not include vowels!

7 שׁ 6 א 5 ר 4 הָ — 3 ד 2 יָ 1 הַ

Use the first word to score bonus points in the Animal Antics game in Lesson Twelve of the Quest for the Golden Kiddush Cup.

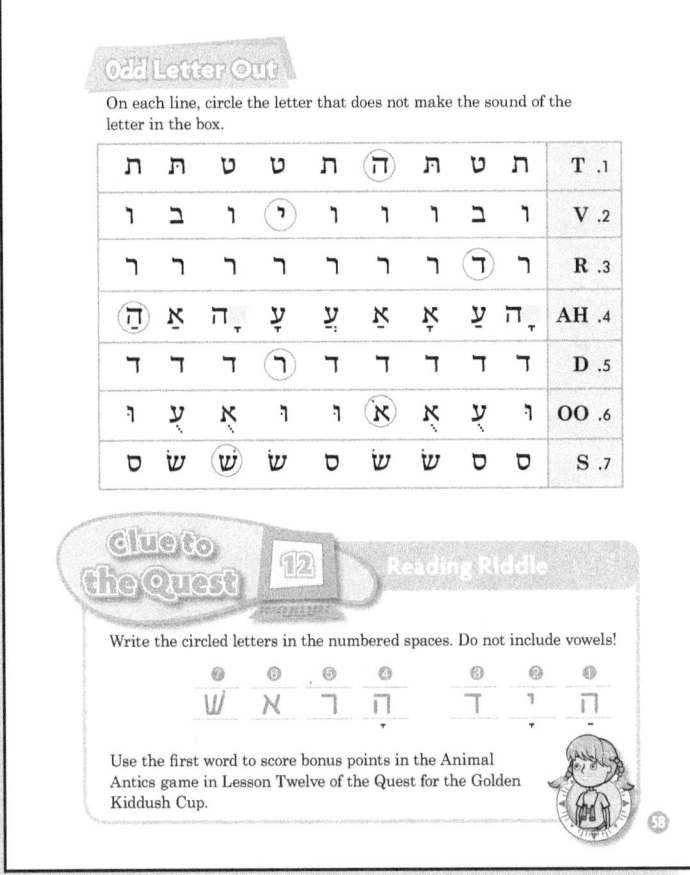

58

Assessment

For information on assessing students' progress, see page 9.

Odd Letter Out

This activity provides additional practice in recognizing multiple letters that represent single sounds. At the same time, it provides practice in making fine visual distinctions. Students practice differentiating between ת ה ו י ד ר ד ה הָ וּ אֻ שׂ שׁ.

Ask a volunteer to read the instructions, then allow students to complete the activity individually. Circulate to provide assistance as needed.

Clue to the Quest: Reading Riddle

Using the answers to the "Odd Letter Out" activity above, students are asked to find two Hebrew words that they have learned. (הַיָּד הָרֹאשׁ)

Ask students to complete this activity individually. Circulate to provide assistance as needed. Students will use the first word to score bonus points in the "Animal Antics" game in Lesson 12 of the digital application.

Challenge students to come to class next time with the answer to the following question. They can find the answer in Lesson 12 of the digital application.

What are two ways you can get to the top of Masada? (*by cable car or walking up the Snake Path*)

If students print out or e-mail their lesson summaries, remind them to do so when they have completed all the activities in this lesson.

Quest for the Golden Kiddush Cup

When students complete this lesson in their digital application, have them color piece #12 on the plate on page 4 of their book. They can also write in the key words and the new letters and vowels for this lesson.

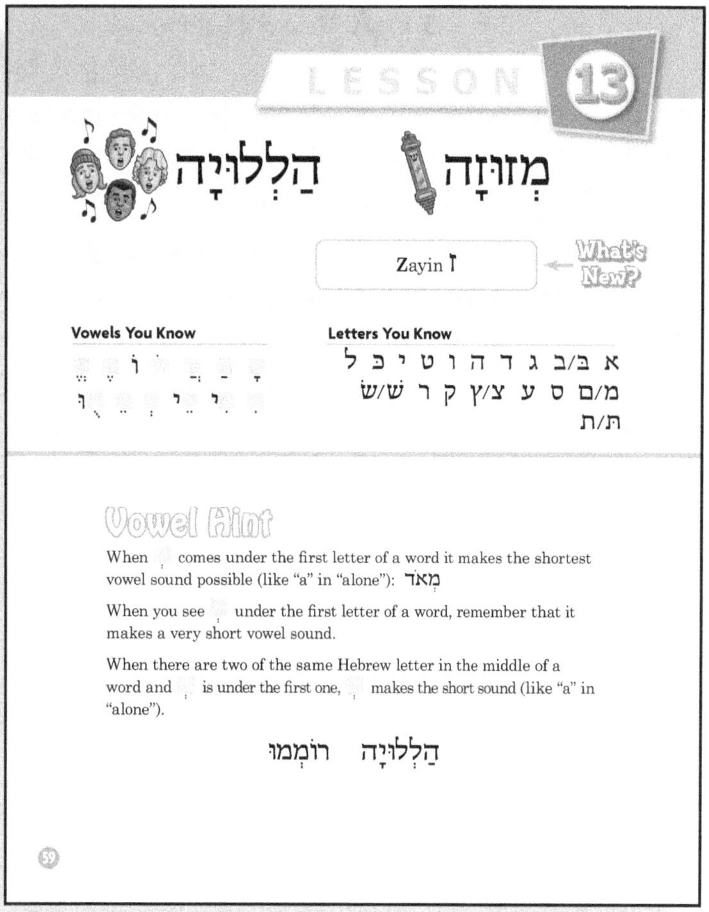
LESSON 13

הַלְלוּיָה מְזוּזָה

Zayin ז ← What's New?

Vowels You Know

Letters You Know

א בּ/ב ג ד ה ו ט י כּ ב ל

מ/ם ס ע צ/ץ ק ר שׁ/שׂ

ת/תּ

Vowel Hint

When ְ comes under the first letter of a word it makes the shortest vowel sound possible (like "a" in "alone"): מְאֹד

When you see ְ under the first letter of a word, remember that it makes a very short vowel sound.

When there are two of the same Hebrew letter in the middle of a word and ְ is under the first one, ְ makes the short sound (like "a" in "alone").

הַלְלוּיָה רוֹמְמוּ

59

Use the word מְזוּזָה to introduce the new letter *zayin* and the voiced version of ְ when it appears in the initial position. Next, introduce the key word הַלְלוּיָה. Consider having students first sing a line from "Halleluyah." (*halelu, halelu, halelu, halelu—halleluyah!*) Point out the voiced version of ְ when it appears under the first in a pair of doubled letters (לְל).

Vowel Hint

Read the information to the class, pausing between sections to discuss and to answer students' questions. Ask students to make their own "*Sh'va* Go Signs," using green construction paper circles, black markers, and glue. Have students glue their signs to the back of their Stop signs.

LESSON 13

Pages: 59–63

Key Words: מְזוּזָה הַלְלוּיָה

New Letter: ז

New Vowel: ְ (voiced)

Recommended Instructional Materials:
Phonics Flash Cards #2, 4–5, 10, 14–15, 30, and 37– 38, including two copies of #10, 14, and 38; Word Cards #26–27; cards for the "Same or Different?" game; the *Sh'va* Stop signs that students made in Lesson 10, and green construction paper circles (enough for the class)

Review Activity

Play the "Same or Different?" game (see page 15 for instructions). Begin with cards that require students to determine if individual letters are the same, then two-letter clusters, and finally three-letter clusters. (Students are not required to read the words.) For example:

ת ה ת ת צ צ צ ע

Then: טל טל טל מל שׁם שׁם שׁם שׂם

Finally: רגל דגל גור גור גור גיר
דגל דגל

Set Induction

Ask students what a red traffic light indicates (*stop*) and what a green light indicates (*go*). Remind students that Hebrew reading also has signs for "stop" and "go."

Introducing the Key Words and Deducing Their Sound-Symbol Associations

Introduce the key word מְזוּזָה by pointing out a mezuzah on the class doorpost or at the entrance to the synagogue. You can also pass around a mezuzah, allowing students to explore it and to examine the parchment (*klaf*) inside it. Tell students that the parchment has the words of the Sh'ma and V'ahavta prayers written on it. Introduce the new letter ז and its sound using the "Multi-Sensory Approach to Hebrew Phonics" described on page 11.

I Can Read Hebrew!

Read these Hebrew words out loud.

1. גְּדָל שְׁמוֹ דְּבַר יְקַר כְּמוֹ
2. רְצֵה כְּבוֹד דְּבַשׁ קְהַל מְאֹד
3. גְּאֻלָּה מְשַׁלֵּם יְרֻשָּׁה יְהוּדָה מְקַדֵּם
4. לְהַגִּיד מְרוֹמִים לְהַדְלִיק מְאוֹרוֹת קְדוֹשִׁים
5. גְּדוֹלָה קְשַׁרְתָּם תְּרוּעָה תְּקִיעָה שְׁבָרִים
6. הַלְלוּ טַלְלֵי רוֹמְמוּ הַלְלוּיָהּ הַלְלוּהוּ

It's a Match

On each line circle all the Hebrew syllables that make the sound of the English syllable in the box.

Zoo	זֻ	וֻ	יוֹ	וֶ	זוּ	זוֹ	וֻ	זֶ	זֻ	זוּ
So	טֹ	ם	סֹ	שׁוֹ	שׁוּ	סוּ	ם	טוֹ	שׁוֹ	שׁוֹ
Vo	כוֹ	בּוּ	וֻ	בוּ	זֻ	כּוּ	בוֹ	זוּ	וֻ	וֹ
Coo	כּוּ	בּוּ	קוּ	בּוֹ	כֻ	כֹּ	בוּ	קוּ	כֻ	בֹּ
Sue	סוֹ	שׁוּ	שֻׁ	טוּ	סֻ	שׁוֹ	סוּ	שׁוּ	טֻ	סוּ

60

I Can Read Hebrew!

Have students read this section immediately after the Vowel Hint on the previous page. Here students practice reading the voiced ְ. In lines 1–4, the second and fifth word are either rhymes or slant rhymes (the vowel rhymes but not the consonant). Ask students to read two, then three words at a time, then to read full lines. Line 6 drills the use of the voiced ְ when it appears under the first in a pair of doubled letters.

As volunteers read, ask the class to hold up their "Go" signs to indicate when they are reading the voiced ְ.

It's a Match

This activity provides additional practice in three skills, two of which are crucial for developing phonological awareness. First, just as there are certain pairs of English letters that can represent the same sound, there are letter and vowel symbols in Hebrew that stand for identical sounds. In this activity students review several letter pairs (ב/ו, ס/שׂ, and כּ/ק) and the vowel pairs ֹ/וֹ and ֻ/וּ. Students also practice making the fine auditory distinction between the *oo* and *oh* vowels.

In addition, students are required to make visual discriminations. For example, in the first row, students distinguish between the visually similar letters ז, ו, and י, as well as the visually similar vowels וֹ/וּ and ֻ/ֶ.

The second and fifth rows ask students to discriminate between the visually similar letters ס/ם/ט and שׁ/שׂ. The third row focuses on ו/ז and כ/בּ/ב, while the fourth centers on בּ/כּ.

Ask a volunteer to read the directions and allow students to complete the activity independently. Circulate to provide assistance as necessary.

Oral Language Lesson (Optional)

Introduce the words and phrases:

בֹּקֶר, בֹּקֶר טוֹב, עֶרֶב, עֶרֶב טוֹב, מַזָּל טוֹב

Show students pictures of the following scenes and ask which greeting they think is most appropriate.

- a person waking up in the morning (בֹּקֶר טוֹב)
- people eating breakfast (בֹּקֶר טוֹב)
- people eating dinner (עֶרֶב טוֹב)
- a bar or bat mitzvah or a bridal couple (מַזָּל טוֹב)

I Can Read Hebrew!

This reading section drills the new letter ז in all three positions within a word (beginning, middle, and end). The first line presents the new letter in the final position, the second in the initial position, and lines 3 and 4 in the medial position. Ask students to read the lines, then columns.

Lines 5 and 6 contain full sentences. Challenge students to read them as smoothly and rhythmically as possible. (*Line 5: Z'evi is Adam and Gila's dog. Line 6: Adam likes/loves Z'evi. Gila likes/loves Z'evi.*)

Sound Advice

This activity provides students with practice in segmenting the initial phoneme of several words using cognates (words that are similar in Hebrew and English). Practicing this skill is crucial because some students have difficulty making fine auditory distinctions. The sounds *z*, *s*, *tz*, and *sh* are similar, and some students confuse them. This activity provides students with practice in making these fine auditory distinctions. If a student struggles with this activity, it may indicate that he or she has difficulty making fine auditory distinctions and needs additional practice in this area.

Have students complete the activity individually. Review as a class.

I Can Read Hebrew!

Read these Hebrew words and sentences out loud.

1. מֵאָז מֶרְכָּז עֹז אֶרֶז רֶמֶז אֱגוֹז
2. זֶה זַמֵּר זֶרַע זֹאת זִיו זְאֵבָה
3. עוֹזֵר אֶזְכֹּר עֻזּוֹ זוּלָתוֹ יִזְכּוֹר מִזְמוֹר
4. עֶזְרִי אֲזַמְּרָה מְזוּזָה מְזֻזוֹת יַעַלְזוּ אֲרָזִים
5. זְאֵבִי הַכֶּלֶב שֶׁל אָדָם וְגִילָה.
6. אָדָם אוֹהֵב אֶת זְאֵבִי. גִּילָה אוֹהֶבֶת אֶת זְאֵבִי.

Sound Advice

The objects below have the same name in Hebrew and English. Cross out all the objects that do not begin with the letter ז.

61

I Can Write Hebrew!

Ask students to trace the letters with their fingers then write the letters in pencil. Review the letter names and sounds as students write them.

Ask students to write the key words for the lesson. Students can also write and/or illustrate the following sentences:

מְזוּזָה שָׁם.
הַלְלוּיָה!

Rhyme Time

Ask a volunteer to read the instructions. Tell the class to listen carefully, and ask a second volunteer to read line 1. Ask which two words rhyme. (זִיבָּה and קְוָה) Tell students to circle these two words. They can complete the activity individually or in pairs. Circulate to provide assistance as necessary.

Stop and Go

Because this activity is complex, it is best completed as a class. Read the directions aloud. Then invite one or two strong readers to read the Hebrew words in the center column. As they read, ask the class to hold up their Stop or Go sign to indicate which type of ְ is being read. After each word, have the readers pause to allow students time to write their answers in the correct blank spaces. Circulate to provide assistance as necessary.

Clue to the Quest: Crack the Code

Here again, the task is more complex than usual, so you may want to complete this activity as a class.

Students will use the word they find (צְדָקָה) to score bonus points in the "Ruin Quest" game in Lesson 13 of the digital application.

Challenge students to come to class next time with the answers to the following questions. They can find the answers in Lesson 13 of the digital application.

1. What was the capital of Israel under Roman rule? *(Caesaria)*
2. How old is the ancient amphitheater in Israel where you can still hear a concert? *(2,000 years)*

If students print out or e-mail their lesson summaries, remind them to do so when they have completed all the activities in this lesson.

Quest for the Golden Kiddush Cup

When students complete this lesson in their digital application, have them color piece #13 on the plate on page 4 of their book. They can also write in the key words and the new letter for this lesson.

Assessment

For information on assessing students' progress, see page 9.

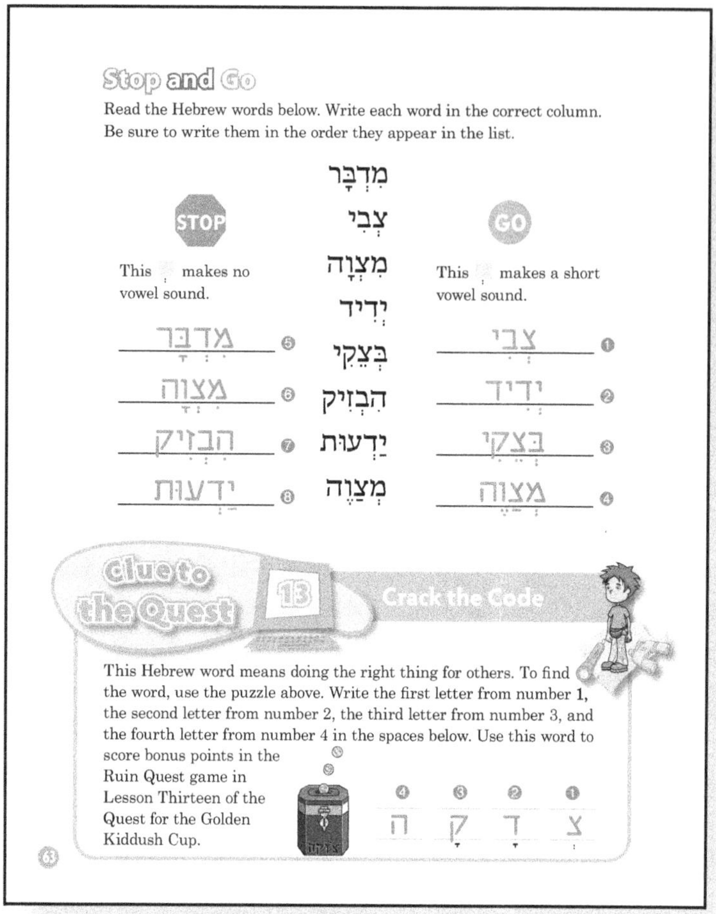

Stop and Go

Read the Hebrew words below. Write each word in the correct column. Be sure to write them in the order they appear in the list.

STOP — This ְ makes no vowel sound.

GO — This ְ makes a short vowel sound.

STOP		Words	GO	
מִדְבָּר	5	מִדְבָּר	צְבִי	1
מִצְוָה	6	צְבִי	יְדִיד	2
הִבְזִיק	7	מִצְוָה	בְּצֵקִי	3
יַדְעוּת	8	יְדִיד	מְצַוֶּה	4
		בְּצֵקִי		
		הִבְזִיק		
		יַדְעוּת		
		מְצַוֶּה		

Clue to the Quest 13 Crack the Code

This Hebrew word means doing the right thing for others. To find the word, use the puzzle above. Write the first letter from number 1, the second letter from number 2, the third letter from number 3, and the fourth letter from number 4 in the spaces below. Use this word to score bonus points in the Ruin Quest game in Lesson Thirteen of the Quest for the Golden Kiddush Cup.

4 ה 3 ק 2 ד 1 צ

63

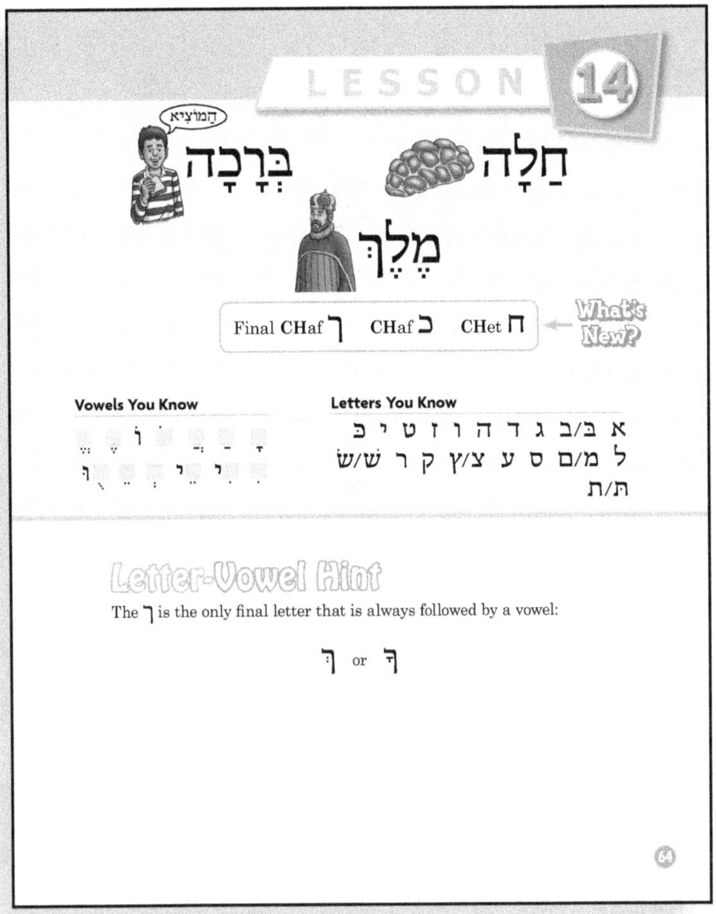
LESSON 14

חַלָּה בְּרָכָה מֶלֶךְ

Final CHaf ך CHaf כ CHet ח

Vowels You Know

Letters You Know

א בּ/ב ג ד ה ו ז ט י כּ
ל מ/ם ס ע צ/ץ ק ר שׁ/שׂ
תּ/ת

Letter-Vowel Hint

The ך is the only final letter that is always followed by a vowel:

ךְ or ךָ

64

LESSON 14

Pages: 64–67

Key Words: חַלָּה בְּרָכָה מֶלֶךְ

New Letters: ח כ ך

Recommended Instructional Materials: Phonics Flash Cards #2, 4–5, 9–10, 14, 17, 23, 30, and 39–41, and an additional copy each of #4 and 17; Word Cards #28-30; cards for the "Concentration" game; a ḥallah and napkins; photos of cake and ice cream, if you are including the oral language component

Review Activity

Play "Concentration" (see page 15 for instructions). Divide the class into groups of up to four students. Distribute sets of cards containing each of the following key words and their matching art:

סַבְתָּא סַבָּא הַבְדָּלָה מִצְוָה טַלִּית תּוֹרָה
רֶגֶל הַלְלוּיָהּ מְזוּזָה קִדּוּשׁ סֻכָּה יִשְׂרָאֵל

Set Induction

Show the class the ḥallah and ask them when we eat this kind of bread. (*Shabbat and holidays*)

Remind students that before we eat bread, we say a בְּרָכָה called הַמּוֹצִיא. Review the blessing with the class, then distribute the ḥallah and allow students to eat it.

בָּרוּךְ אַתָּה, יְיָ אֱלֹהֵינוּ, מֶלֶךְ הָעוֹלָם,
הַמּוֹצִיא לֶחֶם מִן הָאָרֶץ.

Praised are You, Adonai our God, Ruler of the world, who brings forth bread from the earth.

Introducing the Key Words and Deducing Their Sound-Symbol Associations

Introduce the key word חַלָּה as students are eating. Use this word to introduce the new letter ח using the "Multi-Sensory Approach to Hebrew Phonics" described on page 11. Next, introduce the key word בְּרָכָה, emphasizing the new letter כ, using the same approach. Ask students if they can find the word הַמּוֹצִיא on page 64. (*in the drawing of the boy eating bread*) Finally, introduce the word מֶלֶךְ using the same approach, and remind them that this word appears in every בְּרָכָה. Ask: Who does מֶלֶךְ refer to in a בְּרָכָה? (*God*)

Letter-Vowel Hint

Ask a volunteer to read the hint, then direct students to look at the words in the "I Can Read Hebrew!" section on page 65. Ask them to count how many words in this section end in ך. (9) How many contain ךְ? (5) How many contain ךָ? (4)

I Can Read Hebrew!

This reading selection drills the new letters ח, כ, and ך in all three positions within a word (beginning, middle, and end). This sound is often difficult for English-speaking students to recognize and pronounce.

Ask volunteers to read individual words in lines 1–5. Then ask students to read full lines, then columns of five words. Finally, challenge each student to read lines 4 and 5. Line 6 consists of two Hebrew sentences that should be read as fluently and smoothly as possible. (*Adam writes in the notebook. Gila writes Hebrew.*)

Sound Advice

One of the great challenges for native English speakers is learning how to pronounce those sounds that do not occur in the English language such as the sound of the three letters introduced in this lesson, as well as the sound of צ at the beginning of a word (where it occurs only in a very few words that English has borrowed from other languages, such as "tsetse fly").

This activity provides students with practice in segmenting the initial phoneme of several words using cognates (words that are similar in Hebrew and English), and making fine auditory distinctions between the new sound *ch* and *h* and *k*, the two sounds that English speakers are most likely to substitute for the new sound. If a student struggles with this activity, it may indicate that he or she has difficulty making fine auditory distinctions and needs additional practice in this skill.

Ask a volunteer to read the directions and allow students to complete the activity individually. Circulate to provide assistance as needed.

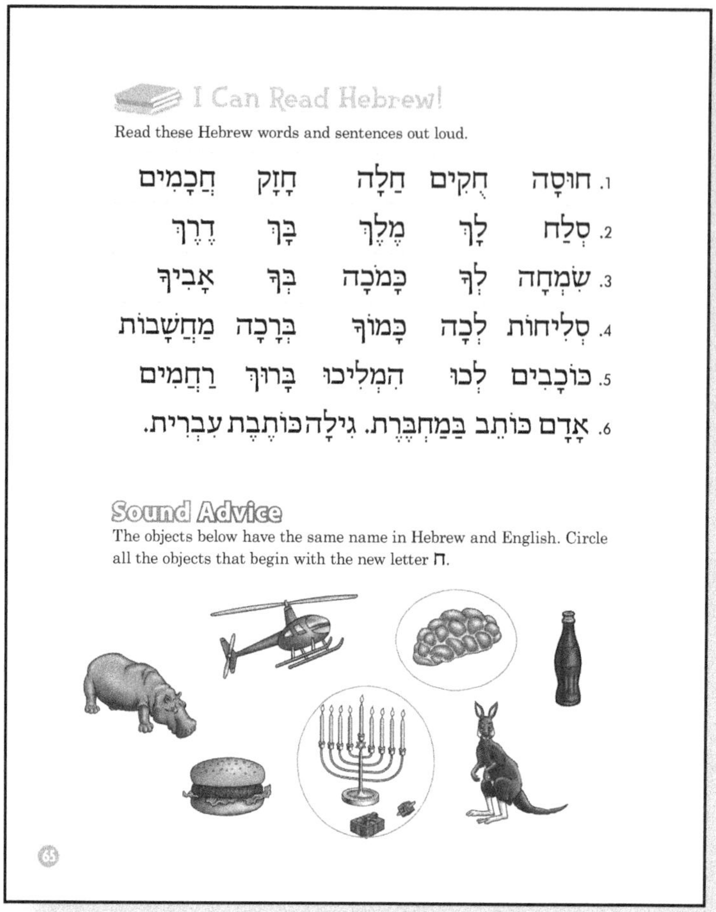

I Can Read Hebrew!

Read these Hebrew words and sentences out loud.

1. חוּסָה חֶקִים חַלָּה חָזָק חֲכָמִים
2. סְלַח לָךְ מֶלֶךְ בָּךְ דֶרֶךְ
3. שִׂמְחָה לְךָ כָּמֹכָה בְּךָ אָבִיךָ
4. סְלִיחוֹת לְכָה כָּמוֹךָ בְּרָכָה מַחֲשָׁבוֹת
5. כּוֹכָבִים לְכוּ הִמְלִיכוּ בָּרוּךְ רַחֲמִים
6. אָדָם כּוֹתֵב בַּמַחְבֶּרֶת. גִילָה כּוֹתֶבֶת עִבְרִית.

Sound Advice

The objects below have the same name in Hebrew and English. Circle all the objects that begin with the new letter ח.

65

Oral Language Lesson (Optional)

Introduce the words: שׁוֹתֶה/שׁוֹתָה
עוּגָה גְלִידָה וְ־/וּ אוֹכֵל/אוֹכֶלֶת

Drill the words using sentences such as:

אָדָם אוֹכֵל עוּגָה. גִילָה אוֹכֶלֶת גְלִידָה.
סַבָּא אוֹכֵל עוּגָה וּגְלִידָה. סַבְתָּא לֹא אוֹכֶלֶת.
אָדָם לֹא שׁוֹתֶה.

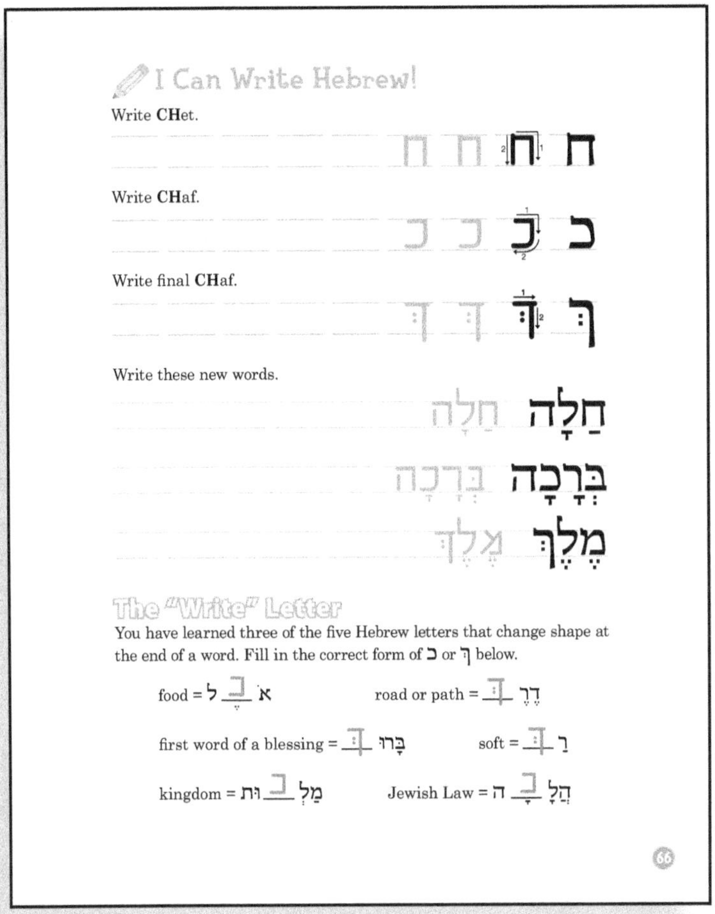
I Can Write Hebrew!

Write **CHet.**

ח

Write **CHaf.**

כ

Write final **CHaf.**

ךְ

Write these new words.

חַלָּה

בְּרָכָה

מֶלֶךְ

The "Write" Letter

You have learned three of the five Hebrew letters that change shape at the end of a word. Fill in the correct form of כ or ךְ below.

food = אֹ ___ ל

road or path = דֶּרֶ ___

first word of a blessing = בָּרוּ ___

soft = רַ ___

kingdom = מַלְ ___ וּת

Jewish Law = הֲלָ ___ ה

66

I Can Write Hebrew!

Ask students to trace the letters with their fingers then write the letters in pencil. Review the letter names and sounds as students write them. This provides auditory reinforcement for the visual and kinesthetic activity.

Ask students to write the key words for the lesson. Students can also write and/or illustrate the following sentences:

חַלָּה שָׁם.

דָּוִד הַמֶּלֶךְ.

The "Write" Letter

Here students practice the regular and final forms of the new letter כ/ךְ. Because writing provides an excellent kinesthetic reinforcement for visual information, practicing the dual forms in isolation can help students remember the concept of final letters.

Ask a volunteer to read the instructions. Ask students to complete the activity individually. Circulate among them to provide assistance as needed.

Sound Check

This activity asks students to identify and match Hebrew homonyms.

Allow students to work with partners in completing this activity. You may choose to assign stronger readers to work with weaker readers on this task. Ask the first partner to read the first word on the top line aloud. The second student should scan the words on the bottom line, identify the match, point to it, and read it aloud. If both partners agree, they should connect the words. If they do not, they should work together to find the correct answer. They should repeat this procedure with the second word, switching roles, and continue, alternating, until they complete the activity.

Clue to the Quest: Reading Riddle

Ask students to work individually or with a partner to complete the page. Circulate to provide assistance as necessary. Students can use the answer word (הַלְלוּיָה) to score bonus points in the "Keep Israel Green" game in Lesson 14 of the digital application.

Challenge students to come to class next time with the answers to the following questions. They can find the answers in Lesson 14 of the digital application.

1. Where can you see pelicans and cranes in Israel? (*the Hula Valley Nature Reserve*)
2. On which river can you go rafting in Israel? (*the Yarden River*)

If students print out or e-mail their lesson summaries, remind them to do so when they have completed all the activities in this lesson.

Quest for the Golden Kiddush Cup

When students complete this lesson in their digital application, have them color piece #14 on the plate on page 4 of their book. They can also write in the key words and the new letters for this lesson.

Assessment

For information on assessing students' progress, see page 9.

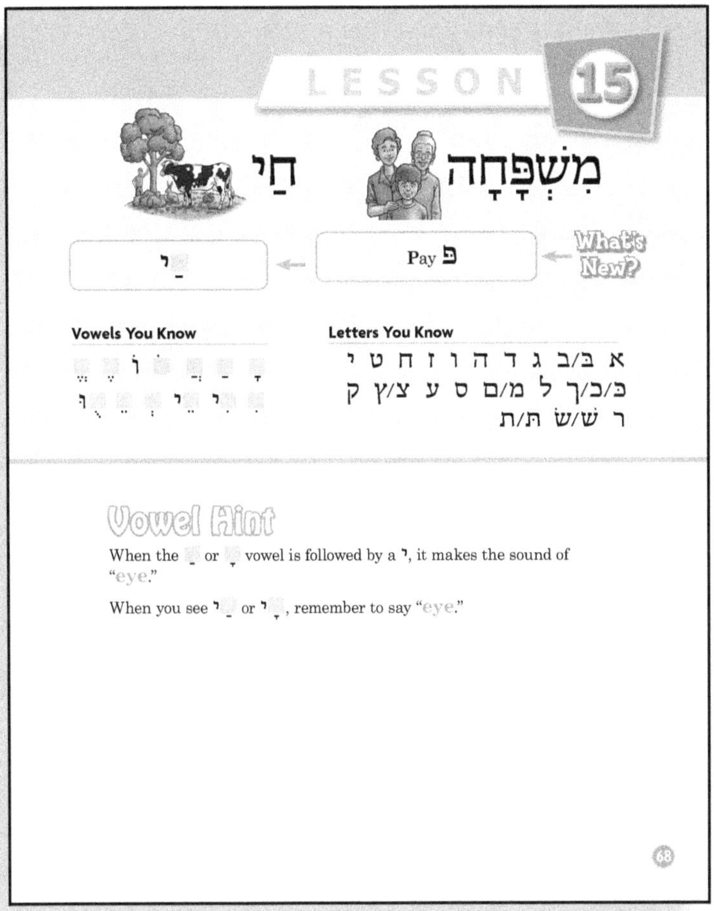
LESSON 15

מִשְׁפָּחָה חַי

What's New?

Pay פּ

יַ

Vowels You Know

Letters You Know

א בּ/ב ג ד ה ו ז ח ט י

כּ/כ/ך ל מ/ם ס ע צ/ץ ק

ר שׁ/שׂ תּ/ת

Vowel Hint

When the ַ or ָ vowel is followed by a י, it makes the sound of "eye."

When you see ַי or ָי, remember to say "eye."

68

LESSON 15

Pages: 68–71

Key Words: מִשְׁפָּחָה חַי

New Letter: פּ

New Vowel: ַי

Recommended Instructional Materials:
Phonics Flash Cards #1–2, 5, 14, 19, 30, 39, and 42–43, and two copies of #4; Word Cards #31–32; a חַי necklace; blue crayons or colored pencils

Review Activity

Play "Beginning, Middle, End" (see page 14 for instructions). Tell students to pay attention to where the target sound falls within each word. Use these words for each target sound.

צ: צְדָקָה מַצָּה מִיץ בֵּיצָה אֶרֶץ
רִיצוּד יִצְחָק

כ, ח: חָזָק דֶּרֶךְ כּוֹכָבִים סְלִיחוֹת חוּסָה
זָח יִצְחָק

ז: זֶבְּרָה זְאֵב תַּמּוּז רֶמֶז חָזָק
תִּזְמוֹרֶת רַמְזוֹר

ק, כּ: כָּבוֹד קוֹבַע יִצְחָק דַּק חָזָק רִיקּוּד
בִּרְכַּת

Set Induction

Pass the חַי necklace around the group, allowing students to feel the letters. Ask if students know what the Hebrew word is and why people might wear it as a necklace. (*life/live, because life is so important, helps people appreciate life*) Tell students that the two key words in this lesson express two important Jewish values.

Introducing the Key Words and Deducing Their Sound-Symbol Associations

Introduce the key word מִשְׁפָּחָה, reminding students that they have already met several members of this group (אִמָּא, סַבָּא, סַבְתָּא, אַבָּא). Use this word to introduce the new letter פּ through the "Multi-Sensory Approach to Hebrew Phonics" described on page 11. Next, introduce the key word חַי by reminding students about the necklace they examined, and use it to introduce the new vowel combination, ַי, using the same approach.

Vowel Hint

Ask a volunteer to read the information. You can add a tactile or kinesthetic association by asking students to point to the outside corner of their eyes when they pronounce each of the new vowels. Such kinesthetic associations can help students recall the auditory and visual associations more readily.

Oral Language Lesson (Optional)

Introduce the words צִפּוֹר חָתוּל מַיִם בַּיִת כֶּלֶב, using pictures to illustrate each word.

Drill these words using sentences such as:

כֶּלֶב בַּבַּיִת. חָתוּל בַּבַּיִת.

צִפּוֹר בַּבַּיִת.

דָּג בַּמַּיִם.

חָתוּל לֹא בַּמַּיִם.

I Can Read Hebrew!

This exercise drills the new letter פּ in both positions in which it can occur within a word (beginning and middle). The letter does not occur at the end in any native Hebrew word, but can appear in those words that are borrowed from other languages, such as קֶטְשַׁאפּ.

Ask volunteers to read individual words then full lines. They can also read columns of five words.

The "Write" Letter

Here students practice two skills: 1) the fine auditory distinction between the sounds of the letters ח and ה, and 2) visual discrimination among ה, ח, and תּ.

Ask a volunteer to read the instructions. Ask students to complete the activity individually. Circulate among them to provide assistance as needed.

I Can Read Hebrew!

Read these Hebrew words out loud.

1. פֶּלֶא פּוֹעֵל פַּחַד פּוֹחֵז פָּשׁוּט
2. פַּרְעֹה פֹּעֲלֵי פְּתַח פֶּסַח פִּלְפּוּל
3. כַּפֵּר אַפּוֹ חִפֵּשׂ תַּפּוּז רֻפָּה
4. כִּפָּה טִפָּה חֻפָּה מִסְפָּר כִּפּוּר
5. מִתְפַּלֵּל יִפֹּלוּ הַפּוֹרֵשׁ מִשְׁפָּחָה כִּפּוּרִים

The "Write" Letter

The objects below have the same name in Hebrew and English. Circle the Hebrew letter that begins each word.

ה ח תּ   ה ח תּ   ה ח תּ   ה ח תּ   ה ח תּ

69

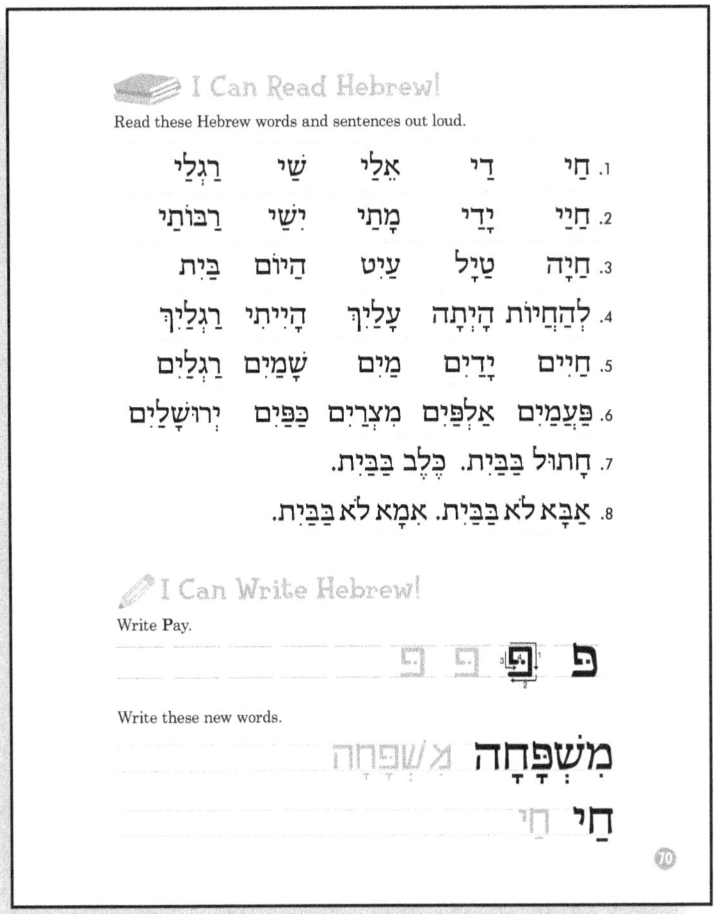

I Can Read Hebrew!

Read these Hebrew words and sentences out loud.

1. חַי דַי אֵלַי שַׁי רַגְלַי
2. חַיַּי יָדַי מָתַי יִשַׁי רַבּוֹתַי
3. חַיָּה טַיָּל עַיִט הַיּוֹם בַּיִת
4. לְהַחֲיוֹת הָיְתָה עָלַיִךְ הָיִיתִי רַגְלַיִךְ
5. חַיִּים יָדַיִם מַיִם שָׁמַיִם רַגְלַיִם
6. פַּעֲמַיִם אַלְפַּיִם מִצְרַיִם כַּפַּיִם יְרוּשָׁלַיִם
7. חָתוּל בַּבַּיִת. כֶּלֶב בַּבַּיִת.
8. אַבָּא לֹא בַּבַּיִת. אִמָּא לֹא בַּבַּיִת.

I Can Write Hebrew!

Write Pay.

פּ

Write these new words.

מִשְׁפָּחָה

חַי

70

I Can Read Hebrew!

Lines 1 and 2 present ַי at the end of a word. Ask students to read the lines in groups of three, then two words. Ask volunteers to read clusters of words then full lines. They can also read columns of six words.

Lines 7 and 8 contain actual sentences, which should be read as fluently and smoothly as possible. (*Line 7: A cat is in the house. A dog is in the house. Line 8: Father/Dad is not in the house. Mother/Mom is not in the house.*)

I Can Write Hebrew!

Ask students to trace the letters with their fingers then write the letters in pencil. Review the letter names and sounds as students write them. Remember that this provides auditory reinforcement for the visual and kinesthetic activity.

For fun, after students have completed writing the letters and key words, ask them to draw a family tree, entitled הַמִּשְׁפָּחָה. They can include their grandparents, parents, and themselves.

As an alternative, they can illustrate the following sentence:

דָּוִד, מֶלֶךְ יִשְׂרָאֵל, חַי!

Consider teaching students the song.

Super Reading Secret #4

This activity provides students with practice in making fine visual distinctions between ַי, ֵי, and ִי.

Distribute blue crayons or colored pencils to the class. Ask a volunteer to read the directions, then ask students to complete this activity individually. Circulate to provide assistance as needed.

Note: Some students may have difficulty remembering the pronunciation of ַי, confusing it with ֵי. In most cases this indicates a difficulty with visual discrimination. Offer these students additional practice in these vowel combinations.

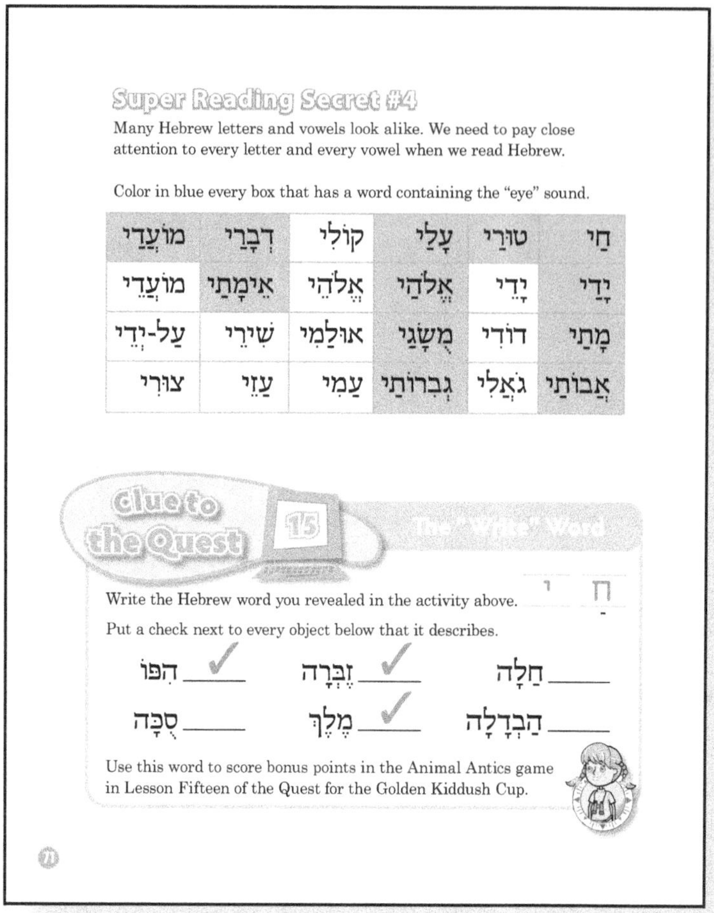

Super Reading Secret #4

Many Hebrew letters and vowels look alike. We need to pay close attention to every letter and every vowel when we read Hebrew.

Color in blue every box that has a word containing the "eye" sound.

מוֹעֲדַי	דְבָרַי	קוֹלִי	עָלַי	טוּרַי	חַי
מוֹעֲדֵי	אֵימָתַי	אֱלֹהֵי	אֱלֹהַי	יָדֵי	יָדַי
עַל-יְדֵי	שִׁירֵי	אוּלַמִי	מְשָׁגַי	דוֹדִי	מָתַי
צוּרִי	עֲזֵי	עַמִי	גְבוּרוֹתַי	גְאַלִי	אֲבוֹתַי

Clue to the Quest 15 The "Write" Word

Write the Hebrew word you revealed in the activity above. ח ַ י

Put a check next to every object below that it describes.

הִפּוֹ ✓ זֶבְרָה ✓ חַלָה ___

סֻכָּה ___ מֶלֶךְ ✓ הַבְדָלָה ___

Use this word to score bonus points in the Animal Antics game in Lesson Fifteen of the Quest for the Golden Kiddush Cup.

71

Clue to the Quest: The "Write" Word

Students should use the answer to the "Super Reading Secret" above (חַי) to complete this activity. Students will experience reading Hebrew with comprehension. (Students who are completing the *Alef Bet Quest Companion Reader* will already have a great deal of experience with this.)

Ask volunteers to read the instructions and each word. The class as a whole can vote whether each item is alive. Students can use the word חַי to score bonus points in the "Animal Antics" game in Lesson 15 of the digital application.

Challenge students to come to class next time with the answers to the following questions. They can find the answers in Lesson 15 of the digital application.

1. How many kinds of animals are protected in the Ḥai Bar Animal Preserve? *(450)*
2. What did the ostrich not do? *(bury its head in the sand)*

If students print out or e-mail their lesson summaries, remind them to do so when they have completed all the activities in this lesson.

Quest for the Golden Kiddush Cup

When students complete this lesson in their digital application, have them color piece #15 on the plate on page 4 of their book. They can also write in the key words and the new letter and vowel for this lesson.

Assessment

For information on assessing students' progress, see page 9.

LESSON 16

נֵר יַיִן

What's New?

Nun נ Final Nun ן

ֵיךָ

Vowels You Know

Letters You Know

א בּ/ב ג ד ה ו ז ח ט י
כּ/כ/ך ל מ/ם ס ע פּ צ/ץ
ק ר שׁ/שׂ תּ/ת

I Can Read Hebrew!

Read these Hebrew words out loud.

1. פֶּן יַיִן מָזוֹן קֶרֶן רָצוֹן
2. חֵן צִיוֹן פִּזְמוֹן פְּרְקָן שָׂשׂוֹן
3. נֵר נִסִּים נְסַפֵּר נְבִיאִים נִזָּכֵר
4. נָטַע נֵלְכָה נֵצַח נַחֲלָה נִשְׂמַח
5. חֲנֻכָּה הַמוֹנָם פָּנַי עֲנָוִים חַשְׁמוֹנַי
6. אֲנַחְנוּ אָבִינוּ פִּינוּ יִתְעַנְּגוּ יְרַנְּנוּ

72

LESSON 16

Pages: 72–77

Key Words: נֵר יַיִן

New Letters: נ ן

New Vowel: ֵיךָ

Recommended Instructional Materials:
Phonics Flash Cards #5, 19, 23, 33, and 44–46, and two copies of #15; Word Cards #1–34; two Shabbat candles and a bottle of kosher wine

Review Activity

Play "Tic-Tac-Toe" (see page 14 for instructions) to review difficult letter and vowel combinations. For example, use ַי, ֵי, ַ, שׂ, and ח/כ/ך words in the center and the four corners of the grid. Use easier items in the remaining squares.

Set Induction

Ask students what Shabbat items they know. *(Answers may include ḥallah, candles, wine, Torah, havdalah set.)* Tell students that most people light two Shabbat candles, while some light a candle for every family member. Introduce the key word נֵר. Explain that נֵר is singular. Pass Shabbat candles around the class. If you choose, tell students that the plural is נֵרוֹת (candles).

Next, discuss wine as a symbol of joy on Shabbat and holidays.

Introducing the Key Words and Deducing Their Sound-Symbol Associations

Highlight the new letter נ in נֵר using the "Multi-Sensory Approach to Hebrew Phonics" described on page 11. Then introduce ן through the key word יַיִן, using the same approach and directly associating the new word with a bottle of kosher wine.

I Can Read Hebrew!

The first two lines in this activity drill final ן, lines 3 and 4 drill נ in the initial position, and lines 5 and 6 provide practice with נ in the middle of the word—the most difficult position for beginning readers. The third and fifth words on each line rhyme. Ask students to read each line in groups of three, then two words, and finally as full lines. For variety, students can also read the words in columns.

Oral Language Lesson (Optional)

Review עַל עֶרֶב בֹּקֶר

Using pictures, introduce לַיְלָה כִּסֵּא תַּחַת. Drill these words using sentences such as:

לַיְלָה בַּבַּיִת.

כֶּלֶב תַּחַת כִּסֵּא. חָתוּל עַל כִּסֵּא.

Consider having students illustrate the sentences.

Super Reading Secret #5

This Super Reading Secret presents an important sight word that students need to know in order to read prayer texts—the abbreviation that is used in place of God's name: יְיָ

Read this passage to the class and ask students to summarize their understanding of its meaning.

Have students practice reading the word יְיָ. Write the opening six words of the blessing formula on the board. If it is customary in your synagogue to refrain from writing and erasing God's name, write אֱ-לֹהֵינוּ in place of אֱלֹהֵינוּ. Call individual students up. Read one of the words, and ask a student to point to the correct word and repeat it. The class should repeat the word if the student is correct. Repeat with the remaining words.

Sound Off

This activity provides students with practice in making associations between Hebrew letter symbols and their sounds. At the same time, it provides practice in making fine visual distinctions.

Have students complete the activity individually. Allow students to check each other's work.

Students should then fill the circled letters in the numbered spaces to find a Hebrew word they know. (מִשְׁפָּחָה)

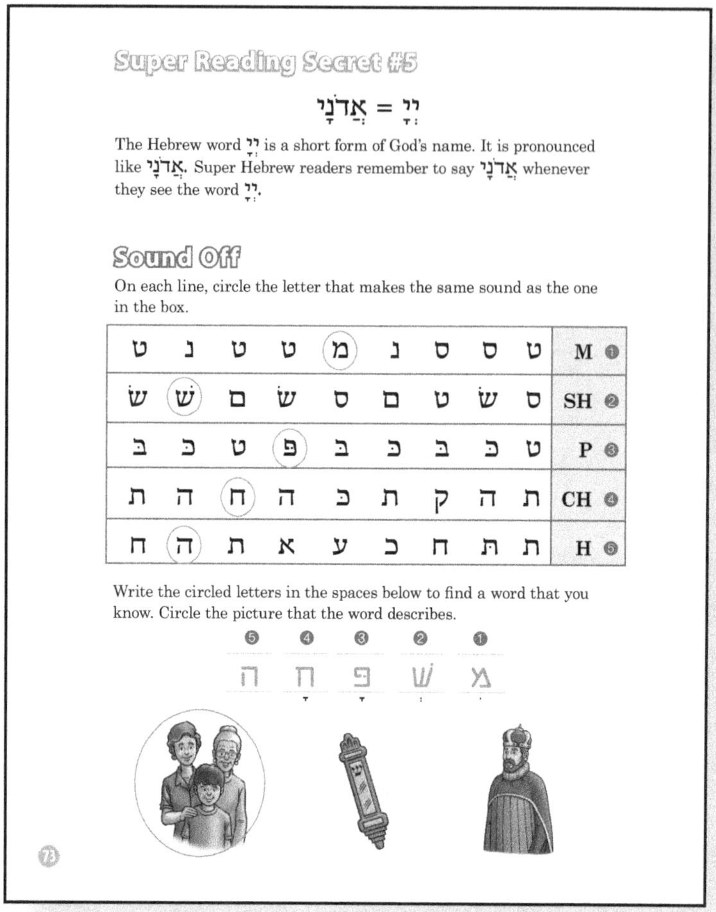

Super Reading Secret #5

יְיָ = אֲדֹנָי

The Hebrew word יְיָ is a short form of God's name. It is pronounced like אֲדֹנָי. Super Hebrew readers remember to say אֲדֹנָי whenever they see the word יְיָ.

Sound Off

On each line, circle the letter that makes the same sound as the one in the box.

ט	נ	ט	ט	מ	נ	ס	ס	ט	M 1
שׂ	שׁ	ם	שׂ	ס	ם	ט	שׁ	ס	SH 2
ב	כ	ט	פּ	ב	כ	ב	כ	ט	P 3
ת	ה	ח	ה	כ	ת	ק	ה	ת	CH 4
ח	ה	ת	א	ע	כ	ח	ת	ת	H 5

Write the circled letters in the spaces below to find a word that you know. Circle the picture that the word describes.

5 4 3 2 1

ה ח פּ שְׁ מִ

73

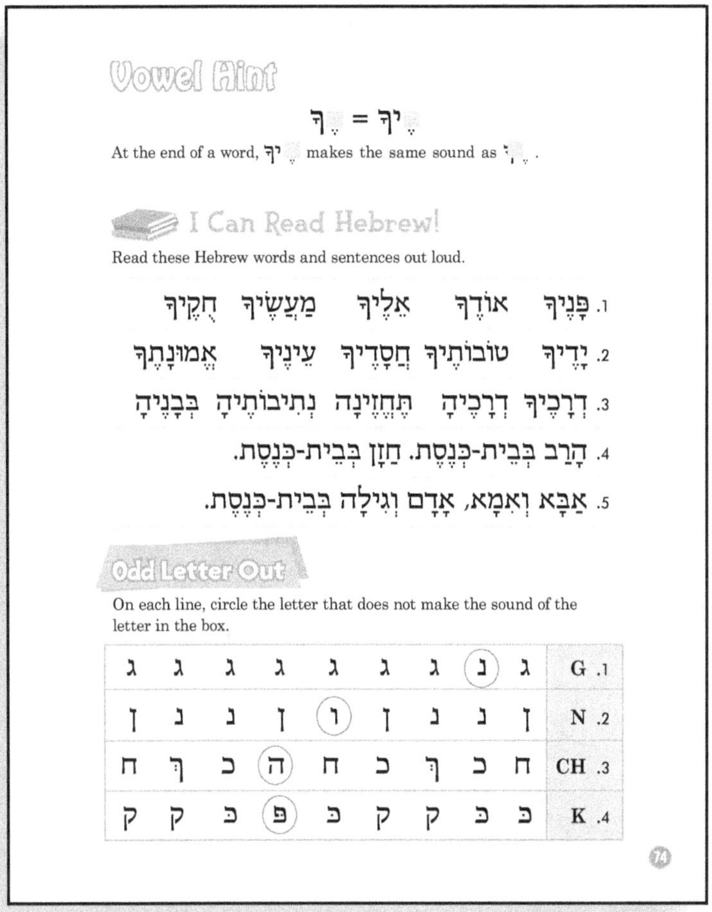
Vowel Hint

ֶיךָ = ֶךָ

At the end of a word, ֶיךָ makes the same sound as ֶךָ.

I Can Read Hebrew!

Read these Hebrew words and sentences out loud.

1. פָּנֶיךָ אוֹדְךָ אֵלֶיךָ מַעֲשֶׂיךָ חֻקֶּיךָ
2. יָדֶיךָ טוּבוֹתֶיךָ חֲסָדֶיךָ עֵינֶיךָ אֱמוּנָתֶךָ
3. דְּרָכֶיךָ דְּרָכֶיהָ תְּחֶזֶינָה נְתִיבוֹתֶיהָ בְּבָנֶיהָ
4. הָרַב בְּבֵית-כְּנֶסֶת. חַזָּן בְּבֵית-כְּנֶסֶת.
5. אַבָּא וְאִמָּא, אָדָם וְגִילָה בְּבֵית-כְּנֶסֶת.

Odd Letter Out

On each line, circle the letter that does not make the sound of the letter in the box.

1. G	ג	נ	ג	ג	ג	ג	ג	ג	ג
2. N	ן	נ	נ	ן	ו	ן	נ	נ	ן
3. CH	ח	כ	ךְ	כ	ח	ה	כ	ךְ	ח
4. K	כּ	כּ	ק	ק	כּ	פּ	כּ	ק	ק

74

Vowel Hint

Display Phonics Flash Card #46 and tell students that this combination can only come at the end of a word. The י is not pronounced in this combination.

I Can Read Hebrew!

Many of the words in this section are longer than students are used to seeing. Ask volunteers to read words individually, then two or three at a time, and finally in full lines.

Lines 4 and 5 contain actual sentences, two per line, which should be read as fluently and smoothly as possible. (*Line 4: The rabbi is in a synagogue. A cantor is in a synagogue. Line 5: Father and Mother, Adam and Gila are in a synagogue.*)

Odd Letter Out

As students progress, they encounter more letters that resemble those they have previously learned. For example, both נ and ן can be confused with several other letters such as ו and ג. This activity provides additional practice in making fine visual distinctions between similar letters. In line 1, students are asked to distinguish between ג and נ. In line 2, students are asked to associate נ and ן with the sound *n*, while differentiating them from ו. In line 3, they are asked to discriminate between ח and ה and to distinguish the *ch* sound. Line 5 asks students to associate כּ and ק with the *k* sound, while distinguishing their shapes from that of פּ.

Ask students to complete this activity individually. Circulate to provide assistance as needed.

I Can Write Hebrew!

Ask students to trace the letters with their fingers, then to write the letters in pencil. Review the letter names and sounds as students write them.

For fun, after students have written the letters and key words, they can draw a picture of a Shabbat table with wine, candles, and ḥallah and entitle their drawing שַׁבָּת. Students should then label all of the items in Hebrew.

The "Write" Letter

This activity gives students additional practice with the regular and final forms of the new letter נ/ן. Because writing provides an excellent kinesthetic reinforcement for visual information, practicing the dual forms in isolation should help students remember the concept of final letters.

Ask a volunteer to read the instructions. Ask students to complete the activity individually. Circulate among them to provide assistance as needed.

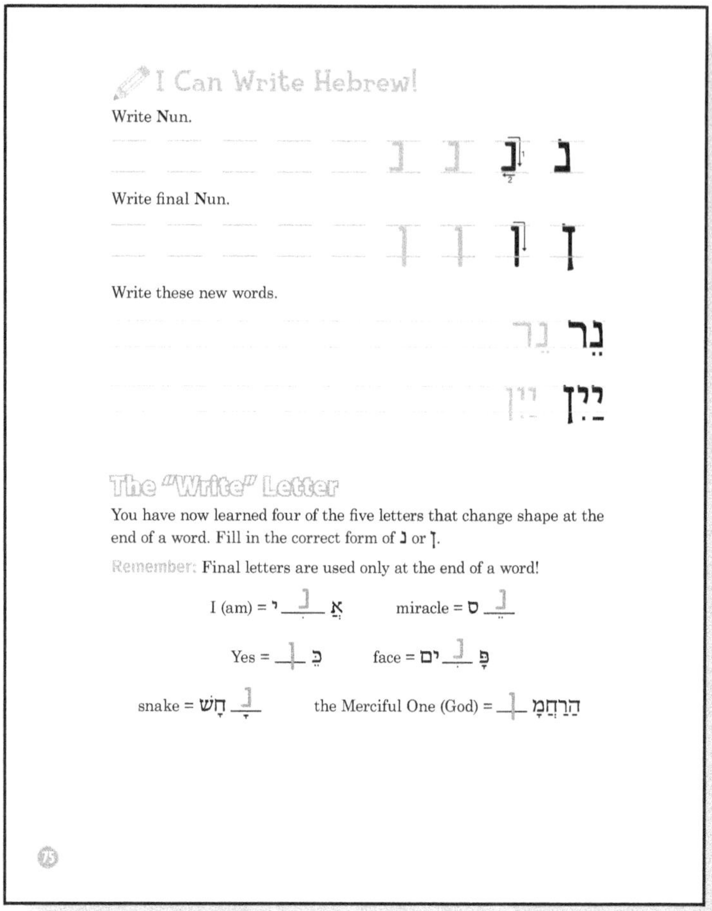

I Can Write Hebrew!

Write Nun.

נ נ

Write final Nun.

ן ן

Write these new words.

נֵר נֵר

יַיִן יַיִן

The "Write" Letter

You have now learned four of the five letters that change shape at the end of a word. Fill in the correct form of נ or ן.

Remember: Final letters are used only at the end of a word!

I (am) = אֲ___י

miracle = ___ס

Yes = כֵּ___

face = פָּ___ים

snake = ___חָשׁ

the Merciful One (God) = הָרַחֲמָ___

75

Just for Fun

Tongue twisters are a fun way to use language. Teach students one of the following Hebrew tongue twisters. You can teach it orally, or you can write it on the board and have students read the words, since they have learned all of the letters and vowels.

גַּנָּן גִּדֵּל דָּגָן בַּגַּן. דָּגָן גָּדוֹל גָּדַל בַּגַּן.

A gardener grew corn in the garden. Big corn grew in the garden.

נָחָשׁ נָשַׁךְ נָחָשׁ נָשׁוּךְ.

A snake bit a bitten snake.

"פַּרְפַּר," פֶּרַח אָמַר,
"הַיּ! רֵד־נָא, שֵׁב־נָא עָלַי!"

"Butterfly," said the flower, "Hi! Please come down and sit on me."

Picture This

Check the words that describe each picture.

- אִמָּא ✓
- סַבָּא ✓
- סַבְתָּא
- מִשְׁפָּחָה ✓
- הַבְדָּלָה
- מְזוּזָה ✓

- חַי ✓
- מִשְׁפָּחָה ✓
- קֶנְגּוּרוּ ✓
- בֵּיצָה
- הַלְלוּיָה
- הִפּוֹ ✓

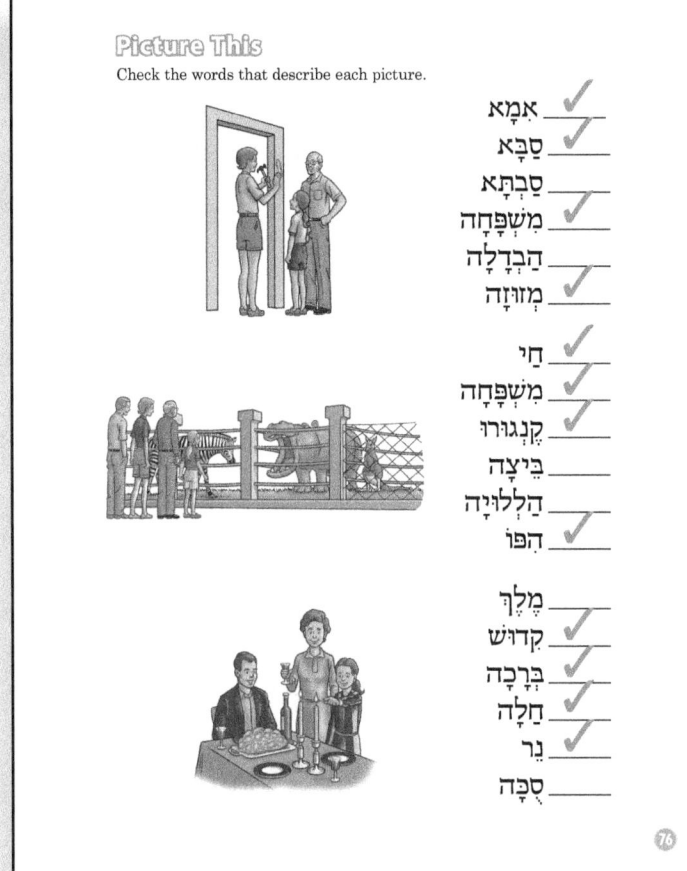

- מֶלֶךְ
- קִדּוּשׁ ✓
- בְּרָכָה ✓
- חַלָּה ✓
- נֵר ✓
- סֻכָּה

76

Picture This

Here students review many of the key words they have learned by putting a check next to each word that describes the picture.

Before students complete the page, you may want to do a full review of the key words they have learned so far. Using four to six cards at a time, display Word Cards 1–34 on the board. Call on students one at a time and read one of the words. The student must then point to the word and read it. If he or she is correct, the class should repeat the word. If the student's choice is incorrect, ask him or her to self-correct.

You can also ask students to find a word according to its meaning. For example, you can display the following words: מְזוּזָה חַלָּה תּוֹרָה טַלִּית סֻכָּה

Ask a student to find the word that: describes where we celebrate the fall harvest holiday (סֻכָּה), identifies what adult Jews can wear when they pray (טַלִּית), names the "book" that contains the story and laws of the Jewish people (תּוֹרָה), marks a house as a Jewish home (מְזוּזָה), describes the bread we eat on Shabbat and holidays (חַלָּה), etc. The student should point to the word and read it. If he or she is correct, the class should repeat the word. If the student's choice is incorrect, the class should remain silent, and the student should try to correct the error.

You can also have students match Word Cards with their pictures.

Complete the first part of the activity together as a class, then allow students to complete the other two parts individually or with a partner. Circulate around the room to provide assistance as needed.

Clue to the Quest: Reading Riddle

Ask a volunteer to read the instructions, which are written in the form of a poem. Allow students to complete the crossword puzzle individually or with a partner. In the numbered spaces below the puzzle, students should fill in the letter from the yellow box that corresponds to the number.

They can use this word (מִצְוָה) to score bonus points in the "Super Water Ski" game in Lesson 16 of the digital application.

Challenge students to come to class next time with the answers to the following questions. They can find the answers in Lesson 16 of the digital application.

1. Where can you snorkel in Israel? (*Eilat*)
2. What can you see when you snorkel in Eilat? (*colorful fish and coral*)

If students print out or e-mail their lesson summaries, remind them to do so when they have completed all the activities in this lesson.

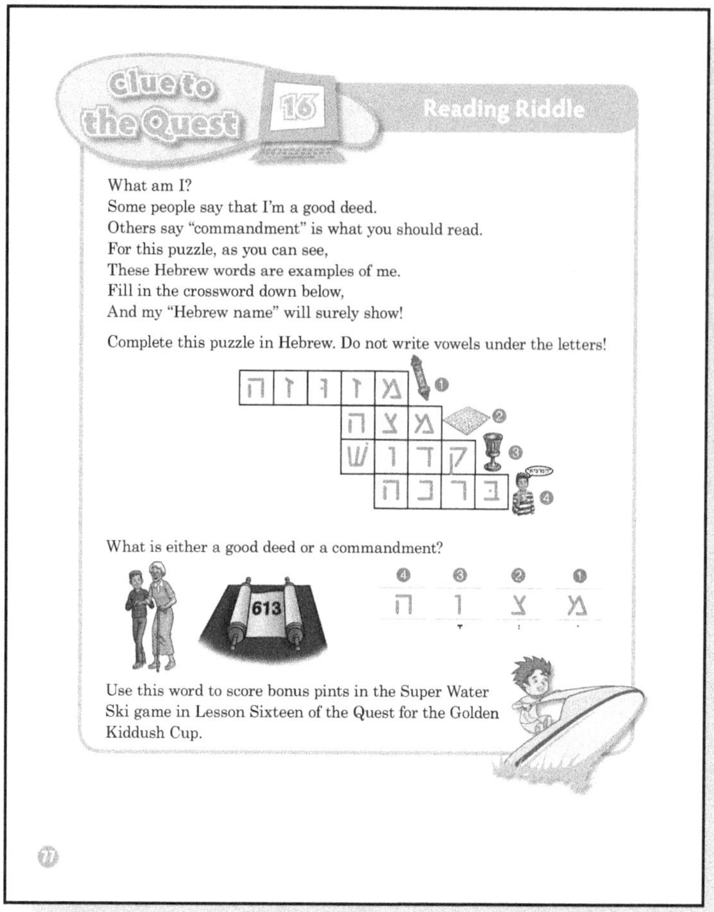
Clue to the Quest 16 Reading Riddle

What am I?
Some people say that I'm a good deed.
Others say "commandment" is what you should read.
For this puzzle, as you can see,
These Hebrew words are examples of me.
Fill in the crossword down below,
And my "Hebrew name" will surely show!

Complete this puzzle in Hebrew. Do not write vowels under the letters!

מזוזה ❶
מצה ❷
קדוש ❸
ברכה ❹

What is either a good deed or a commandment?

❹ ה ❸ ו ❷ צ ❶ מ

Use this word to score bonus pints in the Super Water Ski game in Lesson Sixteen of the Quest for the Golden Kiddush Cup.

77

Quest for the Golden Kiddush Cup

When students complete this lesson in their digital application, have them color piece #16 on the plate on page 4 of their book. They can also write in the key words and the new letters and vowel for this lesson.

Assessment

For information on assessing students' progress, see page 9.

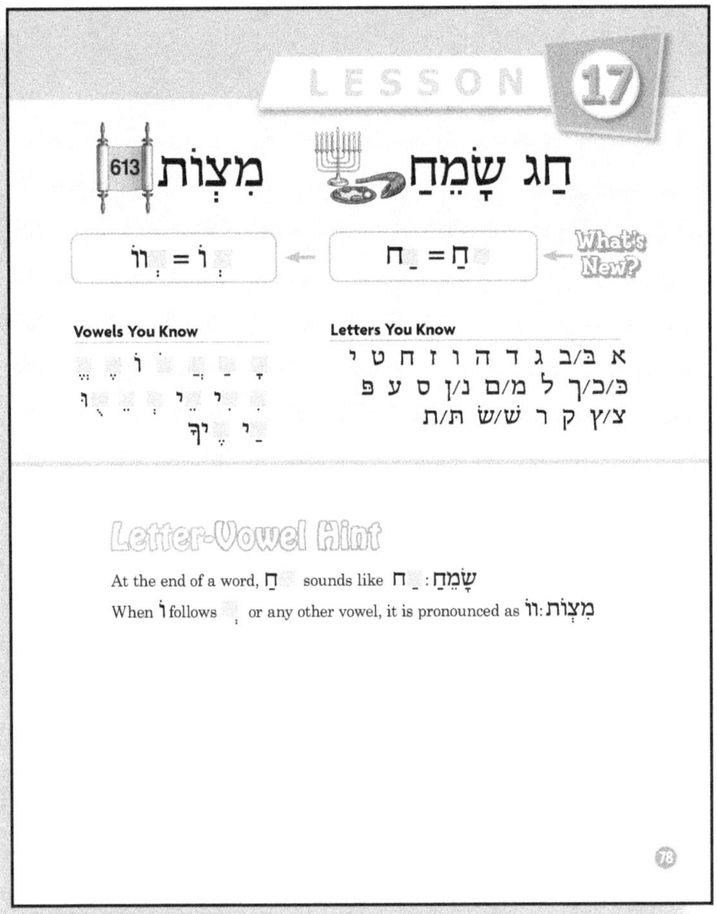

Letter-Vowel Hint

Ask a volunteer to read the passage. You may want to let different students explain the information in their own words.

LESSON 17

Pages: 78–81

Key Words: חַג שָׂמֵחַ מִצְוֹת

New Vowels: חַ וֹ

Recommended Instructional Materials:
Phonics Flash Cards #2, 4, 16, 19, 21, 27, 30, 32–33, and 47–48, and two copies each of #5 and 39; Word Cards #35-36; teacher-made Bingo cards composed of the letters and vowels learned to this point; pictures of various Jewish holidays

Review Activity

Play "Phonics Bingo" (see page 15 for instructions).

Set Induction

Ask students to list all of the English "hello" greetings that they can think of. (*hello, hi, howdy, what's up? how ya' doin' today?, etc.*) Next, ask students to list all of the English "farewell" greetings that they can think of. (*good-bye, see you later, peace out, L8R, etc.*) Tell students that they already know one Hebrew word that is both a greeting and a farewell, and ask them to name that word. (שָׁלוֹם) Ask them if they can think of a special greeting for Shabbat. (שַׁבָּת שָׁלוֹם) Tell the class that one of their new key words is a greeting for holidays.

Introducing the Key Words and Deducing Their Sound-Symbol Associations

Hold up a picture of a Jewish holiday celebration, wave to the class, and say:
חַג שָׂמֵחַ!

Ask the class to repeat the Hebrew phrase. Using the "Multi-Sensory Approach to Hebrew Phonics" described on page 11, introduce the new letter-vowel combination at the end of the word (חַ), its sound, and the way that the letter and vowel reverse position.

Next, introduce the second key word, מִצְוֹת. Highlight the fact that here, וֹ represents both a letter *and* a vowel sound.

Oral Language Lesson
(Optional)

Review לֹא אוֹכֵל/אוֹכֶלֶת

Introduce אֲנִי לֶחֶם פִּיצָה שׁוֹקוֹלָד תַּפּוּז

Drill the words using the following sentences:

אֲנִי אוֹכֵל פִּיצָה. אֲנִי אוֹכֶלֶת לֶחֶם. אַתְּ אוֹכֶלֶת שׁוֹקוֹלָד? כֵּן, אֲנִי אוֹכֶלֶת שׁוֹקוֹלָד. אַתָּה אוֹכֵל תַּפּוּז? לֹא, אֲנִי לֹא אוֹכֵל תַּפּוּז. אֲנִי אוֹכֵל לֶחֶם.

I Can Read Hebrew!

Lines 1–4 drill the *"furtive pataḥ,"* or פַּתָּח גָּנוּב, with the letter ח. In these instances, the vowel sound switches places with the consonant and the *ah* sound is pronounced *before* the *ch—ach*. Note that the last word on lines 1–4 practices the כָה or חָה ending, pronounced *cha,* in contrast to חַ, pronounced *ach.* Lines 5 and 6 present and drill פַּתָּח גָּנוּב when ע is the last letter of the word. Line 7 drills the וֹ combination in various forms of the two words in which it is most commonly found (מִצְוֹת, עָוֹן). In lines 1–7, ask students to read individual words, then full lines. Lines 8 and 9 contain full sentences, which should be read as fluently and smoothly as possible. (*Line 8: The dog is in the house. It is under the table. Line 9: A cat is in the house. It is on the chair.*)

I Can Write Hebrew!

For fun, after students have completed this activity, they can choose to illustrate either מִצְוֹת or חַג שָׂמֵחַ.

I Can Read Hebrew!

Read these Hebrew words and sentences out loud.

1. שָׂמֵחַ פּוֹקֵחַ נוֹבֵחַ מִזְבֵּחַ בְּרֵכָה
2. לוּחַ תַּפּוּחַ לָנוּחַ רוּחַ אֲרוּחָה
3. שָׁלִיחַ אֲבַטִּיחַ לְהָנִיחַ מַצְמִיחַ סְלִיחָה
4. מֹחַ לִסְלוֹחַ נֹחַ מִשְׁלוֹחַ אוֹרְחָה
5. יוֹדֵעַ יָדוּעַ שָׁבוּעַ שָׁמֹעַ יְהוֹשֻׁעַ
6. שׁוֹמֵעַ רָקִיעַ מוֹשִׁיעַ מַשְׂבִּיעַ לְהוֹשִׁיעַ
7. מִצְוֹת מִצְוֹתַי מִצְוֹתֶיךָ עָוֹן עֲוֹנוֹת
8. הַכֶּלֶב בַּבַּיִת. הוּא תַּחַת הַשֻּׁלְחָן.
9. חָתוּל בַּבַּיִת. הוּא עַל הַכִּסֵּא.

I Can Write Hebrew!

Write these new words.

מִצְוֹת

חַג שָׂמֵחַ

Rock, Paper, Scissors

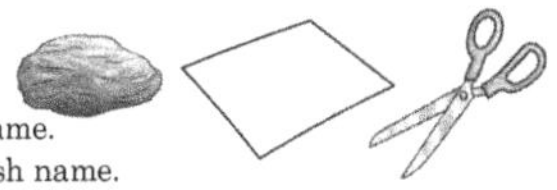

Play this popular Hebrew counting game.
You may already know it by its English name.

אֶבֶן נְיָר מִסְפָּרַיִם–

מִי מְנַצֵּחַ מִן הַשְּׁנַיִם?

אַחַת, שְׁתַּיִם, שָׁלוֹשׁ!

Sound Check

How does each word below end, with a "**cha**" or an "**ach**"? Put a ✓ in the correct column.

ends with a "**cha**"	ends with an "**ach**"	
✓		1. שֶׁלְּךָ
	✓	2. שֶׁלָּךְ
	✓	3. אוֹרֵחַ
✓		4. מַדְרִיכָה
✓		5. כִּנְאֻמֶיךָ
	✓	6. נָשִׂיחַ

80

Rock, Paper, Scissors

Allow students to play "Rock, Paper, Scissors" with a partner. Practice reading the Hebrew verse together as a class. Students can also use this game to select who will go first in reading games or at any other time they need to select one person in a pair.

Sound Check

Determining whether the sound at the end of a word is *ach* or *cha* can be difficult for early readers. "Sound Check" provides students with practice in the important skill of distinguishing between these similar items.

Ask students to complete this activity independently. Circulate around the room to provide assistance as needed and to make sure that students are completing this activity correctly.

Super Reading Secret #6

This activity reviews the וֹ combination, which can be very challenging for beginning Hebrew readers.

Ask a volunteer to read the information at the top of the page, then allow individual students to read the words. Make sure that every student has the opportunity to read several examples. Have students read the words to a partner.

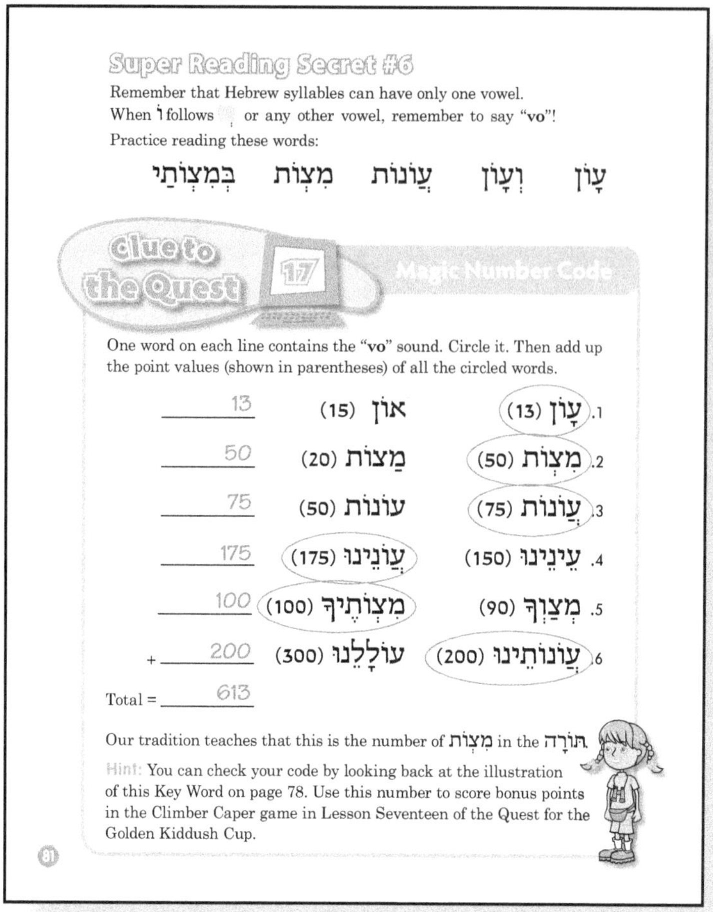

Super Reading Secret #6

Remember that Hebrew syllables can have only one vowel.
When וֹ follows or any other vowel, remember to say "**vo**"!
Practice reading these words:

עָוֹן   וְעָוֹן   עֲוֹנוֹת   מִצְוֹת   בְּמִצְוֹתַי

Clue to the Quest 17 Magic Number Code

One word on each line contains the "**vo**" sound. Circle it. Then add up the point values (shown in parentheses) of all the circled words.

.1	עָוֹן (13)	אוֹן (15)	13
.2	מִצְוֹת (50)	מַצּוֹת (20)	50
.3	עֲוֹנוֹת (75)	עוֹנוֹת (50)	75
.4	עֵינֵינוּ (150)	עֲוֹנֵינוּ (175)	175
.5	מְצַוְּךָ (90)	מִצְוֹתֶיךָ (100)	100
.6	עֲוֹנוֹתֵינוּ (200)	עוֹלָלֵנוּ (300)	+ 200
		Total =	613

Our tradition teaches that this is the number of מִצְוֹת in the תּוֹרָה.

Hint: You can check your code by looking back at the illustration of this Key Word on page 78. Use this number to score bonus points in the Climber Caper game in Lesson Seventeen of the Quest for the Golden Kiddush Cup.

81

Clue to the Quest: Magic Number Code

Here students practice making fine distinctions between words that contain וֹ and similar words that simply contain the vowel וֹ. Ask students to work with partners to complete this activity. You may want to pair a weaker student with a stronger student for this task. Direct the first student to read both words on the line. The second student should indicate which one contains the *vo* sound and should point to that word. If the students agree, they should write the numerical value of the word in the blank provided. Students should alternate roles with each line. At the end, they should add up the numbers. (*613*) (If students are not sure of the correct total, ask them to look back at the illustration of the key word מִצְוֹת on page 78 in their books.)

Students can use this number to score bonus points in the "Climber Caper" game in Lesson 17 of the digital application.

Challenge students to come to class next time with the answers to the following questions. They can find the answers in Lesson 17 of the digital application.

1. Where in Israel do many artists live and work? (*Tzfat*)
2. What kind of painting does Ben like? (*finger painting*)

If students print out or e-mail their lesson summaries, remind them to do so when they have completed all the activities in this lesson.

Quest for the Golden Kiddush Cup

When students complete this lesson in their digital application, have them color piece #17 on the plate on page 4 of their book. They can also write in the key words and the new vowels for this lesson.

Assessment

For information on assessing students' progress, see page 9.

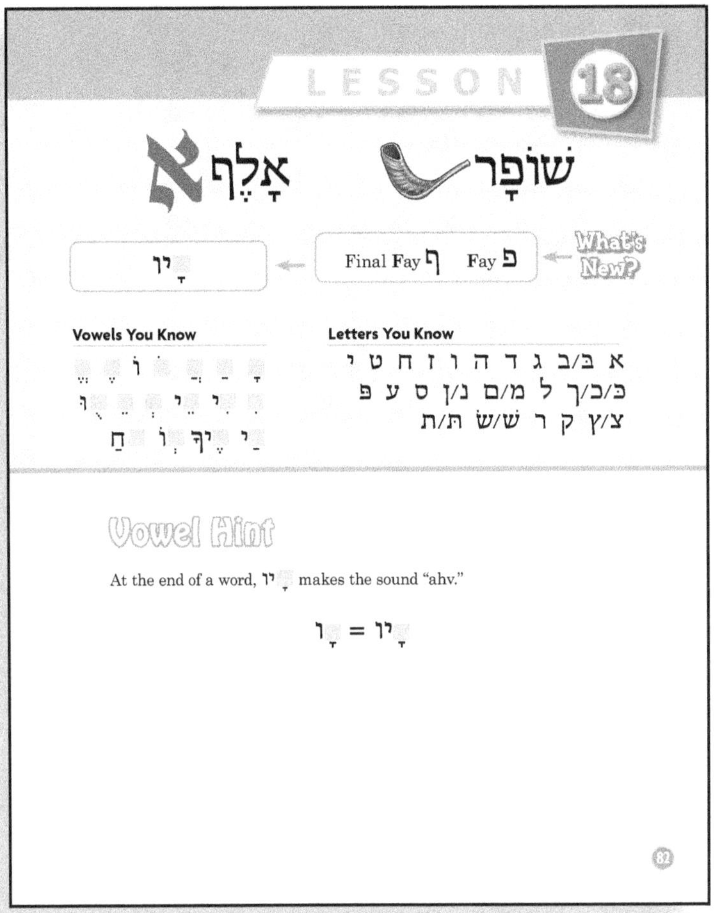

LESSON 18

Pages: 82–86

Key Words: שׁוֹפָר אָלֶף

New Letters: פ ף

New Vowel: ָיו

Recommended Instructional Materials:
Phonics Flash Cards #1, 4, 7, 10, 13, 17, 23, and 49–51; Word Cards # 1, 3, 5, 11–13, 17–19, 21–22, 24–26, 28, 30, 33–38; a shofar; an *alef-bet* poster

Review Activity

Play "Categories" (see page 14 for instructions) using Word Cards #1, 3, 5, 11, 12, 13, 17, 18, 19, 21, 22, 24, 25, 26, 28, 30, 33, 34, and 35. Tell students what categories they should look for:
Greetings (חַג, שָׂמֵחַ, שָׁלוֹם)
Synagogue Items (בִּימָה, טַלִּית, מְזוּזָה, תּוֹרָה)
Shabbat (נֵר, חַלָּה, יַיִן, קִדּוּשׁ, הַבְדָּלָה)
People (סַבָּא, סַבְתָּא, מֶלֶךְ, אִמָּא, אַבָּא)
Holiday Items (שַׁמָּשׁ, מַצָּה, סֻכָּה)

Set Induction

Pass the shofar around the class. Ask students if they know what this object is called (*shofar*) and on which holidays we use it (*Rosh Hashanah and Yom Kippur*). If you can make the three types of shofar blasts (*t'ki'ah, t'ru'ah, sh'varim*), demonstrate them for the students, or invite the rabbi, cantor, or someone else to demonstrate blowing the shofar.

Introducing the Key Words and Deducing Their Sound-Symbol Associations

Introduce the key word שׁוֹפָר and associate it directly with the actual shofar. Highlight the new letter, פ, using the "Multi-Sensory Approach to Hebrew Phonics" described on page 11.

Introduce final ף through the key word אָלֶף using the same approach. Since students have now learned all the letters, you can show them an *alef-bet* poster, directly associating the new word with the letter א. Now would be a good time to teach one of the many *alef-bet* songs to the class.

Vowel Hint

Ask a volunteer to read the passage, and invite one or more students to explain the information in their own words. Emphasize that the י is not pronounced.

Oral Language Lesson
(Optional)

Review: אֲנִי אַתָּה אַתְּ הוּא הִיא
עַל יֶלֶד יַלְדָּה תַּלְמִיד תַּלְמִידָה טוֹב

Introduce: יְרָקוֹת שֻׁלְחָן טוֹבָה

Drill the words using the following sentences:

יְרָקוֹת עַל הַשֻּׁלְחָן.
אָדָם יֶלֶד טוֹב וְגִילָה יַלְדָּה טוֹבָה.
הוּא יֶלֶד טוֹב. הִיא יַלְדָּה טוֹבָה.
הַפִּיצָה עַל הַשֻּׁלְחָן. הַפִּיצָה טוֹבָה.

I Can Read Hebrew!

The letter פ appears only at the beginning of Hebrew words that are borrowed from other languages, such as פִּלְפֵּל and פּוֹטוֹ. This first reading page drills the new letter פ/ף in both of the positions within a word in which it can occur naturally in Hebrew (the middle and the end). The first three lines drill the final form of the new letter ף, and lines 4–6 provide practice with פ embedded within the word. This is the most difficult position for beginning readers. The second and fifth words on each line rhyme. Ask students to read each line in groups of two then three words, and finally as full lines. For variety, students can also read the words in columns.

I Can Write Hebrew!

Ask students to trace the letters with their fingers then write the letters in pencil. Review the letter names and sounds as students write them.

Ask students to write the key words for the lesson. Students can also write and/or illustrate the following sentences:

שׁוֹפָר עַל הַטַּלִּית.
אָלֶף אָדָם.

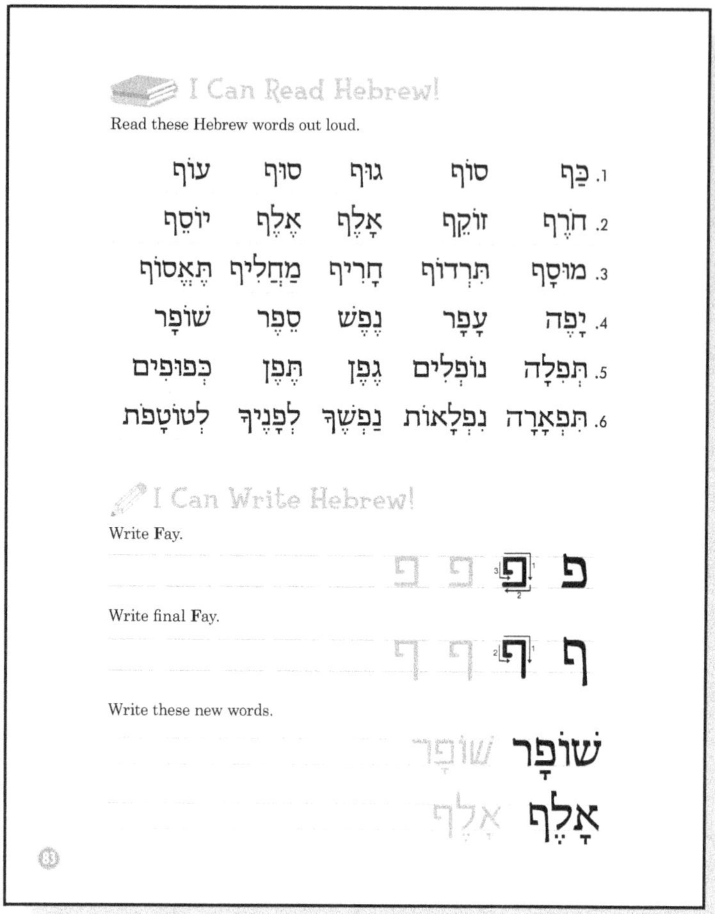
I Can Read Hebrew!

Read these Hebrew words out loud.

1. כַּף סוֹף גּוּף סוּף עוֹף
2. חֹרֶף זוֹקֵף אָלֶף אֶלֶף יוֹסֵף
3. מוּסָף תִּרְדּוֹף חָרִיף מַחֲלִיף תֶּאֱסוֹף
4. יָפֶה עָפָר נֶפֶשׁ סֵפֶר שׁוֹפָר
5. תְּפִלָּה נוֹפְלִים גֶּפֶן תֶּפֶן כְּפוּפִים
6. תִּפְאָרָה נִפְלָאוֹת נַפְשֶׁךָ לְפָנֶיךָ לְטוֹטָפֹת

I Can Write Hebrew!

Write Fay.

פ

Write final Fay.

ף

Write these new words.

שׁוֹפָר

אָלֶף

83

I Can Read Hebrew!

Read these Hebrew words and sentences out loud.

1. עָלָיו בָּנָיו יַחְדָּו פָּנָיו עַכְשָׁו
2. אֵלָיו עֵינָיו עֲבָדָיו רַגְלָיו רַחֲמָיו
3. מַעֲשָׂיו חֲסִידָיו לְפָנָיו כְּנָפָיו יְצוּרָיו
4. אֹהֲבָיו מְשָׁרְתָיו דְּרָכָיו גְּבוּרֹתָיו מִצְוֹתָיו
5. אֵיפֹה הַסֵּפֶר? הַסֵּפֶר תַּחַת הַמַּחְבֶּרֶת.
6. אֵיפֹה הַמַּחְבֶּרֶת? הַמַּחְבֶּרֶת עַל הַשֻּׁלְחָן.
7. אֵיפֹה הַשֻּׁלְחָן? הַשֻּׁלְחָן בַּכִּתָּה.
8. אֵיפֹה הַכִּתָּה? הַכִּתָּה בְּבֵית-הַסֵּפֶר.

The "Write" Letter

You have now learned all five letters that change shape at the end of a word. Fill in the correct form of פ or ף.

Remember: Final letters are used only at the end of a word!

1. כֶּסֶף silver, money
2. גֶּפֶן grape vine
3. קְלָף Torah parchment
4. סֵפֶר book
5. יוֹסֵף Joseph
6. שָׂפָה language, lip

84

I Can Read Hebrew!

The first four lines of this second reading selection drill יו ָ . Refer students back to the Vowel Hint on page 82 in their book. Ask a volunteer to reread the passage, then allow students to read the words in the activity individually, then in full lines.

Lines 5–8 contain full sentences. Challenge students to read them as fluently and smoothly as possible. (*Line 5: Where is the book? The book is under the notebook. Line 6: Where is the notebook? The notebook is on the table. Line 7: Where is the table? The table is in the classroom. Line 8: Where is the classroom? The classroom is in the school.*)

The "Write" Letter

Making a decision about whether to use פ/ף helps students remember the concept of final letters.

Ask a volunteer to read the instructions. Ask students to complete the activity individually. Circulate among them to provide assistance as needed.

Just for Fun

Tongue twisters and rhymes are a fun way to use language. You can teach the following lines orally or enlarge the words, post them on the board or a wall, and have students read them. Or allow individual or groups of students to recite the lines in front of the class. Give students a few minutes to practice first.

אוּרִי כְּדוּרִי מְלָפְפוֹן
הוּא בָּלַע כַּדּוּר גָּדוֹל.

Uri Kaduri cucumber,
he swallowed a big pill.

הַנִּימוּס עוֹלֶה בְּזוֹל
וּמֵבִיא שָׂכָר גָּדוֹל.
לְהוֹסִיף "בְּבַקָּשָׁה"
לֹא צָרִיךְ לִהְיוֹת כָּל־כָּךְ קָשֶׁה!

Manners are inexpensive
but they bring a big reward.
To add "please"
should not be so hard!

Super Reading Secret #7

For the first time, students are given the opportunity to read whole prayer passages, in this case the Shabbat blessings. On the first line of each blessing, the short two-word phrases have been set apart by commas. The second and third lines each contain single phrases. You may want students to practice fluent phrase reading by asking them to read the individual phrases while drawing a smooth arc in the air from right to left (see page 54). Practice the phrases so that every student in class has the opportunity to read several of them. Then allow students to read the full passages as a group and individually.

When students have read the passages several times, ask a volunteer to read the instructions at the top of the page. Invite students to complete the matching activity individually. Circulate to provide assistance as needed.

Super Reading Secret #7

בְּרָכוֹת שֶׁל שַׁבָּת

Blend Hebrew words into smooth phrases and sentences. Then blend phrases and sentences into whole passages.

Read each of the blessings below out loud. Then connect the blessing to its matching drawing.

1. בָּרוּךְ אַתָּה, יְיָ אֱלֹהֵינוּ, מֶלֶךְ הָעוֹלָם,
אֲשֶׁר קִדְּשָׁנוּ בְּמִצְוֹתָיו
וְצִוָּנוּ לְהַדְלִיק נֵר שֶׁל שַׁבָּת.

2. בָּרוּךְ אַתָּה, יְיָ אֱלֹהֵינוּ, מֶלֶךְ הָעוֹלָם,
בּוֹרֵא פְּרִי הַגָּפֶן.

3. בָּרוּךְ אַתָּה, יְיָ אֱלֹהֵינוּ, מֶלֶךְ הָעוֹלָם,
הַמּוֹצִיא לֶחֶם מִן הָאָרֶץ.

85

Word Search

Find four words hidden in the puzzle below. They may go from right to left or top to bottom. Then write the words below their pictures.

מ	ם	ק	שׁ	ו	ל	ה	ג	בּ
צ	א	ח	א	ה	ח	פּ	שׁ	מ
ו	ל	א	ר	שׁ	י	ר	ם	צ
ה	ב	ס	י	מ	י	י	ע	וֹ

Write the circled letters to find the Hebrew greeting we use on holidays.

חג שמח!

Use this greeting to score bonus points in the Ruin Quest game in Lesson Eighteen of the Quest for the Golden Kiddush Cup.

86

Word Search

Ask a volunteer to read the instructions at the top of the page. Tell students that there are no vowels included under the letters in the grid, but the vowels are included below the blank lines under the pictures. Ask students to complete the activity individually. Circulate to provide assistance as needed.

Clue to the Quest: Crack the Code

Read the instructions to the class and together find the correct letter to fill in the first space on the right. Allow students to work with partners to complete the rest of the activity.

They can use this phrase (חַג שָׂמֵחַ) to score bonus points in the "Ruin Quest" game in Lesson 18 of the digital application.

Challenge students to come to class next time with the answers to the following questions. They can find the answers in Lesson 18 of the digital application.

1. How many cities does Jerusalem consist of? (*2*)
2. Where in the Israel Museum did Ben and Batya find a piece of the plate? (*in the sculpture garden*)

If students print out or e-mail their lesson summaries, remind them to do so when they have completed all the activities in this lesson.

Quest for the Golden Kiddush Cup

When students complete this lesson in their digital application, have them color piece #18 on the plate on page 4 of their book. They can also write in the key words and the new letters and vowel for this lesson.

Assessment

For information on assessing students' progress, see page 9.

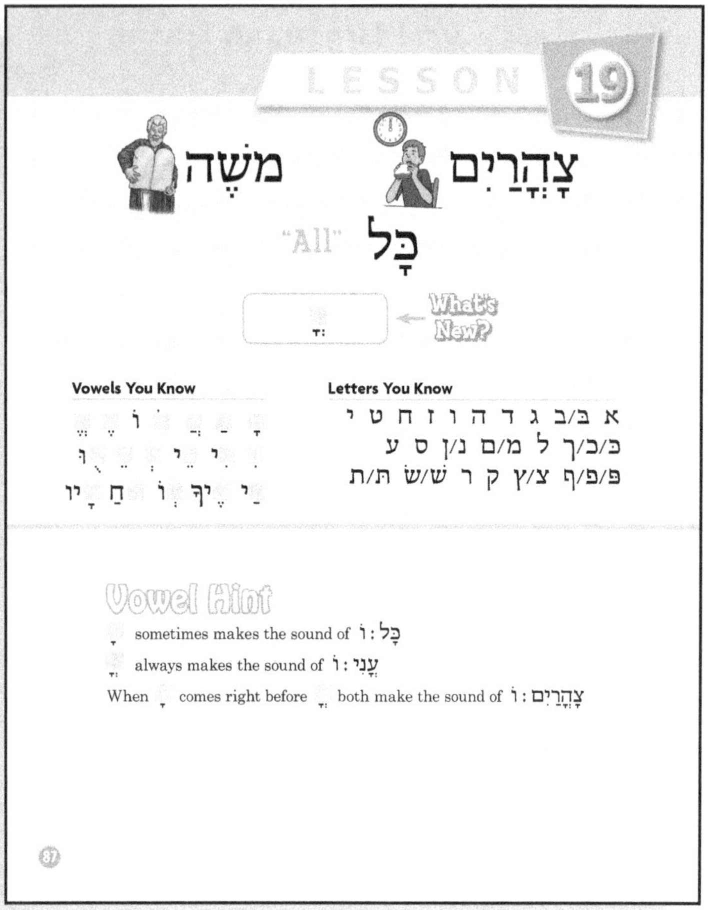

LESSON 19

Pages: 87–91

Key Words: צָהֳרַיִם מֹשֶׁה כָּל

New Vowel: ֳ

Recommended Instructional Materials:
Phonics Flash Cards #1–5, 10, 12, 14–15, 17, 19, 21, 23, 34, and 52; Word Cards #39–41; teacher-made cards for the "Same or Different?" game

Review Activity

Play "Same or Different?" (see page 15 for instructions). Begin with cards that require students to determine if individual letters are the same, then two-letter groups, and finally three-letter groups. Students can simply call out "Same" or "Different." For example:

Individual letters: ח ח ח ה ט מ ט ט ק ף ף ף כ ב כ כ ז ו ו ן ז ן ח ת ר ר ף ר

Two-letter groups: כך פּך תף חף שׁו שׁן פך פּך

Three-letter groups: טבז מבז חנן חנן כּכף פּגף גזר גור

Set Induction

Ask students to name different English words in which a vowel looks the same but is pronounced differently (example: a—apple, are, ate). Explain that in this lesson students will be learning a different pronunciation for the ָ vowel.

Introducing the Key Words and Deducing Their Sound-Symbol Associations

Introduce the new vowel and sounds of each key word using the "Multi-Sensory Approach to Hebrew Phonics" described on page 11. Be sure to pronounce the words correctly (*tzohorayim, moshe, kol*).

To introduce the key word צָהֳרַיִם, draw and write the following on the board: a sun rising on the horizon, labeled 7:00; a sun high in the sky, labeled 12:00; a moon rising on the horizon, labeled 6:00. Point to the first sun and say בֹּקֶר, point to the moon and say עֶרֶב, then point to the middle sun and say צָהֳרַיִם. Use this word to introduce the new vowel ֳ.

To introduce the key word מֹשֶׁה, write the following holiday names on the board:

חֲנֻכָּה פּוּרִים פֶּסַח שָׁבוּעוֹת

Ask students to name the heroes of each holiday. (*Judah Maccabee, Esther and Mordecai, Moses [leaving Egypt], Moses [receiving Ten Commandments]*) Ask which hero is associated with two holidays. (*Moses*) Explain that Moses does "double duty." Next, write מֹשֶׁה on the board and ask students to try to figure out what the first vowel is. (*oh*)

Next, write the key word כָּל on the board. Tell students that the ָ in this word (and any of its related forms, such as בְּכָל) is pronounced as *oh.*

Vowel Hint

Ask a volunteer to read the passage. Make sure that everyone understands the information by writing a number of examples on the board and asking students to identify the sounds of the vowels.

I Can Read Hebrew!

Read these Hebrew words and sentences out loud.

Hint: Every ◌ָ in these lines sounds like "oh."

1. כָּל בְּכָל לְכָל מִכָּל כְּכָל וְכָל
2. קָדְשִׁי גָּדְלוֹ גָּדְלֶךָ בְּגָבְהֵי קָדְשׁוֹ קָדְשֶׁךָ
3. חָפְשִׁי אָזְנַיִם זָכְרֵנוּ שָׁכְבֵנוּ קָרְאֵנוּ עֳנִי
4. נָעֳמִי צָהֳרַיִם אָהֳלוֹ אָהֳלֶךָ מָחֳרַת פָּעֳלוֹ

Challenge: Circle both words with the "oh" sound in this line.

(כָּל) הַמִּשְׁפָּחָה בַּבַּיִת. שַׁבָּת (שָׁלוֹם)!

Sound Check

Circle the letter that ends each word.

1	שׁ	ר	ף	(ם)	צ	ז	ץ	ךְ	ק	ט
2	י	(ן)	ץ	ם	ס	ל	ף	ר	מ	ךְ
3	מ	ל	ף	ן	ט	ם	ץ	(ךְ)	ק	ס
4	שׁ	ל	ף	ס	ט	ן	(ץ)	ה	ק	ת
5	פּ	ל	(ף)	ם	ס	ן	ץ	ךְ	ב	ת

88

Sound Check

In previous activities, students have had an opportunity to practice segmenting the initial phoneme of Hebrew words and cognates. This activity provides students with practice in segmenting the final phoneme of several words. This is a more difficult position for most students to hear sounds than the initial position. At the same time, this activity provides students with practice on the final letters that they have learned.

Ask a volunteer to read the directions, and allow students to complete the activity individually while you circulate to provide assistance as needed.

Oral Language Lesson

(Optional)

Review כִּתָּה מוֹרֶה/מוֹרָה גִּיר תַּפּוּז עַל תַּחַת שֻׁלְחָן

Introduce לוּחַ בֵּית־סֵפֶר תַּפּוּחַ אֵיפֹה? סֵפֶר עִפָּרוֹן מַחְבֶּרֶת

Practice using questions and answers such as:

אֵיפֹה הַסֵּפֶר? הַסֵּפֶר עַל הַשֻּׁלְחָן.
אֵיפֹה הָעִפָּרוֹן? הָעִפָּרוֹן תַּחַת הַמַּחְבֶּרֶת.
אֵיפֹה הַגִּיר? הַגִּיר עַל הַלּוּחַ.
אֵיפֹה הַמּוֹרָה? הַמּוֹרָה בַּכִּתָּה.
אֵיפֹה הַכִּתָּה? הַכִּתָּה בְּבֵית־סֵפֶר.

I Can Read Hebrew!

This first reading selection provides practice with the new vowel ◌ֳ and the pronunciation of ◌ָ as *oh*, as well as the combination ◌ֳ ◌ָ (in which both vowels are pronounced *oh*). Line 1 presents various forms of the word כָּל, while line 2 and most of line 3 provide practice with specific examples of words in which ◌ָ is pronounced *oh*. Note that in all of these words ◌ָ is followed immediately by ◌ְ. The last word on line 3 contains ◌ֳ in isolation, while all the words on line 4 contain the combination ◌ֳ ◌ָ.

Ask a volunteer to read the information at the top of the page, and allow students to practice reading individual words, then full lines. Ask students to complete the challenge activity as a class or individually. If they complete it individually, circulate to provide assistance as needed.

Super Reading Secret #8

The "double-duty dot" indicates whether a ש is pronounced שׁ or שׂ, and it also indicates the vowel *oh*. Ask a volunteer to read the information. Help students understand the concept by writing several examples of the double-duty dot on the board. Choose words from the reading section that follows. Invite students to come up, circle the double-duty dot, and read the words. The class should repeat if the student is correct. If the class is silent, the student should try to self-correct.

I Can Read Hebrew!

This second reading passage focuses on the double-duty dot. The first two lines are composed of words that contain the double-duty dot as part of שׁ. Lines 3 and 4 are composed of words that contain the double-duty dot as part of שׂ. Ask volunteers to read individual words then full lines.

I Can Write Hebrew!

Ask students to trace and then write the key words.

For fun, after students have completed writing the key words, they can illustrate either צָהֳרַיִם or מֹשֶׁה and label their drawings with the correct key word.

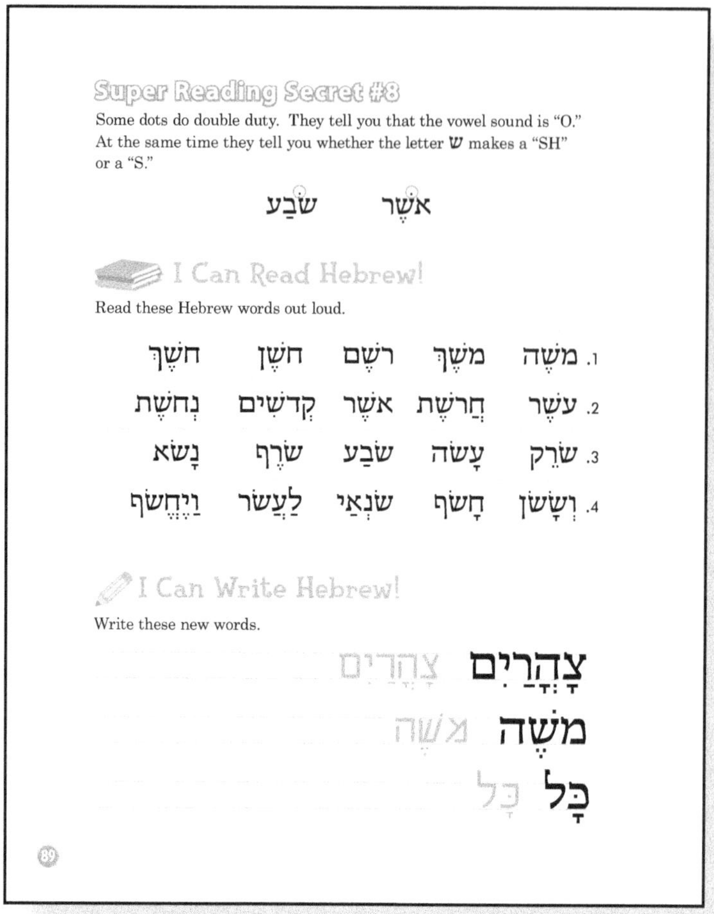

Super Reading Secret #8

Some dots do double duty. They tell you that the vowel sound is "O." At the same time they tell you whether the letter ש makes a "SH" or a "S."

שֹׂבַע אֹשֶׁר

I Can Read Hebrew!

Read these Hebrew words out loud.

1. מֹשֶׁה מֹשֵׁךְ רֹשֶׁם חֹשֶׁן חֹשֶׁךְ
2. עֹשֶׁר חֲרֹשֶׁת אֹשֶׁר קְדֹשִׁים נְחֹשֶׁת
3. שֹׂרֵק עָשׂה שֹׂבַע שֹׂרֶף נָשֹׂא
4. וְשָׂשׂן חָשׂף שֹׂנְאַי לַעֲשֹׂר וַיֶּחֱשֹׂף

I Can Write Hebrew!

Write these new words.

צָהֳרַיִם צָהֳרַיִם
מֹשֶׁה מֹשֶׁה
כָּל כָּל

89

> **Super Reading Secret #9**
>
> Remember that the ָ vowel makes the sound of וֹ in the word כָּל.
>
> The ָ vowel sometimes makes the sound of וֹ when it is followed by ְ : חָפְשִׁי
>
> **הַתִּקְוָה**
>
> הַתִּקְוָה is the name of Israel's national anthem. It means "The Hope." In two of the words in הַתִּקְוָה the ָ vowel makes the sound of וֹ. Write those two words:
>
> חָפְשִׁי and כָּל
>
> Hint: See lines 1 and 7.
>
> 1. כָּל עוֹד בַּלֵּבָב פְּנִימָה
> 2. נֶפֶשׁ יְהוּדִי הוֹמִיָּה,
> 3. וּלְפַאֲתֵי מִזְרָח קָדִימָה
> 4. עַיִן לְצִיּוֹן צוֹפִיָּה.
> 5. עוֹד לֹא אָבְדָה תִּקְוָתֵנוּ,
> 6. הַתִּקְוָה בַּת שְׁנוֹת אַלְפַּיִם,
> 7. לִהְיוֹת עַם חָפְשִׁי בְּאַרְצֵנוּ,
> 8. בְּאֶרֶץ צִיּוֹן וִירוּשָׁלַיִם.
>
> 90

Super Reading Secret #9

Ask a volunteer to read the information about ָ when it is followed immediately by ְ. To make sure that the class fully understands this concept, you may want to write several examples on the board and allow students to come up, circle the vowel that makes an *oh* sound, and read each word. The class should repeat if the student is correct. If the class is silent, the student should try to self-correct. You can find many examples of ָ followed immediately by ְ in *I Can Read Hebrew* (Behrman House) on page 88.

הַתִּקְוָה

Here, for the second time, students are given the opportunity to read a long Hebrew passage, in this case Israel's national anthem, הַתִּקְוָה. This version of הַתִּקְוָה is sung in Israel and may be different from the version that is printed in some prayer books and other North American texts. Specifically, the inclusion of the word בַּת in line 6 is necessary to make the Hebrew grammatically correct.

This passage also provides students with the opportunity to practice reading ָ as *oh* in a complete passage. See line 1 (כָּל) and line 7 (חָפְשִׁי). Students may notice that the third word on line 5 (אָבְדָה) does not follow the rule presented in Super Reading Secret #9, as ָ is followed immediately by ְ but the pronunciation remains *ah*. Point out that there are exceptions to this rule, and אָבְדָה is one of them.

Ask a volunteer to read the information, and ask students to read lines individually and the full passage as a group. Students can work with partners to complete the activity while you circulate to provide assistance where needed.

מַה נִּשְׁתַּנָּה?

This is the third full passage that students can read, and it is an important one, especially if they arrive at this stage of instruction before Passover. You may want to assign the class to practice reading it at home in their digital application so that they can recite it for the class during the next session.

Ask individuals to read full lines or sentences. Practice reading the passage as a group. You can also divide the class into two groups (table A and table B, boys and girls, etc.). Ask one group to read the first sentence, then alternate sentences. When the group has finished reading, repeat the passage with groups reading the lines they did not read the first time.

Clue to the Quest: Four Questions Quiz

Ask a volunteer to read the information at the beginning of this section, then allow students to work with a partner to answer the questions. Circulate to provide assistance as needed.

Students can use the word שֶׁבְּכָל to score bonus points in the "Keep Israel Green" game in Lesson 19 of the digital application.

Challenge students to come to class next time with the answers to the following questions. They can find the answers in Lesson 19 of the digital application.

1. What kind of stone is used to build in Jerusalem? (*Yerushalayim stone*)
2. What color is that stone when the sun hits it? (*golden*)
3. What do some people call Jerusalem? (*the City of Gold*)
4. What is the holiest place in the Jewish world? (*the Kotel or Western Wall*)

If students print out or e-mail their lesson summaries, remind them to do so when they have completed all the activities in this lesson.

מַה נִּשְׁתַּנָּה?

You can now read the Four Questions at your Passover seder!

מַה נִּשְׁתַּנָּה הַלַּיְלָה הַזֶּה מִכָּל הַלֵּילוֹת?

שֶׁבְּכָל הַלֵּילוֹת אָנוּ אוֹכְלִין חָמֵץ וּמַצָּה,
הַלַּיְלָה הַזֶּה כֻּלּוֹ מַצָּה.

שֶׁבְּכָל הַלֵּילוֹת אָנוּ אוֹכְלִין שְׁאָר יְרָקוֹת,
הַלַּיְלָה הַזֶּה מָרוֹר.

שֶׁבְּכָל הַלֵּילוֹת אֵין אָנוּ מַטְבִּילִין אֲפִילוּ פַּעַם אֶחָת,
הַלַּיְלָה הַזֶּה שְׁתֵּי פְעָמִים.

שֶׁבְּכָל הַלֵּילוֹת אָנוּ אוֹכְלִין בֵּין יוֹשְׁבִין וּבֵין מְסֻבִּין,
הַלַּיְלָה הַזֶּה כֻּלָּנוּ מְסֻבִּין.

Clue to the Quest 19 Four Questions Quiz

Sometimes a prefix added to the word כָּל makes the כּ change to כ:

שֶׁבְּ- + כָּל = שֶׁבְּכָל

How many times does a variation of כָּל appear in the Four Questions? 7

Hint: כֻּלּוֹ and כֻּלָּנוּ are variations.

Which variation of כָּל appears four times? שֶׁבְּכָל

Use this word to score bonus points in the Keep Israel Green game in Lesson Nineteen of the Quest for the Golden Kiddush Cup.

91

Quest for the Golden Kiddush Cup

When students complete this lesson in their digital application, have them color piece #19 on the plate on page 4 of their book. They can also write in the key words and the new vowel for this lesson.

Assessment

For information on assessing students' progress, see page 9.

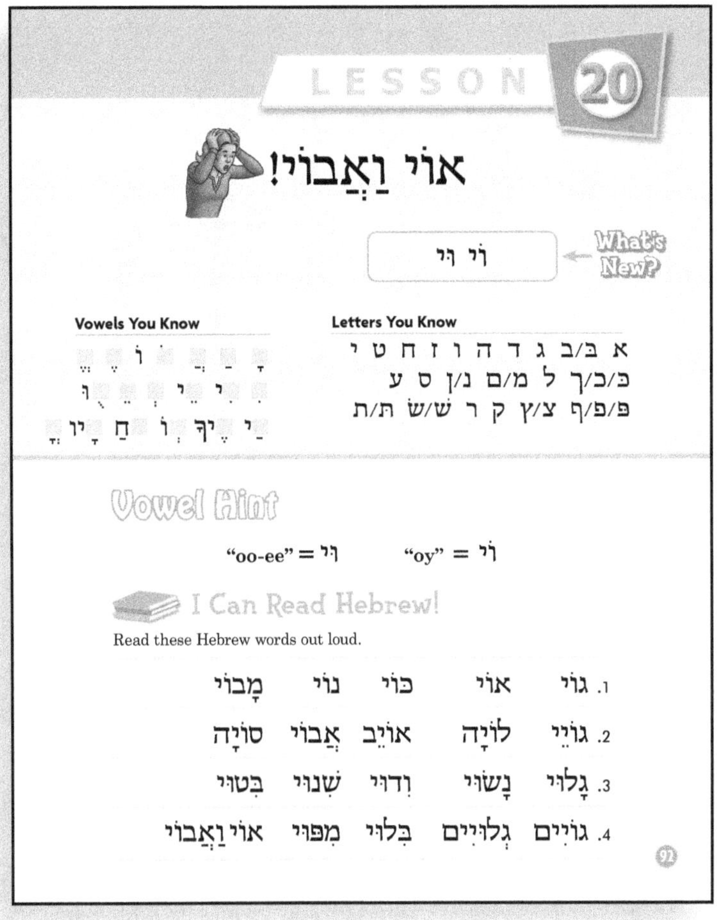

LESSON 20

אוֹי וַאֲבוֹי!

What's New? וֹי וּי

Vowels You Know

Letters You Know

א בּ/ב ג ד ה ו ז ח ט י

כּ/כ/ך ל מ/ם נ/ן ס ע

פּ/פ/ף צ/ץ ק ר שׁ/שׂ תּ/ת

Vowel Hint

"oo-ee" = וּי   "oy" = וֹי

I Can Read Hebrew!

Read these Hebrew words out loud.

1. גוֹי אוֹי כּוֹי נוֹי מָבוֹי

2. גוֹיֵי לוֹיָה אוֹיֵב אֲבוֹי סוֹיָה

3. גָלוּי נָשׂוּי וִדוּי שִׁנוּי בִּטוּי

4. גוֹיִם גְלוּיִים בִּלוּי מִפּוּי אוֹי וַאֲבוֹי

92

LESSON 20

Pages: 92–94

Key Words: אוֹי וַאֲבוֹי!

New Vowels: וֹי וּי

Recommended Instructional Materials:
Phonics Flash Cards #5–6, 28–29, and 54, and two copies of cards #7 and 53; Word Cards #2, 4, 6–7, 9–10, 14–17, 23, 25, 27, 29, 31–32, 35, and 37–42; Stop and Go signs from Lessons 10 and 13

Review Activity

Play "Musical Words" (see page 14 for instructions) using all of the Word Cards listed above, except #42.

Set Induction

Ask students if they have heard the Yiddish expression *"Oy vey!"* and when a person might say that. Tell students that today they are going to learn the Hebrew version of that expression.

Introducing the Key Words and Deducing Their Sound-Symbol Associations

Introduce וֹי through the key words אוֹי וַאֲבוֹי! using the "Multi-Sensory Approach to Hebrew Phonics." Then introduce the other new vowel וּי using the word וִדוּי.

Vowel Hint

Ask a volunteer to read the two vowels. Ask students to brainstorm English words that contain these vowels (e.g., *boy, Roy, soy, toy; dewey, gooey, Huey, Louie,* etc.).

I Can Read Hebrew!

Ask students to read each line in groups of two then three words, and finally as full lines. For variety, students can also read the words in columns.

Oral Language Lesson
(Optional)

Review שׁוֹתֶה/שׁוֹתָה

בַּ- עַל בַּיִת כֶּלֶב צִפּוֹר אוֹכֵל/אוֹכֶלֶת

Introduce בֵּית־כְּנֶסֶת הַצָּגָה

Super Reading Secret #10

Here students learn how to read two *sh'vas* in a row (ְ ְ). Ask a volunteer to read the information. In order to help students understand the concept, you may want to distribute their Stop and Go signs, which were previously used in Lessons 10 and 13. They can use these signs to indicate when they should stop at ְ or go (short vowel), as they hear and read the words in the reading section that follows.

I Can Read Hebrew!

Here students practice reading words that have two *sh'vas* in a row (ְ ְ). The first word on line 1 also reviews the special rule that students learned in Super Reading Secret #9 (ָ = *oh*).

Before reading this word (קָדְשְׁךָ), you may want to have students review Super Reading Secret #9 on page 90 in their books.

Ask volunteers to read individual words then full lines. Fun fact: The last word on line 3 is the longest word in the prayer book (it is found in the מַעֲרִיב עֲרָבִים prayer).

Sound Check

Allow students to work with partners to complete this activity. You may choose to assign stronger readers to work with weaker readers. Ask the first partner to read the first line aloud. The second student should scan the words on the line, identify the words that sound the same, point to them, and read them aloud. If both partners agree, they should circle the words that sound the same. If they do not agree, they should work together to find the correct answer. They should repeat this procedure with the second line, switching roles, and continue, alternating, until they complete the activity.

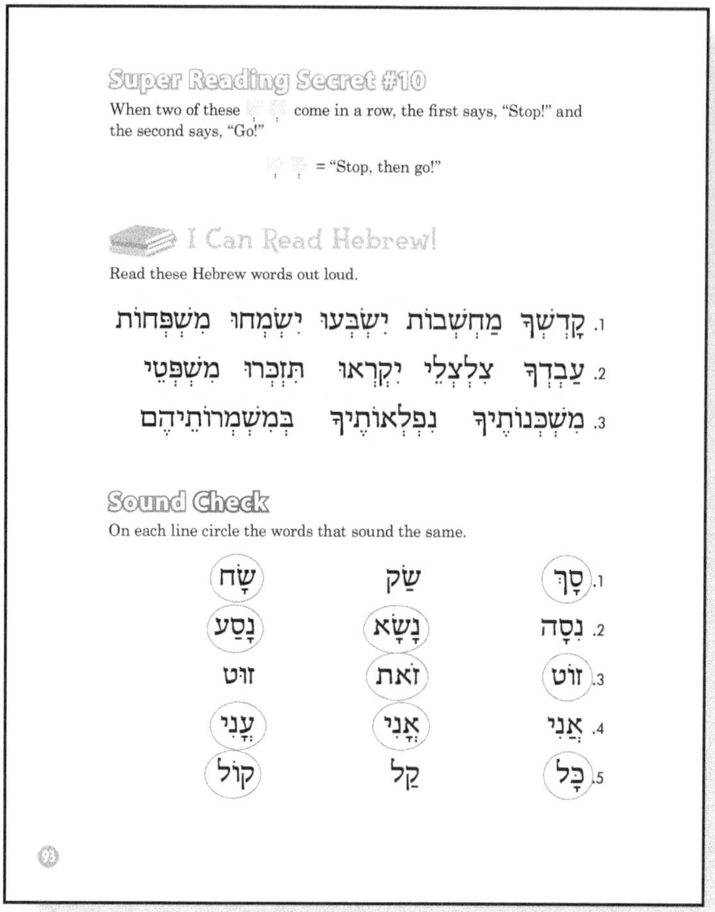

Super Reading Secret #10

When two of these ְ ְ come in a row, the first says, "Stop!" and the second says, "Go!"

ְ ְ = "Stop, then go!"

I Can Read Hebrew!

Read these Hebrew words out loud.

1. קָדְשְׁךָ מַחְשְׁבוֹת יִשְׁבְּעוּ יִשְׂמְחוּ מִשְׁפְּחוֹת
2. עַבְדְּךָ צִלְצְלֵי יִקְרְאוּ תִּזְכְּרוּ מִשְׁפְּטֵי
3. מִשְׁכְּנוֹתֶיךָ נִפְלְאוֹתֶיךָ בְּמִשְׁמְרוֹתֵיהֶם

Sound Check

On each line circle the words that sound the same.

1. סָךְ שַׂק שָׁח
2. נִסָּה נָשָׂא נָסַע
3. זוֹט זֹאת זוּט
4. אֲנִי אֳנִי עֳנִי
5. כָּל קַל קוֹל

93

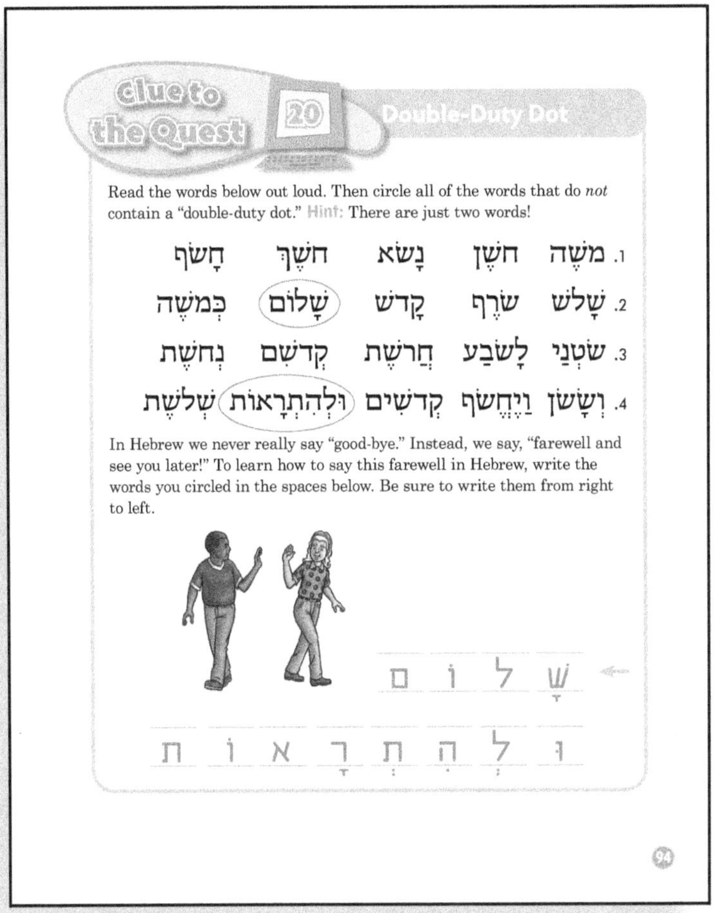
Clue to the Quest 20 Double-Duty Dot

Read the words below out loud. Then circle all of the words that do *not* contain a "double-duty dot." Hint: There are just two words!

1. מֹשֶׁה חֹשֶׁן נָשֹׂא חֹשֶׁךְ חָשֹׁף
2. שָׁלֹשׁ שֹׁרֶף קָדֹשׁ שָׁלוֹם כְּמֹשֶׁה
3. שֹׁטְנַי לָשֹׁבַע חֲרֹשֶׁת קְדֹשִׁם נְחֹשֶׁת
4. וְשָׂשֹׁן וַיֶּחֱשֹׁף קְדֹשִׁים וּלְהִתְרָאוֹת שְׁלֹשֶׁת

In Hebrew we never really say "good-bye." Instead, we say, "farewell and see you later!" To learn how to say this farewell in Hebrew, write the words you circled in the spaces below. Be sure to write them from right to left.

שָׁ ל וֹ ם

וּ לְ הִ תְ רָ א וֹ ת

94

As your students complete *Alef Bet Quest,* celebrate their new Hebrew literacy with a special מְסִיבַּת סִיּוּם. Involve the students in planning the celebration so that they will feel that it is theirs. You may want to include any of the following activities as part of the celebration:

- Invite parents, the education director, rabbi, and/or cantor.
- Complete the last activity on page 94, then recite the שֶׁהֶחֱיָנוּ blessing.
- Serve refreshments and recite the appropriate blessings.
- Read or act out a story from the *Alef Bet Quest Companion Reader.*
- Sing Hebrew songs (including הַתִּקְוָה, which is found on page 90 of the student text).
- Play Hebrew games, either individually or in teams.
- Give out certificates of completion (see the last page of this guide).

Clue to the Quest: Double-Duty Dot

This final activity provides students with additional practice in reading words that contain a double-duty dot, and in identifying words that may contain a שׁ, a שׂ, or an *oh* vowel, but which do not contain a double-duty dot.

Ask a volunteer to read the information at the beginning of this section. You can either allow students to work with a partner on this activity while you circulate to provide assistance, or you can ask the class to work on it as a whole. Answer: שָׁלוֹם וּלְהִתְרָאוֹת

Challenge students to come to class next time with the answers to the following questions. They can find the answers in Lesson 20 of the digital application.

1. In what part of Jerusalem do סַבָּא and סַבְתָּא live? (*the Jewish Quarter*)
2. What is the real treasure? (יִשְׂרָאֵל—*the Land of Israel*)

If students print out or e-mail their lesson summaries, remind them to do so when they have completed all the activities in this lesson.

Quest for the Golden Kiddush Cup

When students complete this lesson in their digital application, have them color piece #20 on the plate on page 4 of their book. They can also write in the key phrase and the new vowels for this lesson. Their plate is complete. Wish students mazal tov!

Assessment

For information on assessing students' progress, see page 9.

Wrap It Up! מְסִיבַּת סִיּוּם

Upon completing a course of study, it is customary to celebrate with a מְסִיבַּת סִיּוּם. This custom dates back to Talmudic times (fourth century CE), when Rabbi Abbaye would hold a celebration, a סִיּוּם, whenever one of his students completed a tractate of Talmud.

APPENDIX A: PHONICS FLASH CARDS BLACK-LINE MASTERS

מ 2	שׁ 1
ָ 4	ם 3
ֲ 6	ַ 5
ע 8	א 7
ל 10	בּ 9

ד
11

◌ֹ
12

וֹ
13

ה
14

י
15

ג
16

◌ֶ
17

◌ֱ
18

◌ִ
19

◌ִי
20

ץ 22	צ 21
י ◌ֵ 24	ר 23
תּ 26	ט 25
ב 28	ת 27
◌ְ 30	ו 29

שׁ 32	ס 31
כּ 34	◌ֵ 33
◌ֻ 36	ק 35
ז 38	וּ 37
כ 40	ח 39

פּ 42	ך 41
נ 44	◌ַי 43
◌ֶיךָ 46	ז 45
◌ְוֹ 48	◌חַ 47
ף 50	פ 49

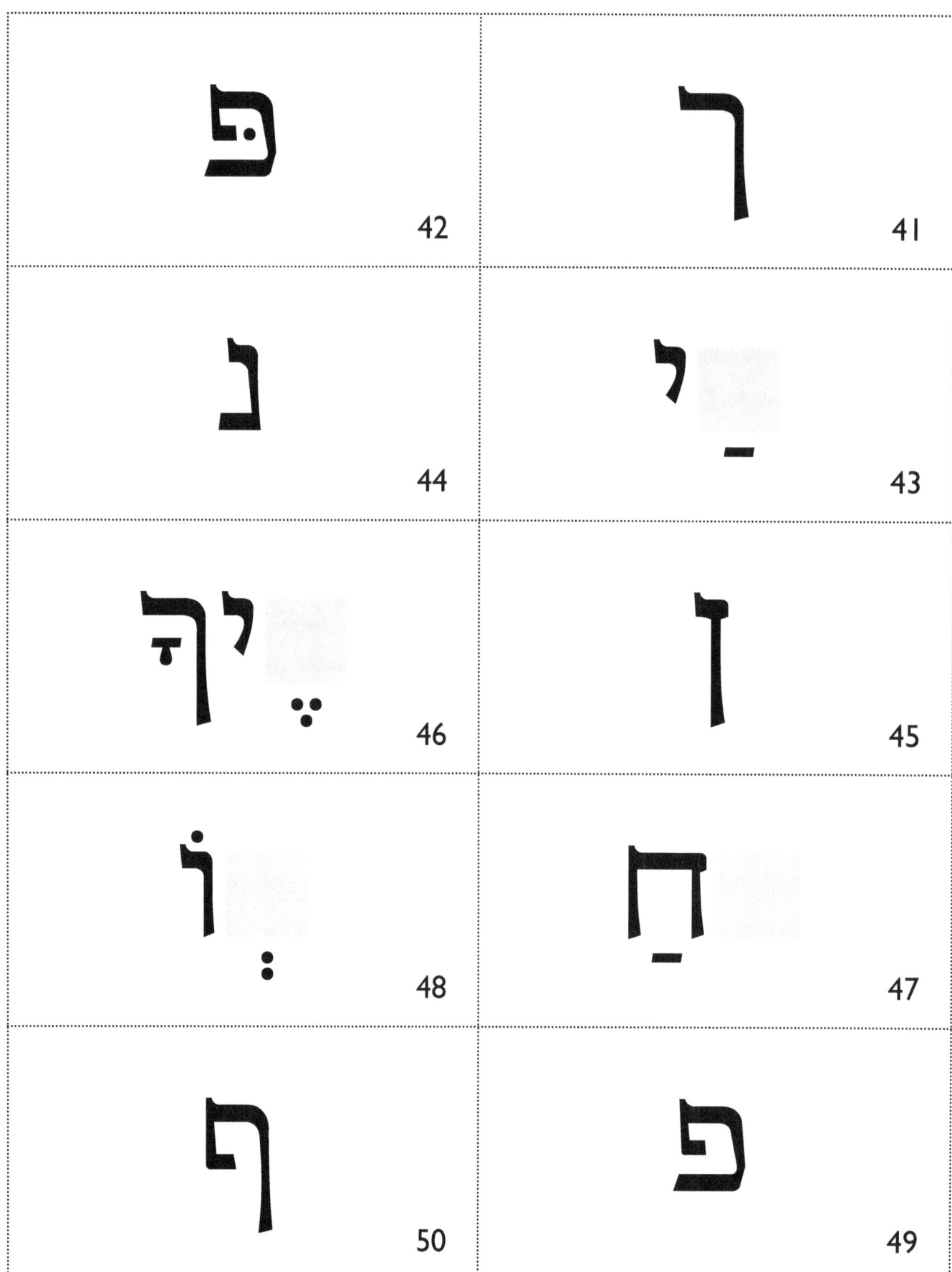

ֳ 52	ָין 51
וּי 54	וֹי 53

APPENDIX B: WORD CARDS BLACK-LINE MASTERS

שַׁמָשׁ

1

שָׁם

Alef Bet Quest © Behrman House, Inc.

2

אַבָּא

Alef Bet Quest © Behrman House, Inc.

3

עַם

Alef Bet Quest © Behrman House, Inc.

4

שָׁלוֹם

Alef Bet Quest © Behrman House, Inc.

5

אָדֹם

Alef Bet Quest © Behrman House, Inc.

6

יָד

Alef Bet Quest © Behrman House, Inc.

7

הַר

Alef Bet Quest © Behrman House, Inc.

8

גֶשֶׁם

Alef Bet Quest © Behrman House, Inc.

9

שֶׁמֶשׁ

Alef Bet Quest © Behrman House, Inc.

10

1

2

3

4

5

6

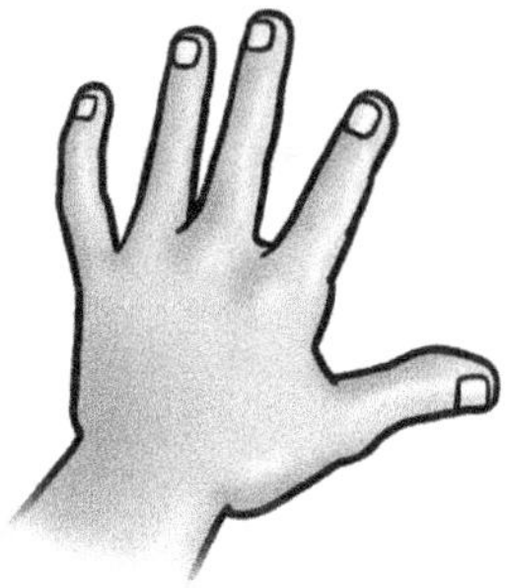

7

The

8

9

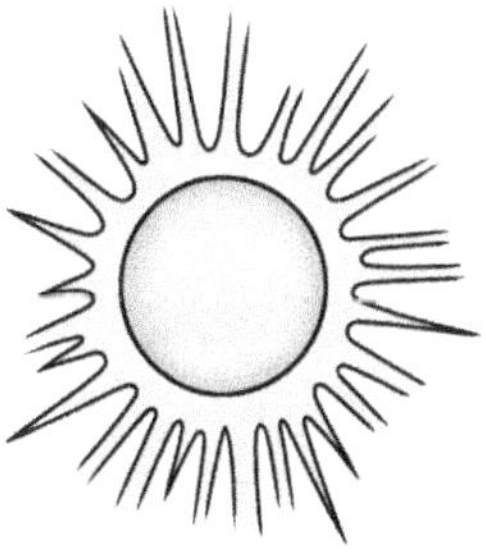

10

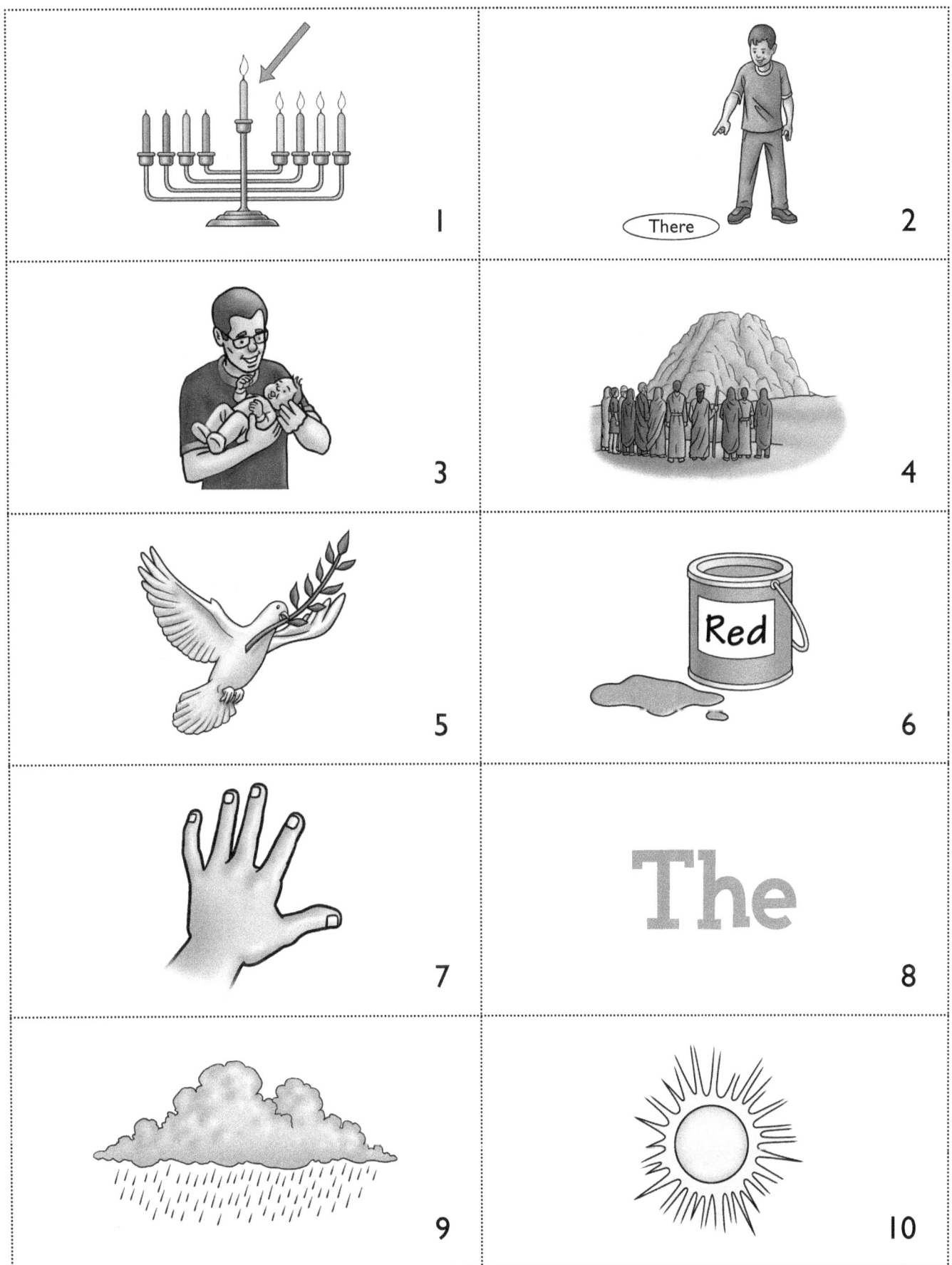

בִּימָה

11

אִמָא

12

מַצָה

13

מִיץ

14

רֶגֶל

15

בֵּיצָה

16

טַלִית

17

תּוֹרָה

18

הַבְדָלָה

19

מִצְוָה

20

11

12

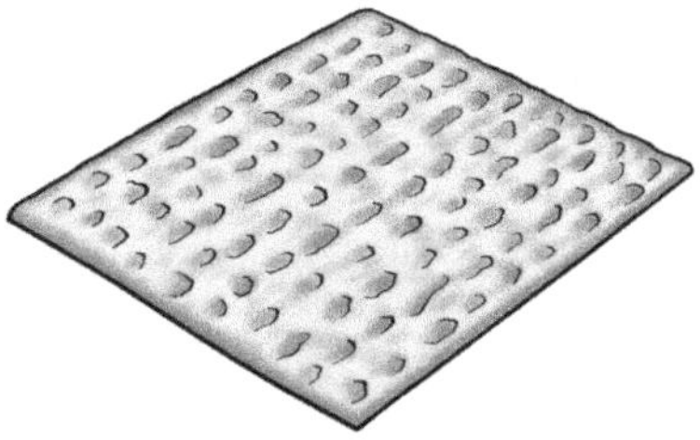

13

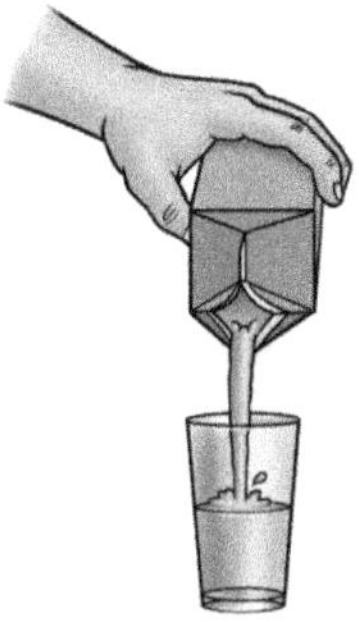

14

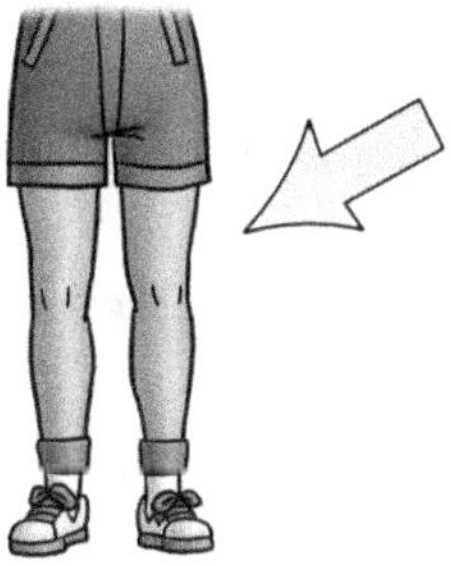

15

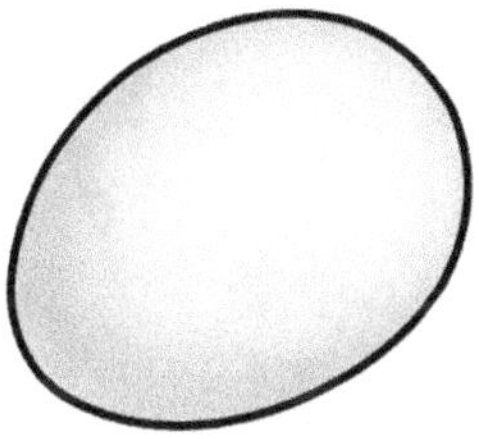

16

17

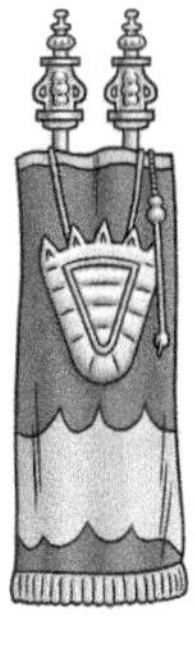

18

19

20

סַבָּא

21

סַבְתָּא

22

יִשְׂרָאֵל

23

סֻכָּה

24

קִדוּשׁ

25

מְזוּזָה

26

הַלְלוּיָה

27

חַלָה

28

בְּרָכָה

29

מֶלֶךְ

30

21

22

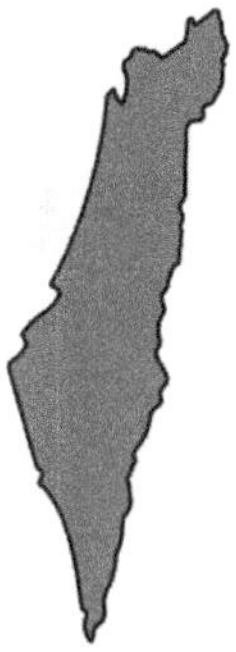

23

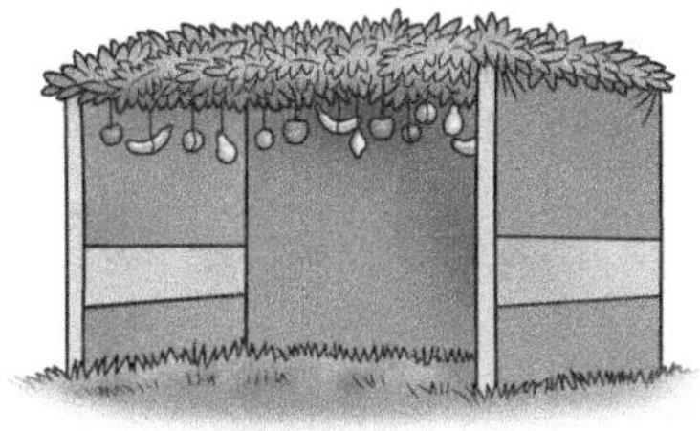

24

25

26

27

28

29

30

מִשְׁפָּחָה

31

חַי

32

נֵר

33

יַיִן

34

חַג שָׂמֵחַ

35

מִצְוֹת

36

שׁוֹפָר

37

אָלֶף

38

צָהֳרַיִם

39

מֹשֶׁה

40

31

32

33

34

35

36

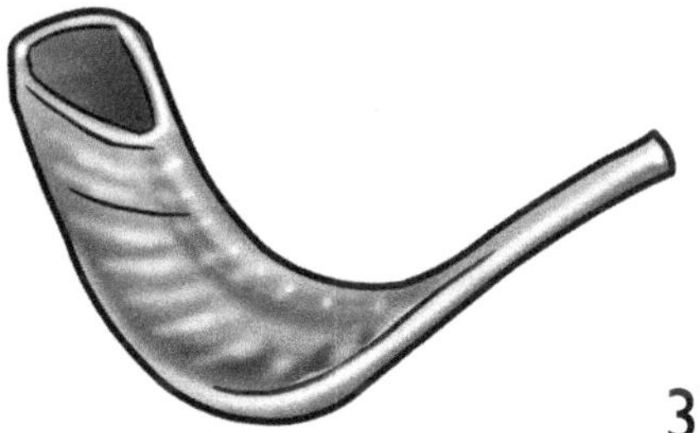

37

א

38

39

40

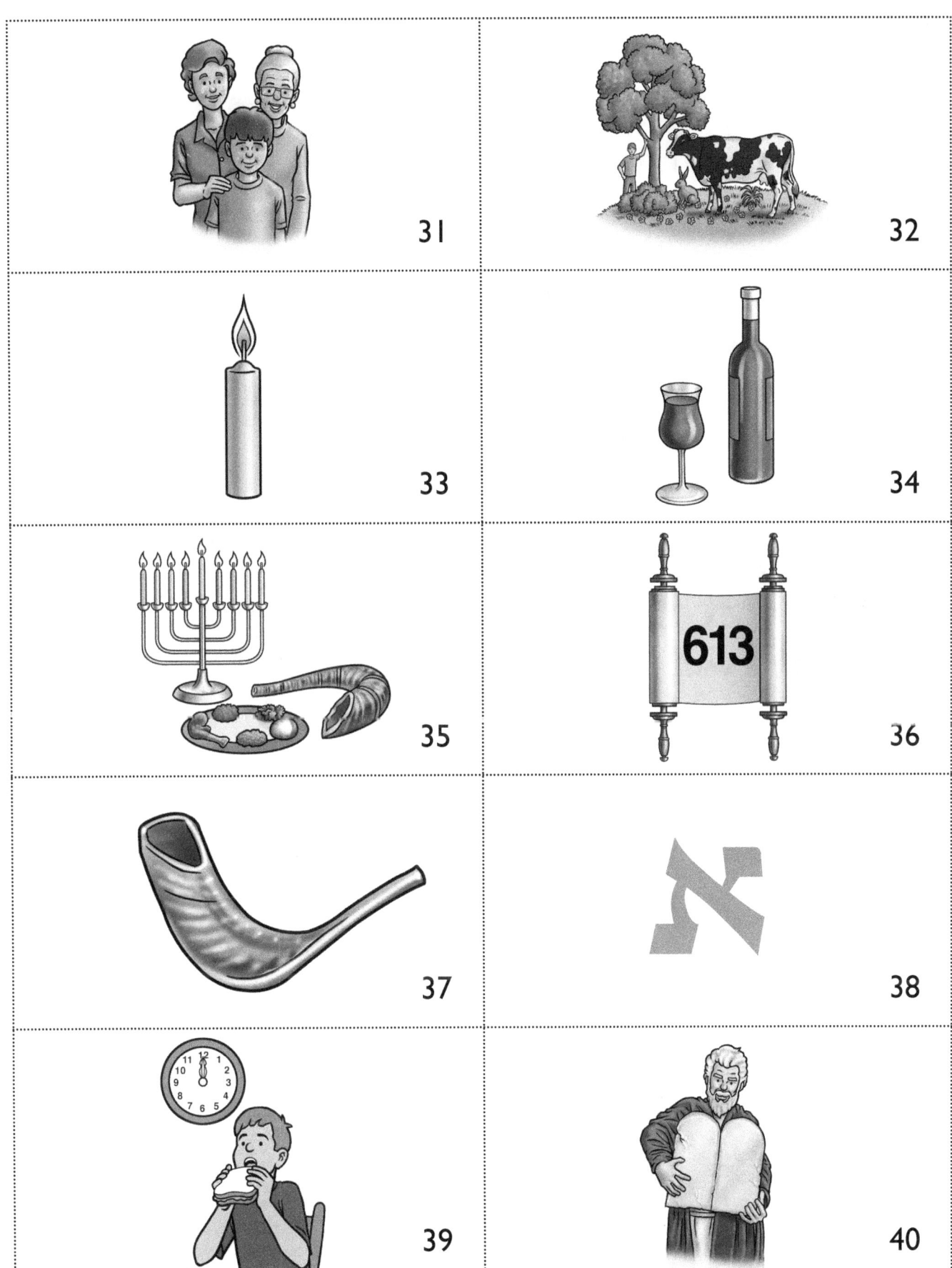

כָּל

41

אוֹי וַאֲבוֹי!

42

All 41	 42

APPENDIX C: ASSESSMENT SHEETS

PLACEMENT TEST

Name ______________________ Date ______________

	Lesson		Lesson		Lesson
27. כַּפַּי	15	14. תּוֹרָשָׁה	9	1. שָׁמַם	1
28. לְתַקֵן	16	15. עֲטֶרֶת		2. בָּא	2
29. נוֹרְאֹתֶיךָ		16. עִבְרִית	10	3. עֲמָם	
30. פּוֹתֵחַ	17	17. שַׁלְוָה		4. אֹם	3
31. מִצְוֹתַי		18. סִוֵג	11	5. לַעֲמוֹד	
32. נִתְכּוֹפֵף	18	19. עֵשֶׂב		6. הַיוֹם	4
33. כְּנָפָיו		20. כֻּלָם	12	7. לֶאֱגוֹד	5
34. מִכָּל	19	21. קוּמִי		8. שֶׁלֶג	
35. אָהֳלֶךָ		22. זְאֵב	13	9. אִם	6
36. יֹשֶׁר		23. יְהַלְלוּ		10. עֲמִידָה	
37. נוֹי	20	24. חֲכָמִים	14	11. צָמִיג	7
38. כָּפוּי		25. מַדְרִיךְ		12. אֹמֶץ	
39. נַפְשְׁךָ		26. יוֹדֵךְ		13. הֲרֵי	8

Comments: ____

____

ASSESSMENT: Lessons 1–5

Name ____________________________________

	Lesson 5	Lesson 4	Lesson 3	Lesson 2	Lesson 1	
	גַג	יָם	דַל	עָשׂ	שָׁ	.1
	דַאָג	יָעַד	אֹם	בָּא	מַ	.2
	גֹדֶל	יוֹם	עוֹד	בָּם	מַם	.3
	עָגֹל	יָדוֹ	עֹל	עָשַׂשׂ	שָׁשׁ	.4
	שֶׁלֶג	הוֹד	דוֹד	עַמָא	שָׁם	.5
	בֶּגֶד	הֲדֹם	אָדָם	עֲמָם	שַׁשָׁם	.6
	אֶלָא	אֲהָל	מָשַׁל	אֲשַׁם	שָׁמַם	.7
	אֹהֶל	שֹׁהַם	שָׁלוֹשׁ	בָּאַשׁ	מַמָשׁ	.8
	אֱיָל	הַיוֹם	מַעֲמָד	שַׁעַם	מָשׁשׁ	.9
	לֶאֱיוֹם	יַהֲלוֹם	לַעֲמוֹד	מַבָּע	שַׁמָשׁ	.10
Score						
Date						

ASSESSMENT: Lessons 6–10

Name ______________________________

	Lesson 10	Lesson 9	Lesson 8	Lesson 7	Lesson 6	
	אָבוֹת	טַל	רָץ	מַצָה	אִי	.1
	אֲוִיר	אַט	גִיר	גַהָץ	בָּה	.2
	יֹבֶשׁ	אוֹת	צַבָּר	צָמֹג	עִם	.3
	וַעֲדָה	טִירָה	רָגִיל	שֶׁמֶץ	גִילָה	.4
	מִצְרִי	תֹּמֶר	שֶׁרֶץ	צֶמֶד	מוֹדָה	.5
	עֶגְלָה	בֵּיתֵי	רוֹצָה	צִיץ	דָגִים	.6
	אַשְׁרֵי	צִיצִית	הָרֵי	אֹמֶץ	שִׁשָׁה	.7
	גִבְעוֹל	מַעֲטֶה	עֲדֵי	דִיצָה	הוֹעִיל	.8
	הִשְׁתַּטָה	עֲתֶרֶת	שַׁעֲרֵי	הַצָגָה	הֶעֱלִיל	.9
	מִשְׁמֶרֶת	שִׁבֹּלֶת	עֵילוֹם	עֲצִימָה	הֲלִימָה	.10
Score						
Date						

ASSESSMENT: Lessons 11–15

Name ______________________________

	Lesson 15	Lesson 14	Lesson 13	Lesson 12	Lesson 11	
	פָּז	חֶקֵי	זִיו	אִבּוּק	שָׂרַט	.1
	אֲזַי	זֵכֶר	לוּז	כֶּבֶשׂ	יוֹבֵל	.2
	צָרַי	לְכֶם	בַּרְוָז	מֶסָק	סִוֵג	.3
	רֶפָּא	חֲסְדֵי	אֱגוֹז	עֹתֶק	סוֹבֵל	.4
	פָּסוּל	שִׂמְחָה	עֶזְרָה	קֶבּוּץ	עֵשֶׂב	.5
	אַפַּיִם	לְבָרֵךְ	כְּתֻבָּה	שִׁכּוּל	מֵלִיץ	.6
	מְחַיֶה	זַרְעֲךָ	מְשׁוּרָה	תִּקְוָה	לִסְטֵם	.7
	פְּעֻלָּה	סְלִיחוֹת	זְאֵבִיּוּת	הִשְׂכִּיל	מִצְטַעֵר	.8
	פּוּרִים	יְהַלְלוּךָ	יְהַלְלוּ	כּוֹרְעִים	תַּעֲשִׂיָה	.9
	מִשְׁפָּטִים	אֶשְׁתַּחֲוֶה	הִתְעוֹרְרִי	הִתְכַּוֵן	הִשְׁתַּמֵשׁ	.10
Score						
Date						

ASSESSMENT: Lessons 16–20

Name ________________________________

	Lesson 20	Lesson 19	Lesson 18	Lesson 17	Lesson 16	
	הוֹי	כָּל	קוֹף	כֹּחַ	נָשִׂיא	.1
	בִּזוּי	וְכָל	שָׂפָה	שִׂיחַ	חַנּוּן	.2
	טָפּוּי	חשֶׁן	יָדָיו	וְכּוּחַ	הִנְנִי	.3
	הַגּוֹי	עֳנִי	חֲפָף	עוֹן	נִרְקוֹד	.4
	עוֹיֵן	גָּבְהֵי	קְפִיץ	בּוֹקֵעַ	רַחֲמָן	.5
	נַפְשְׁךָ	אָזְנֵי	רְפוּאָה	מַבְטִיחַ	פַּרְנָסָה	.6
	נִשְׂמְחָה	כְּמֹשֶׁה	מְכֻשָּׁף	לַמְנַצֵּחַ	הִתְכּוֹנֵן	.7
	קָדְשְׁךָ	כִּנְשׂא	לְפָנֶיךָ	הוֹכִיחַ	בְּבָנֶיךָ	.8
	שָׁכְבְּךָ	קָדְשֶׁךָ	לִפְלֵיטָה	בְּמִצְוֹתַי	פְּשָׁעֶיךָ	.9
	גָּלֻיּוֹתֵינוּ	אָהֳלִים	בְּמִצְוֹתָיו	עֲוֹנוֹתֵינוּ	נֶעֱרַכְתָּ	.10
Score						
Date						

Certificate of Completion

____

Student's Name

Has successfully completed *Alef Bet Quest* and
is a certified Hebrew reader

מַזָל טוֹב!

____

Date

____________________ ____________________

Teacher | Education Director